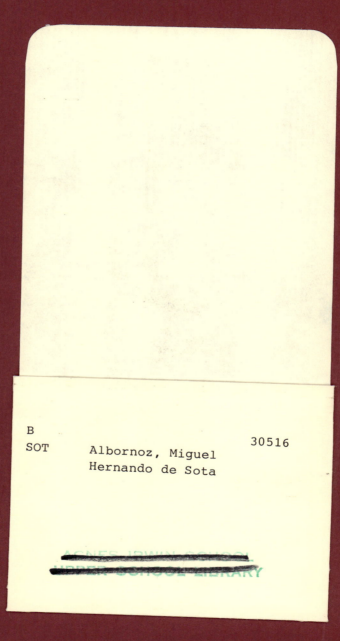

HERNANDO
DE SOTO

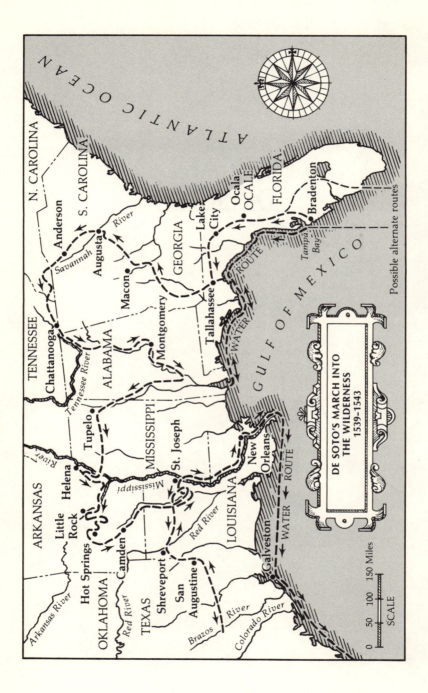

To the memory of Atahualpa,
the Inca from Quito, my hometown,
of whom de Soto was a
loyal friend and defender.

Table of Contents

PROLOGUE
AMADIS ONCE MORE ON SCRUTINY

There are several ways of assessing the extraordinary importance of the part which our America has played in fashioning, through the interplay of many successive and concomitant acts of responsibility, the web of human solidarity we now call the Universal History of Civilization.

Some scholars have elected to highlight and praise the valor of the great indigenous builders who lived before the conquest and of the heroes who fought to repel it. Nexahualcoyotl, Atahualpa, Caupolicán and Cuauthemoc are the frequent subjects of their studies. Reading such works, the mestizos, ever more numerous on our continent of Latin expression, take great pride in recalling that they carry the same blood which once ran in the veins of these men of bronze, men of God, men of war, stoics all, trained from childhood to live up to their high ideals of sacrifice, integrity and manhood.

Other, better informed historians have delved into the records, trusting the written word rather than mere tradition, statues, bas-reliefs and, at times, indecipherable stelae, to discover the true nature, the courage, the tenacity and the adventurous spirit of the men of iron who, aided by their considerable equipment, startled and defeated the bronze people, ever at a disadvantage with their inferior battle tactics, their political rivalries and even their own prophecies that foretold their doom.

Such scholars tell of Hernán Cortés, of the Pizarro brothers, of Almagro and so many others who, with the sword and the cross—or just the cross of the sword—opened up the New World to Western civilization. Today, their lessons give our local people all at once encouragement, confidence and strength. One of our poets said, "We are a race of eagles, a race of lions. Therefore, take heart!" This is the group of writers to which the author of this book belongs: Miguel Albornoz, an Ecuadorean of penetrating spirit, natural style, effective prose and solid information. To his earlier book, *Orellana*, he now adds a biography of Hernando de Soto, "The Amadís of Florida."[1]

How unique this fiery Hernando is! A man of the Renaissance, still bound by feudal loyalties recalling the Middle Ages, yet all the while driven by ambitions which at times far exceed plain Renaissance expansiveness. He wants fortune, power and love. But when he gains love—and the peace that love, fortune and power bring—he allows himself to be seduced once more by the lure of adventure.

For more than twenty years he takes part in the most dangerous forays. We see him fighting in Darién, in Panama, in Nicaragua and in Peru. He has to serve—sometimes reluctantly—under the command of intolerant and unscrupulous chiefs. The implacable Pedrarias Dávila orders the execution of Núñez de Balboa. This arouses Hernando's indignation. But Pedrarias is not only the man he has sworn to obey, he is also the father of the woman he loves and will eventually marry after many years of anguish and danger. He meets Atahualpa and holds him in high esteem, but he also must abide by the decision of a chief, Francisco Pizarro. And—this we consider less honorable—he agrees to join in the sharing of the Inca's ransom. Gold in the hand of a knight is outright villainy!

Once he becomes a rich man—and gains the aura of success as a conqueror—he returns to Spain and marries the woman who has been waiting for him, Doña Isabel de Bobadilla. He enjoys a season of happiness, first in Segovia, then in Seville, where he makes his home. His joy, however, clouds over now and then with a nostalgic longing for danger and a lust for glory that the knight can only satisfy through achieving success under arms. Eighteen months after his marriage he takes on a new commission which Emperor Charles V gives him in recognition of his strength and boldness.

On April 6, 1538, he sails from Sanlúcar, with the titles of Adelantado and captain general, in command of a fleet which is to divide in America, part sailing on to the Mexican coast, the rest bound for the land referred to as Florida, where Spanish dominion was to be established. It was, in the mind of the ambitious explorers, a region much larger than the peninsula we know today. This time, Hernando is not traveling alone; his wife is with him. As the author of the book puts it, Oriana accompanies the tireless Amadís to his fate.

Cuba was the ideal choice as a base, to ensure the success of the undertaking. That is why Charles V favored Hernando with the added title of governor of the island. After leaving Oriana in Cuba, as governor of the place, Amadís starts off on an expedition brilliantly recounted by Albornoz, which leads de Soto to discover the Mississippi. He dies of malaria on the banks of the river, in 1542, after contracting the disease in the unhealthy miasma then prevailing in those regions. Inside a tree trunk which became his casket, his body was laid to rest at night in the waters of the river. The swift current would carry him to an unknown destination, a boundless and silent mansion, that the readers of this book will call by the admirable name of posthumous glory. The glory of a man who, when young, could well have been dubbed "The Youth from the Sea."

This, then, is the short account of the theme which the distinguished Ecuadorean writer has turned with enthusiasm not only into an interesting book, but also into a living and eloquent study. True, novels of chivalry have been the targets of witty and famous criticism, but let us not forget Cervantes's immortal pages. . . .

This book does not aim at rivaling any such prodigious novel, though some of its chapters seem to carry something of the scent of such works. In this case, fortunately, facts prevail over fantasy and, whenever available, the document corrects the dream. That is why the author deserves honor and applause.

Jaime Torres Bodet
Former Director General
of UNESCO, Foreign
Minister and Minister
of Education of Mexico

THE CENTURY OF CHIVALRY

I

*The quiet life, comfort and ease, were meant for
mild courtiers; but labor, discomfort, and the
weapons of war were invented and made only for
those whom the world calls knights-errant.*[1]

Cervantes,
Don Quijote

As the curtain rose on the sixteenth century, there prevailed in Europe a bold spirit of confidence in the capacities of men, comparable, perhaps, to the casual manner in which the generations of the latter half of our own century have embarked upon the space age. This Renaissance attitude was called "humanism," but its outstanding feature was a plethora of geographical discoveries, accompanied by fantastic tales about the explorers who had just changed the traditional map of the world. Other major feats were being accomplished simultaneously, such as the victory of Christendom over the Moors and the consolidation of a monarchy in each state. This was a first step toward the integration of Europe with the New World.

Among the peoples living in the year 1500 there was much more than a mere sense of coming out of the Middle Ages. Medieval ideas were still valid, though imbued with the modern spirit of adventure. The religious wars were intended as true crusades. The same bold zeal that launched the brigantines toward exotic kingdoms took people to the wars in Europe, whatever the cause might be, in search of fame and booty.

This philosophy was expounded in the favorite literature of the times: novels of chivalry, which filled the heads of imaginative lads, reminiscing old men and romantic maidens alike. The advent of the printed word had made books fashionable, and the adventures of the knights influenced not only the style of conversation but the whole way of life. The life of the knight errant had wide appeal, whether to improve a modest social position, to channel patriotism or revolutionary fervor or to give form to one's heroic or poetic tendencies.

There was even an element of democracy in the institution of chivalry, since, in the words of Raimundo Lulio in the twelfth century, "knights receive honor and authority from the people in return for guidance and protection." So the institution of chivalry was based on the choice of the knight as the worthiest man from his district, the horse as the noblest and most suitable animal, weapons as tools for the defense of honor, an equerry to attend the knight and an estate to finance his needs. Becoming an equerry was the first step in a training process for the most admired occupation of the times, whose goal was defending the Christian Church to safeguard the spiritual order. The emperor was the head of all the knights, and under him were the kings and knights through the various ranks of nobility. Honor and loyalty were the essential virtues of the knight, committed as he was to defending "widows, orphans and the poor."

The most popular and influential book in sixteenth-century Europe was called *The Virtuous Knight Amadís of Gaul.* Rescued from the waters in infancy like Moses, Amadís's adoptive father gives him the name of The Youth from the Sea. As a knight he falls in love with Oriana, the daughter of King Lisuarte of England, who will not consent to the marriage until Amadís has been tested by going through the most preposterous adventures.[2]

In this century of chivalry, emperors and popes, kings and princes, captains and soldiers shared the same conceptions of honor, faith and ambition, and of war as a means of settling disputes. Great lords emerged from successful trading ventures to become protectors of the arts in Florence, Rome or the great cities of France. At the same time, Venice, Castile and Portugal were creating another field of chivalrous activity on the seas, both in adventures of discovery and in fights against the pirates. The "Sea Dogs" appeared first in small parties, either from Europe or the Moslem countries, but they grew into large fleets like Barbarossa's, which defeated the imperial fleet of Spain. At the end of the century Don Juan of Austria burned the Islamic galleys at the Battle of Lepanto.

A typical story of sixteenth-century chivalry is that of King Fernando and Queen Isabel of Spain, whose goal was to gain unity in their country as a first step toward a united Europe—an ambition almost fulfilled by their grandchildren. The life of Queen Isabel is itself a novel of chivalry. Her half brother Henry IV treated her as a poor relation, and tried to force her into several marriages which were repugnant to her. She secretly obtained a portrait of Don Fernando, prince of Aragon, whose looks appealed to her. She communicated her feelings to him, and eloped with him to escape the persecution of her royal brother. In 1467, the groom, disguised as a muleteer, was met by his bride-to-be and her protector, Cardinal Carrillo, who arrived to conduct the ceremony at the head of three hundred knights in full armor. Eager to make peace with her brother the king, the pope intervened through a young Spanish cardinal, twenty-three-year-old Rodrigo Borgia who, as Alexander VI, was to become pope himself. Seven years later, Isabel became queen.

She was a fighting woman, always at her husband's side in affairs of war. On one occasion, she traveled from town to town dressed in armor to recruit an army of forty thousand men to fight in a war against Portugal. She practically lived in the saddle for the ten years it took to expel the Moors from Spain, and vowed never to change her shirt until Granada was conquered. Granada fell in January 1492, at the same time that a sailor, cartographer and dreamer by the name of Columbus was waiting for his plans to be approved. When the crusade was over, the queen fulfilled her promise to Columbus to finance his fantastic plans, and America was discovered in the same year.

Thus began the sixteenth century in Europe, a century suspended between two chivalresque novels, *Amadís of Gaul* at its beginning and *Don Quijote* at its close.

In the year 1500 were born two children of note: one in Gaunt, Flanders, to Doña Juana the Mad and Philip the Handsome; he would become Charles the First of Spain and the Fifth of Germany; the other in Jerez de los Caballeros,[3] Spain; he would be Don Hernando de Soto, knight-errant of Panama, Nicaragua, Peru and Florida, and discoverer of the Mississippi.

THE YOUTH FROM THE SEA

II

Let me tell you that he whom you found in the sea will be the flower of the knights of his time. He will make strong men tremble, will undertake and accomplish things in which all others have failed.

Amadís of Gaul,
bk. I, chap. 11

Jerez de los Caballeros was named after the Knights Templar and was a typical town of Extremadura. It had an old Roman tradition, a long-standing Arabian connection and little agricultural importance. The main "crop" was of daring youths, eager to join in the new expeditions and triumph in adventure wherever it was to be found.

The family life of the noble house of Francisco Méndez de Soto was presided over by his wife Doña Leonor Arias Tinoco. In accordance with tradition she elected that her eldest son, Juan, would inherit the estate together with the name of Méndez de Soto, and protect his sisters, Catalina and María. The second son, Hernando, would use only the name de Soto. He was a favorite of his mother's, who hoped he would become a man of letters or a churchman. But the child grew up hearing fabulous stories of adventure, in particular those about a neighbor of theirs, Vasco Núñez de Balboa, who had already gone to the Indies. Everybody in town knew him, and many spread rumors about his deeds. When Hernando learned to read, he seemed more interested in novels of chivalry than in grammar or rhetoric. He was a strong boy, skilled at children's games and contests, always ready for any adventurous excursion on foot or on horseback with the other lads of his town. Those were the days when all Spain was talking about the deeds of the "Great Captain,"

Gonzalo de Córdoba, and his companion from Extrema-dura, Colonel Gonzalo Pizarro.[1]

In Jerez de los Caballeros, the boys used to imitate the Knights Templar as they played among the ruins of the ancient castle and fortress, built when the military orders were fighting holy wars which were to make them so strong as to cause envy among the kings of France and Spain, until the Order of Templars was suppressed in the fifteenth century by Pope Clement V.

The house of Francisco Méndez was a regular stopping place for travelers between Spain and Portugal, all of whom related stories of the constant competition between the two countries vying for supremacy as discoverers. Their respective kings were using navigators and captains of both nationalities. The Portuguese Magellan was to make discoveries under the Castilian flag, while several Spanish sailors joined the Portuguese expeditions of Cabral. Also veterans of the Moorish and Italian wars frequently visited. Some had seen the Northern Sea [the Atlantic Ocean] and known Admiral Christopher Columbus. They hinted that since 1495 the kings had been granting free exploration permits for the Indies, setting aside, of course, the vague boundaries of the land assigned to the admiral. Columbus had died in 1506 in Valladolid, two years after the death of Queen Isabel the Catholic, queen of the Americas. He was buried in the main church in Seville, and King Fernando had had his tombstone inscribed with the well-deserved and now famous epitaph:

> *A Castilla y a León*
> *Nuevo Mundo dio Colón.*

> *(Columbus gave a New World*
> *to Castile and to León).*

By that time, it was common belief that the newly discovered lands were not the Indies, nor did they lead to China, but they were a new world. This was shown in the maps which Amerigo Vespucci had sent to his illustrious friend and former employer, the banker Lorenzo Pier Francesco de Medici, one of the rivals of Lorenzo the Magnificent. Vespucci was a loyal friend of Columbus's. All Europe was aware of Amerigo's prestige as a cartographer of the heavens, and as the discoverer of the coastlands of Brazil and Argentina, but none had guessed that through the casual work of German mapmakers, the whole New World would bear his name.

One afternoon in 1508, a group of Méndez' friends were discussing the latest news as they sat around a table overlooking the garden. The boys, Juan and Hernando, were serving the wine, but not missing a word of the travelers' boastful tales, recounted in the true Castilian style. There must be an ocean passage to India and the spice-producing kingdoms, but it was yet to be discovered.[2]

One of the men told of his journeys with Amerigo Vespucci and the master navigator Juan de la Cosa, searching for the strait in the Darién area. While they were unsuccessful in finding a way to reach India, they at least found some gold "in the Atrato River area. It was obtained by imitating the local people, who sifted the sands of the riverbanks through a kind of basket or net." And the narrator continued, displaying some gold flakes in his handkerchief,[3] "But my lord de la Cosa was more interested in gathering data for his maps, and Signor Amerigo said that facts about the stars, the climate, the plants and animals were worth more than gold."

The flakes were being passed from hand to hand among the older men. Finally one of them, realizing the fascination they held for Hernando, whose eyes were shining, placed the gold into his hands.

"Here, boy, touch the gold of the Indies. One day you will follow in the footsteps of other Extremadura men; for there is ample land to be discovered, and few people live there."

To Hernando, the golden flakes in his hands seemed to sparkle like a reflection of those remote lands. They were concrete proof of the existence of countries which were beckoning to him with a mixture of fact and fantasy.

"Balboa, our countryman, is there," said Francisco Méndez. "I used to know his father, who had no use for travels and adventures as a life for his son. But the boy went off with Rodrigo de Bastidas, and we've heard nothing about him except that he settled in Hispaniola [Santo Domingo].[4] They say those are dangerous lands; they talk of Indians who eat human flesh and shoot poisoned arrows, whom they call Caribs."

"He must surely be in Hispaniola still, with that carefree fellow Alonso de Ojeda," said the traveler. "He is well liked and respected, since his successful defense of Admiral Columbus against the Indian chieftain Caonabo, in Santo Domingo. And there are other Extremadura men in those parts, such as Hernán Cortés of Medellín, and Francisco Pizarro of Trujillo."

As the stories went on, Hernando had to take ever more frequent trips to the cellar for more wine. But his head was full of dreams of the fabulous New World, with its golden flakes, clement weather and gaudy parrots, where the pearls in the sea were the size of nutmegs. He thought too of his daily routine as stable and shepherd boy in Jerez, and contrasted it with the adventures of Amadís, which he had read and discussed with his friends in the village.

At his mother's insistence, the young Hernando studied the humanities; history, grammar, logic and rhetoric were a must to prepare him for a future as a prominent figure in the Church, as would be fitting for the second son. His father was hoping that the boy would find a patron so that he could pursue his studies in Salamanca. But the local director of studies, the Franciscan Friar Diego, was not encouraging. His father knew, too, that Hernando spent too much time with the horses in the stables, and wandering to the nearby river or the ruined castle.[5]

At fourteen he looked nineteen. He was a strong lad, and taller than average; he felt well fitted for his ambition of joining the Italian regiments in search of adventure. This was not what his father had envisioned for him, but the family was in financial difficulties, and manual labor was out of the question for a provincial nobleman. To join the wars abroad seemed to be the best course, so despite the tearful protests of the rest of the family, he decided to allow his son to leave. Friar Diego provided letters of introduction for the Franciscan friar who was the assistant to Don Pedrarias Dávila, one of the king's most renowned servants. De Soto took the letters to Seville.

In 1514, Seville was a teeming political center as it was a ships' outfitting port and point of departure for the fabled lands of the Indies, or for the wars in Italy which continued under the leadership of the "Great Captain."[6] The navigators would guide their ships down the Guadalquivir River and through the bar of Sanlúcar, and then return to the city. The inns were crowded with people on their way to or from the New World, all of whom were well informed on the subjects of gold, pearls and cannibals.

The Armada for the Crusade against the Infidels had also been organized in Seville—in fact, the African coast had been conquered only four years earlier. Colonel Pedrarias Dávila had served with the famous Pedro Navarro, and had now been entrusted with the governorship of Castilla del Oro by the king. As the husband of Doña Isabel de Bobadilla[7] y Peñalosa, he had great influence in the Court.

Since the new Darién project had been widely advertised, it had already attracted three thousand men, now anxious to depart. Some had sold their lands, houses and jewelry in order to pay their way. This was in striking contrast with earlier expeditions, where criminals or political prisoners were pressed into going.

Deliveries to the twenty ships were coming from all over Seville—powder kegs and provisions, doublets, guns, crossbows, swords, lances, pikes, bucklers, ropes, iron, lead, spades, bells and religious ornaments, flour and wine, dried fruits and smoked hams—everything, indeed, that such an enterprise might require.

Hernando de Soto arrived in Seville that morning in March riding his horse Lucero through the gate of the Macarena. Still fresh in his memory were the tears of his mother and sisters, and the advice his father had given him the day before. Soon he reached the house where Bishop Quevedo was busy preparing for the long voyage.[8] A throng of knights, sailors and peasants was waiting for the departure in the chambers and hallways of the mansion, but at last Hernando managed to catch the eye of one of the bishop's page boys and communicate the motive for his visit. Friar Diego's letter acted like a passport; soon the bishop received him. His expression was at once kind and alert, and his face swarthy from years in the Indies. His approval guaranteed the interview with Don Pedrarias Dávila.

Hernando was admitted to his room in the inn and saw an old soldier writing at a high oak desk.[9] His white hair, haughty frown and aristocratic profile suggested how handsome he must have been in his youth, when he was known as "The Gallant." He was a tall man, with wide shoulders and a military bearing. Although he was seventy years old, he looked about fifty, and his steadfast gaze showed that he was still a tremendously determined man.

Pedrarias took on de Soto as a page.

The three page boys of the Pedrarias household with whom Hernando now lived were well-born lads from other parts of Spain. They were all under the command of Gaspar de Morales, who instructed them in their duties, and, equally important, helped them to recognize everyone of importance in the expedition.

Pedrarias was surrounded by important men: Lieutenant Don Juan de Ayora, captain general and second-in-command of the expedition; the camp marshal, Hernando de Fuen Mayor; the two chief pilots, Juan Serrano and Juan Vespucci, who was a nephew and disciple of the cartographer and navigator Amerigo;[10] the cosmographer Antonio Romano; Alonso de la Puente, the treasurer; the chief net master, Juan de Albornoz; the victualler, Juan de Tebira; the overseer of gold melting, Gonzalo Fernández de Oviedo; and various captains and soldiers such as Francisco Dávila, Gonzalo Fernández de Lago, Diego de Bustamante, Francisco Vázquez de Coronado, Diego de Almagro, Sebastián de Benalcázar, Bernal Díaz del Castillo and many others who were to make names for themselves in America.

By the 22d of January the armada was ready to sail. The governor was anxious to avoid further delay;[11] he had already taken leave of the king; all that remained was the *alarde*, or final parade, through the streets of Seville. In April they were all ordered to go to Sanlúcar de Barrameda and board the ships.

The page boys prepared the governor's chambers in the flagship for the arrival of his family, the illustrious Doña Isabel de Bobadilla and two of her daughters, Isabel and Elvira.

The flagship set sail on the Sunday of carnival week, but things started badly: a storm forced the whole fleet to return to Sanlúcar. During the wait for better weather, many halfhearted members of the party fell away, disillusioned by seasickness during the trial run. Finally the weather improved, and on Tuesday, April 11, the ships sailed toward the island of Gomera. For Hernando, the last sight of the coastline of Spain ended a chapter of his life. His childhood was over, and manhood was beginning in the school of the sea.

Like most youths of his time, Hernando must have had, among his scant possessions together with a few shirts, a well-worn copy of *Amadís of Gaul*. While gazing at the waves, he must have imagined that he was Amadís, the "Youth from the Sea," who was "only twelve, but whose strong physique made him look fifteen."[12] How could he not remember the heroic deeds of his idol, at Firme Island, and compare them with the dangers of his present voyage?

Hernando now had a master and a cause to serve. He would become an equerry, a soldier and finally a knight with a horse and armor, provided that he comported himself with bravery and honor, as his father had told. Looking toward the horizon, book in hand, he must have felt that Amadís was his companion in a journey to lands of adventure in the West Indies.

THE SCHOOL OF THE NEW WORLD

III

And surely if the terrestrial paradise
be in any part of this earth, I esteem that
it is not far distant from these parts.[1]

Amerigo Vespucci

T he crossing proceeded calmly. Everything about life on board ship was novel and interesting to the young page boy: the sailors' work, the names of all the ship's parts and the mysterious science of the sea. Juan Vespucci, the navigator, had taken a liking to him, and would answer any question that his adolescent curiosity could suggest. He told Hernando about his great-uncle Amerigo, who had died only two years earlier, leaving him all his papers and maps. Juan had made copies of them to sell to other navigators.

"That is how I ended up in this armada," the young Florentine said. "I want to see the lands I have heard so much about from my uncle—the coast of Tierra Firme, called Venezuela, where my maps show 'the Valley of Amerigo.' With the help of Díaz de Solís, who is now the chief pilot, I have made corrections and additions to the master map at the Casa de Contratación in Seville."

"Surely, sir, this great armada must have cost a fortune!" exclaimed Hernando.

"Our lord king has provided fifty-four thousand ducats," answered the navigator. "But what we have done with it is worth three times that sum. You'll have noticed that the ships are not overloaded—there are no more than one hundred men on each, apart from the flagship, of course."[2]

Hernando inspected the ship from the bow to stern. In the course of his chores he also gathered information about Darién, and exchanged his news and impressions with his fellow worker Diego San Martín. He wanted to learn all he could about his countryman Balboa.

De Soto asked Bishop Quevedo about Vasco Núñez de Balboa at the first opportunity, and discovered that Balboa had been in the area since 1501, first with Alonso de Ojeda, and later with Martín Fernández de Enciso, who had left in 1510. Balboa, who had made his last trip to Darién hidden in a barrel of pork, to avoid his creditors, had assumed command, and the Crown later confirmed him as governor. But his enemy Enciso was traveling with Pedrarias and stirring up animosity against him. Apparently, too, the king was most interested in Balboa's rumored plan to cross the country in search of the Southern Sea [the Pacific Ocean]. The Indians knew all about this, as the shrewd Spaniard maintained most cordial relations with their chieftains. He had written to the king asking for one thousand men for this enterprise.

Hernando was gathering knowledge about men. Not all of them were honest or noble. Hatred and rivalries abounded. Several times he had seen Enciso in suspicious-looking groups, evidently plotting something. He realized that a false move on his part could be dangerous, particularly since he lacked name and fortune. He decided to watch and listen and try to keep his mouth shut, and warned his garrulous companion, San Martín, that he would do better to stick to his chores than voice his opinions.

Hernando could let down his guard, however, when the noble Doña Isabel chatted with him and asked him questions during her walks on the deck with her daughters. These were pleasant occasions for both of them: they discussed life aboard ship and a multitude of other things as Isabel, nine years old, and her seven-year-old sister Elvira amused themselves close by. Their mother had not wanted to leave them in Spain, as she had done with their two older sisters, and had finally managed to obtain a permit from the governor, her husband, to bring them with her. To Hernando, she seemed the prototype of the great ladies and princesses in his books of chivalry, but her ideas and teachings also reminded him of his own mother, when she spoke of virtue, duty, loyalty or religion. From her he was learning courtly manners, elegance and poise, and cultivated tastes in colors, clothing and etiquette. He could hardly have found a better teacher in these matters, for Doña Isabel was undoubtedly one of the most prominent ladies in Spain.[3]

During the voyage he developed lasting friendships with Vespucci and San Martín. He learned that their course followed the African coastline southward down to the Canary Islands, which had already been Castilian territory for a century. Here they would stop to take on water and provisions.

San Martín was more interested in other subjects. He gathered political gossip, and was constantly referring to the private life of the governor, whom he had served since the African wars five years earlier. He spoke of the likes and dislikes of the old man, of his ferocity in battle and his rancorous temper. He managed to give the impression of knowing terrible secrets about his master.

"He will destroy Balboa in the end," he would say. He felt the letters to the king explained some of Balboa's actions, but the evil rumors spread by his associate Enciso made a greater impression at Court.

The hatred directed against Balboa may be explained by the fact that the capital of Darién, Santa María la Antigua, was founded by Balboa and Enciso together, but Balboa took over the government of the region and ignored Enciso and Colmenares, who was also a member of the party.

Balboa wrote a letter to the king, dated January 20, 1513, saying that Alonso de Ojeda and Diego de Nicuesa "thought they could rule from their beds,"[4] whereas he had traveled in swamps and jungles until he had discovered thirty rivers containing gold particles. "When the floods subside, the river beds are left full of nuggets the size of oranges, and [his] friend the Indian Chief Davaive has set one hundred men to work smelting gold."[5]

The letter also mentioned the sea on the other side of the country, where even more gold and pearls are to be found.[6]

A popular leader, Balboa had been elected mayor by his troops and he had asked the king for confirmation of his appointment.

San Martín told Hernando[7] of Pedrarias's tyrannical ways with his family and subordinates, and shocked the page by revealing that he always traveled with a coffin, which he kept under his bed. Once a year he spent a night in it, meditating and praying, and believed it was thus that he outlived his enemies.

Pedrarias wrote the king[8] that everything was ready and gave a sailing date of February 26, to be preceded by a solemn religious service with thirteen priests and eleven friars, who were a part of the expedition under Bishop Quevedo. Delayed by a storm, the fleet then set sail on April 11, heading for a point considerably south of Hispaniola, as the king had instructed that they should not touch port at Caribbean islands or in areas inhabited by cannibals. The voyage lasted throughout the month of April.

Finally, the coast of the Canary Islands was sighted, and de Soto was told that the fleet would put in at Gomera. Next day, they disembarked, and Hernando's master and family were greeted by the local authorities with every demonstration of courtesy and respect. The ladies managed several excursions, though the air hung warm and humid over the town. Hernando received his orders from Morales, as head of the governor's household: there would be two weeks in which to check over the ships and make repairs for the long ocean voyage which lay ahead of them. The king's officers ashore had already prepared stores of dried fish, cheese, meats, water, timber, seeds for planting and horses. The crew was only too glad to rest ashore for a while, since many had suffered from seasickness. They set sail again on May 9.

Undoubtedly, Vespucci was aware of the letter from his uncle Amerigo to Piero Soderini, which described in detail the fabulous features of his four trips to the New World. New adventures and opportunities were beginning to open up for Hernando in a setting of the brilliant coastlands of new kingdoms and rivers.

At last the presence of birds announced that land was near; the air was growing warmer, and trees could be seen on the horizon. They had crossed Columbus's Northern Sea, and were approaching the dreaded cannibal islands.

It was Saturday, June 3, the eve of Pentecost, when the fleet reached the Lesser Antilles and anchored off the island of Dominica, before unfamiliar lush green mountains which fascinated the travelers accustomed to the barren landscape of Castile. A wide river which "was a joy to behold," so mentioned by several descriptions of the time, flowed into the sea close by them. The governor gave orders to land and get fresh water and grass for the horses, and to explore the coastal lands. Pedrarias was to hold council with his senior officers to decide on a plan of action, and the bishop wanted to celebrate a Pentecostal Mass on land. De Soto and San Martín were kept busy following Morales' orders. Pedrarias had made it clear that while on land his second-in-command was to be his friend Juan de Ayora.

Pedrarias named the landing place Fonseca Bay, in honor of the chairman of the Royal Council of the Indies, a friend of his and an important prelate in the Spanish Court.

As soon as the religious services were over, the governor called his commanders to a council under the trees. The banner of Their Catholic Majesties, Tanto Monta,[9] waved in the breeze, and guards kept away all lesser officers and the ship's crew. Included in the meeting were the bishop, the lieutenant general, the quartermaster, the mayor, the cabin master and navigators Serrano and Vespucci, as well as a dozen captains from the other ships and other senior officers.

Pedrarias spoke sternly and forcefully about the royal instructions in his possession, describing them in detail, from the simplicity with which the party should dress to the kindness and honesty they were to employ in their dealings with the natives of the new lands. He reminded them that his authority as captain general and governor was in force on land as well as at sea, and he could found cities and grant land and houses to the settlers in accordance with their services.

Bishop Quevedo then added that the main purpose of the armada was that everybody was to learn to live peaceably together in the region formerly known as the Mainland, but to be called thenceforth Castilla del Oro, or Castilla Aurifia, meaning "Golden Castile." In order to give the best possible example to the natives, and "so that none would harm another, nor cause scandal, enmities or blasphemy,"[10] no one was to play cards or indulge in gambling games such as dice. In a subtle manner, the bishop suggested that before taking any action the governor would do well to consult with him and the officers, the treasurer and the accountant.

The commanders returned to their boats and were rowed back to the ships. Hernando accompanied the ladies to the flagship and asked permission to return to the island to look for San Martín, who had not been seen for some time that day. Failing to find him, Hernando joined Juan de Ayora and his party about midnight, worried by tales of poisoned arrows and cannibals. The lieutenant general was in an ill humor, and reprimanded the night watch for not having found the governor's servant. It was one o'clock in the morning when San Martín finally appeared, as cheerful and self-assured as if he were returning from a stroll in the park. But Hernando's friend and companion was about to be subjected to the terrible justice of Pedrarias. San Martín was taken ashore and hanged from a tree.

Hernando went ashore with the others and stood by the tree as the soldiers took down the body and dug a grave; the friar uttered the words of the funeral service. As de Soto touched the hand of his friend, he must have felt that he was in contact with the forces of life and beyond; the mystery of his own destiny in a world of terrible passions. He took a spade and worked vigorously to cover the grave under the hanging tree. A cross was hurriedly made and left there. Throwing a cape across Hernando's trembling shoulders, Oviedo pushed the boy toward the boat. The ships raised anchor as day was breaking, and he could see the little cross on the shore. His first landing had not shown him rivers of gold, but the awesome revelation of death. He had arrived in the New World.[11]

THE GATEWAY TO THE SOUTHERN SEA

IV

Vasco Núñez de Balboa, who holds on our behalf the Captaincy and Governorship of this province, writes us that he has discovered new lands near the Southern Sea; for which we offer thanks to Our Lord, that He deems fit to reveal places which have been hidden and enshrouded in mystery to the men of our times.[1]

Letter from King Fernando
to Pedrarias, 1514

It took them a week of sailing to reach the mainland. Hernando applied himself diligently to his tasks, realizing the value of his nautical experiences; and the kind Doña Isabel favored the boy even more following the tragedy at Dominica. There was comfort and an unspoken warning in her attitude toward de Soto, and he paid heed to it. The day before reaching land, Morales assigned him the task of guarding the ladies with a halberd. This was his first weapon.[2]

By dawn on June 12, the coastline could be seen clearly ahead of the flagship. Everyone on board was anxiously watching the new land of Castilla del Oro, where Pedrarias's governorship would begin. They were rounding the Needle Cape, heading for the port of Santa Marta—in Colombia today—and by ten in the morning had dropped anchor, when they saw several figures on the shore. They were the dreaded warriors of the Indies, wearing feathered headdresses and brandishing bows and arrows.

Pedrarias summoned his advisers to his ship, and upon agreement with the bishop and other commanders, he ordered three boats to land. Following the king's orders, one man on board, Fernández de Oviedo, was carrying a copy of the Requerimiento. This famous document, frequently referred to in the royal instructions, was intended to protect the natives of the Indies from violence and exploitation at the hands of the conquerors. Such abuse had already depopulated the first Spanish dominions in America, such as Hispaniola and Cuba where about 90 percent of the original population had been eliminated, and in reaction Bartolomé de Las Casas, Córdoba and other friars had preached against the unchristian behavior of the invaders. So Pedrarias's orders were "to appeal to the Indians through kind deeds, so that they may view the Christians with love and friendship."[3] They were not to make war against the natives unless attacked by them, and even then must first read them three times the instructions in the Requerimiento, which was a kind of entreaty.

Pedrarias knew that this was a matter of grave concern at Court, where it was stressed that formalities be strictly followed; he also knew that between the procedures dictated by the metropolis and the Indians' warlike attitude in defense of their lands, the distance was as vast as the ocean that separated them.

Nevertheless, Juan de Ayora landed with his sixty men, ready to act as carefully as possible. The Indians were shouting and making menacing gestures: about a hundred of them, adorned in feathers, bodies painted red and glistening with coconut oil. Ayora had with him an Indian who had been in Spain, who tried to translate the main points of the warning document. For a moment there was silence as the natives tried to understand what the bearded men wanted to convey to them. But soon it became clear that neither the interpreter nor the white men knew how to communicate with them, so without further delay they waded out, shooting arrows over the boats.

Ayora ordered one of the soldiers to return to the flagship and report the event to the governor; he also ordered that the harquebus be shot twice into the air, and proceeded to land. The noise of the shots drove the Indians away, so that by the time Pedrarias arrived, his soldiers were already in formation. The governor was relieved that violence had been avoided, and as was the custom on a first landing, took out his sword and cut branches from some trees to symbolize possession of the lands on behalf of Their Majesties, reaffirming their rights over the Indies, both islands and mainland in the Ocean Sea. He ordered an act drafted and signed, and sent an exploring party inland which returned three hours later without having met a soul. They had found dwellings, and brought back items from them such as cotton clothing, hammocks and fishing nets. Pedrarias ordered them back to the ships.

Next morning he ordered another landing to continue exploring, and instructed Oviedo to proceed *in scriptis* with the document, that is to read the entire Requerimiento, as this had not yet been done. Morales gave de Soto permission to accompany Oviedo, who had the bulky document in a leather envelope under his coat. It referred to King Fernando as "the tamer of barbaric peoples," and went on to describe the origin of man, five thousand years earlier, the life of Christ and the institution of Saint Peter as the first pope. From Rome, "the most fitting place to rule the world," the last pope had granted the islands and mainland of the Indies to Their Majesties. If the Indians would accept this peacefully, they would not be disturbed, nor made to become Christians except by their own free will. But if they would not submit, they would be subdued by force, enslaved and stripped of their possessions for their disobedience. All this would be certified by the royal scribe, who was to be ready to sign the act.

The party was under the command of a nephew of the governor, Pedrarias the Younger. They found three villages, all deserted, and started looting, collecting parrot feathers, hammocks and a few pieces of gold. Suddenly, battle cries were heard, and armed Indians appeared on all sides. Young Pedrarias had about thirty men with him, including de Soto, who was embarking upon his first skirmish in the Indies. After throwing stones down on the Spaniards, the Indians descended from a nearby hill, shooting arrows. These were answered by shots from Spanish harquebuses, but there were casualties: a soldier by the name of Arroyo was hit in the knee by an arrow, and died in convulsions three days later, due to the poisoned tip.

Reaching the top of the hill, the Spaniards saw the Indians fleeing, but managed to capture several women, one of whom was clearly a person of some importance. Plantations of corn stretched out before them; soon the governor arrived with an army which swelled their numbers to thirteen hundred. In an abandoned village of no more than twenty huts, the Spanish commanders met for a brief council. The cunning Oviedo took advantage of the occasion to return the Requerimiento to the governor.

"My lord, it seems that these Indians do not agree with the theology of this document. Have it put away until we get one of these Indians in a cage where we could explain it slowly, and our good lord bishop could interpret it."[4]

Pedrarias had to smile at the overseer's clever manipulation of the situation. He had known Oviedo since the old days, during the surrender of Granada, when both men had been friends of Columbus.

The soldiers were taking their siesta when the watchmen gave the alarm, signaling that about a thousand men were about to attack. Pedrarias remained calm and prepared the troops for battle. He ordered his men not to shoot, but had a cannon made ready, and one salvo put the attacking Indians to flight. The captains were free to go hunting for some wild boar for dinner.

The next day they visited several more abandoned villages, and as well as blankets and clothing found some gold pieces, a large sapphire and some emeralds. By the time the governor gave the order to embark, the treasurer estimated the value of the booty at some seven thousand gold castilians.[5] There was horror as well as triumph, for in some of the houses they had found pots containing boiled human limbs, smoked hands and feet, and over some of the doorways were skulls on stakes to commemorate some tribal war. They were glad to set sail for Darién, the ultimate destination of the armada.

The ladies questioned Hernando eagerly about his adventures on land, and he would tell the story with a peculiar grace and optimism. The women were especially curious about the Indian girl prisoner, who had been sent to another ship. It seemed that the other Indians held her in the utmost respect, and cast their eyes down when they addressed her.

A brief storm prevented them from stopping in Cartagena, so the fleet continued toward Darién in the Gulf of Urabá. Hernando pondered what he had learned about Balboa during the voyage. He already felt some sympathy for him, perhaps because he was coming to realize that those plotting against him were the most sinister characters on the expedition. By contrast, the honest and open-minded men in the party were increasingly frank about their good opinion of Balboa.

Soon Vespucci announced that they were about to enter the Gulf of Urabá. It was actually the huge mouth of the San Juan River, discovered by Balboa four years earlier. The pilot also observed that there were dwellings built on pylons; the river was so powerful that at low tide the gulf filled with fresh water. It was known that Balboa had made friends with all the caciques in the area, and that they had supplied him with workers, gold and food; it was even said that some important chiefs had been baptized. Like Hernando, Vespucci was clearly attracted by this resourceful man, and his ability to overcome adversity.

The fleet entered the San Juan River and proceeded upstream, toward the city of Santa María del Darién, six miles inland. When the town was in sight, the governor gave the order to drop anchor. His commanders and the bishop were already on board the flagship. The cunning old general had decided to announce his arrival to Balboa without letting him know how he felt about him, so he sent his cousin Morales on the apparently harmless, though delicate, mission. Morales chose de Soto and two others, with a couple of sailors to man the boat. In a few minutes they stood before Balboa in their fine breeches and velvet coats with the badge of the house of Pedrarias. Morales was wearing his feathered cap and gold-handled sword; this was his Court dress, designed to placate the difficult mayor of Darién.

A group of Indians and Spanish settlers were waiting at the precarious wharf, to find out who the newcomers were and to discover their intentions. The flags had already announced this was a powerful armada from Castile. The settlement consisted of some hundred houses and huts, where over five hundred Spaniards were living. Morales came ashore, followed by the boys, and was surrounded by ragged, bearded adventurers, one of whom led them to the dwelling of Don Vasco Núñez de Balboa.

They arrived at a modest bungalow, edged by trees in a small garden. A group of Indians were busy repairing the roof, on top of which stood a strong-looking man with brown hair and clear eyes which contrasted sharply with his sunburned complexion. The brown-haired man jumped nimbly down the ladder and approached the visitors with a smile. He wore a simple cotton shirt, rope sandals and wide knee-breeches.

A beautiful dark-haired woman came out of the house and stood by Balboa's side as if to protect him. She was Anayansi, the daughter of the powerful cacique Careta, who had first met Balboa on the battlefield, but was now his ally and father-in-law.

Pedrarias's landing orders showed his military caution and his feeling for courtly pageantry. The members of the council were to land together, followed by the ladies and their maids. Pedrarias escorted Doña Isabel de Bobadilla across the deck, followed by her elegantly dressed ladies-in-waiting. On the riverbank the halberdiers were already in formation, while the trumpeters announced the arrival of a governor sent from the king. Pedrarias, wearing tall boots and an ornamented Toledan sword, advanced proudly, with Doña Isabel at his side. His expression was haughty, and his bearing formal and military. Behind him followed Bishop Quevedo, Lieutenant General Ayora and other personages of importance; then came Isabel and Elvira, accompanied by their maids and the ladies-in-waiting and guarded by de Soto and the other page boys, conscious of their gleaming halberds.

Pedrarias took the opportunity to display the finery he was fond of wearing: a short cape, billowing silk breeches and a rich sword sheathed in a velvet-covered scabbard, all of which he was entitled to wear by virtue of his rank and privileges; he was followed by Doña Isabel dressed in elegant brocade. The bishop dressed in purple for the parade.[6]

The governor had Enciso introduce Balboa to all the leaders of the armada, including the noblemen and the navigators, all of whom were eager to meet the legendary Extremenian.

Following Balboa's example, all the settlers opened up their homes to the newcomers. For some of the Spaniards this was the second visit to the Indies; others recognized old friends among the settlers, or met people from their own part of Spain. But for many of them, the arrival was full of disappointments. The hot humid weather did not suit them, and the colonists' humble shacks hardly tallied with the stories of golden rivers which had fired their imaginations when they had decided to forgo glory in the Italian wars in order to join the armada and make their fortunes in "Golden Castile."

The next morning Pedrarias called Balboa to a lengthy

meeting at which Fernández de Oviedo acted as scribe. The governor demanded detailed information on the major events of the colony, and on gold-bearing rivers, gold mines and the friendly caciques on whose cooperation Balboa depended.

Balboa responded, describing as mere duties what were in fact heroic deeds. He explained how he had discovered the Southern Sea after hearing about it from his friends the caciques. Setting out from the town of Santa María del Darién, he had subdued the Indians, doing so by force only when necessary. Two of them, Comogre and his son Paquiano, had told him of an enormous sea to the west, beyond the mountains. In September of 1513, the year before Pedrarias's arrival, he had taken a brigantine and 10 canoes, 190 Spaniards and 810 Indians, toward Acla in San Blas, the land of Cacique Careta. Careta had become a Christian, taking the name Don Fernando, and had given his daughter Anayansi to Balboa as a companion; he had two thousand warriors under him. Balboa went from village to village, receiving help from the chiefs and leaving behind numerous sick men, and on September 25 he finally reached the summit of a hill from which he was able to see the Southern Sea. His scribe had made a list of his sixty-five remaining companions, headed by Francisco Pizarro. Father Andrés de Vera had then sung the Te Deum. He named the gulf he had seen from the hilltop "the Gulf of San Miguel," and reached the coast on September 29. Holding the flag and royal banner of Castile and León, he had waded out into the sea with twenty-six men, and, sword in hand, had taken possession of the seas, lands, coast, ports and islands on behalf of the Crown. They had tasted the salty water, and followed the custom of cutting branches from the trees and erecting crosses as a symbol of possession. Balboa had remarked how *pacific* were the waters of that sea.

Balboa spoke of the lands of Cacique Cuquera, where he had been shown the method of fishing for pearls. He had sailed the new ocean southward for two days, taking sixty men and discovering several islands where he had gathered information about the gold-bearing rivers. He had seen much gold among the Indians, and had exchanged several pieces for knives and beads. They then returned to the Northern sea overland, and rested at his friend Careta's port. A galleon from Hispaniola was waiting there, and had taken them back to Darién.

Pedrarias agreed that Balboa had accomplished great things and he asked him for a full report, giving names of rivers and villages, the places that should be explored, both inland and on the coast, the points where gold is to be found, and the names of the Indian chiefs—or caciques—with whom he had entered into friendly agreements.

Balboa produced all this information the next morning.

Pedrarias also inquired of Balboa whether it was true that his dog Leoncico was receiving part of the booty, as a soldier, to which Balboa replied that it was so, the troops having decided to treat Leoncico in this manner, since they estimated that the dog was worth several fighting men.

CAPTAIN
OF LANCERS

V

*The knight is given a lance as a symbol
of Truth. For the Truth is a straight
thing that cannot be twisted, and Truth
overrides falsehood.*[1]

Raimundo Lulio,
Book of the Order of Chivalry

Two days later Vasco Núñez Balboa gave Pedrarias a lengthy report on his expeditions and discoveries near the Southern Sea, describing the rivers, passes, coastlands and islands, listing the names of the twenty Indian chieftains with whom treaties had been concluded, who had given him gifts and maintained peace. As he was leaving the governor's house he met the young halberdier.

"Hernando," he said in a friendly manner, "how would you like some fencing lessons?"

"Nothing could please me more, Don Vasco."

"Well, come to my house tomorrow morning. We will take half an hour every day. I want my old friend Francisco Méndez to know I have taught you some tricks," smiled Balboa, lunging like a swordsman.

"I am much obliged to you, sir, the more so because all Spain is aware of your prowess as a fencer."[2]

The first class started at dawn the next day. Balboa was waiting in the yard outside his hut in his shirtsleeves. The morning chill invited exercise; he put a sword into Hernando's hands and began explaining technique. Now and then he would make some encouraging comment about his pupil's movements, which were at first clumsy and futile, but little by little became more precise and coordinated.

But the training period was not to last long. A few days later the settlers of Santa María del Darién were shocked to learn from a proclamation, read in several corners of the village, that Governor Pedrarias had started proceedings for a "trial of residency" against Balboa. A long list of charges had been drawn up by the governor himself, based on unfavorable information supplied by Enciso and attributed to the early settlers: Balboa was accused of being responsible for the death of Nicuesa, and ordered to pay a fine of several thousand gold castilians. In the meantime he was to be imprisoned. Balboa offered no resistance, but made it clear that he was sure that such was not the king's justice. He was convinced that following his discovery of the Southern Sea he could count on royal support.[3]

The imprisonment caused havoc in the little settlement. Most of the Darién veterans sided with Balboa, whose popularity only infuriated the choleric governor further. Enciso and Colmenares were doing all they could to discredit the prisoner, but he had friends among the newcomers too, such as Bishop Quevedo and Doña Isabel. These influential people understood proper recognition of merit in service, and on the practical level realized that Balboa's authority over the soldiers and the local people was a direct result of his energy and charisma. Under his leadership, Darién had three very successful years: the villages were at peace, and there was work and food enough for everybody.

The bishop managed to convince Licentiate Gaspar de Espinosa, the new mayor, that Pedrarias was exceeding the limits of his authority in trumping up the charges; the mayor exonerated Balboa of all guilt, but ordered him to pay the fine to Enciso. Pedrarias made an attempt to have Balboa sent to Spain in chains, but finally gave in to the views of the bishop and agreed to release the prisoner, hoping to find some sort of mission to send him away from the town and his many friends.

So Balboa was free, but things had changed in the colony. There was a widespread uneasiness among the settlers, not only because of the controversy over Balboa, but also because feelings of frustration and disappointment were developing as people came to realize that the easy gold they had dreamed of was nonexistent. They had to face the fact that there was hostility in this country: the Indians were no longer bringing gifts as they had before Balboa's imprisonment, the climate was oppressive and gold was very difficult to obtain. To add to their problems, a fire destroyed the storehouse, while other foods brought from Spain rotted and had to be thrown away. At first the rich silks and velvets had been bartered in exchange for gold and pearls, but as time wore on, food became the main concern and the travelers returned the gold to the original settlers in exchange for any kind of victuals. One man was seen crying in the streets from starvation, dying under the gaze of the onlookers. Others, still in their elegant garb, went out to the fields to eat grass. Only a few understood that work could alleviate the situation, and went to the woods to get timber which they could sell. The busiest men in the colony were the gravediggers.

Pedrarias was deeply disappointed by his first months in the colony.[4] For a while, he considered returning to Spain and leaving the administration of Darién to his associates, but the members of the council opposed this course. His health was suffering, a new experience for the man with the "constitution of iron." To reduce the number of complaining Spaniards around him, he ordered a ship to sail to Cuba with all those who were dissatisfied; others he sent on missions of exploration under various leaders, Balboa included; and, following medical advice, he arranged for himself and his family to move to a place by the Corobari River, a few miles from Darién, where the air was said to be healthier.

Several of de Soto's friends left on the ship for Cuba,

among them Juan Vespucci, the navigator, and Bernal Díaz del Castillo, a soldier. Hernando moved to the new site with his master, and continued his daily discovery of the New World in all its aspects, and of the violent and disparate human elements with which he must now deal. It must have seemed to him like living on the third day of creation. The land was swampy and torrential tropical rains were a daily occurrence, creating a very different landscape from the sparsely covered plains of Extremadura. The jungle fascinated the Spaniards, inspiring them with feelings of awe and terror. The strange fauna and luxuriant vegetation were all of unfamiliar shapes and colors; the variety of butterflies, hummingbirds and exotic flowers were a constant source of delight to their astonished eyes. There were nettles and ferns of gigantic size, monumental trees such as the royal palm, the balsa tree, laurel and redwood and the silk cotton tree, jumbled together in dense thickets of reeds and enormous canes. There were enticing fruits: mammee, guanabana, guava, avocado. Palm trees abounded, from which the Indians made strong, lightweight lances and water pipes; from the rubber tree they extracted a strange white sap they put to many uses. Great armies of ants paraded through the jungle, sometimes devouring an entire copse or plantation. Trees were covered with parasites, orchids and lianas that sheltered a shrewdness of chattering monkeys and companies of parrots that kept up a continuous performance. Beneath them, the earth was covered with leaves, roots and dead trees, rotting in a dank, oppressive atmosphere and seeming to feed on the air itself.

In this environment man was clearly inferior to nature, and the white man to the Indian. The Spaniards could hold their own in war and in hunting the larger animals, but simply could not deal with insects and reptiles, or the diseases that terrified them. The mysterious tropical nights were filled with superstitious horror as the men thought of malaria, mosquitoes, vampires, pythons, deadly spiders and locusts, while the water held the famous "serpent with legs," as Vespucci had described the alligators he had once exhibited in Florence, and the piranha fish, which attacked both animals and men.

Such was the jungle that the white men had to contend with in a struggle which was to continue for centuries and is not over to this day. To the Indians, the jungle was a great ally; to the Spaniards, it was a testing ground for their stamina and a daily challenge. So it was not surprising that by the end of 1514, less than half of the members of the once brilliant fleet remained: more than five hundred had died and hundreds more had returned to Spain or gone to more clement parts of the Indies.

The remaining captains developed a hatred for the new surroundings that were proving so hostile. Rather than adapting to the environment as Balboa had done, they decided that violence would be the easiest and most profitable course. This was the very opposite of Balboa's philosophy, shared by most of the old settlers and by Bishop Quevedo. So there gradually evolved in the colony a split into two political parties, even though Balboa had been set free and the governor made a show of seeking his opinion in the organization of several expeditions.

Hernando's fencing was progressing well, and he was benefiting, too, from the drill that Morales had set for all Pedrarias's halberdiers. De Soto stood out among them, and had earned the praise of Morales and the respect of Doña Isabel and her daughters, to the point where he was regarded almost as a member of the family rather than a servant. To the girls, he appeared as a young hero, always in good spirits and prepared to organize games and excursions, or bring home exotic flowers and fruits, animals and birds.[5]

Pedrarias recovered from his illness and was able to work again, organizing exploratory parties to the areas around the coasts of the Southern Sea. He sent Juan de Ayora with four hundred men to found three new towns, but the lieutenant general was more interested in fast results and easy looting, and in a short time he had destroyed all the goodwill that was left among the natives, and that amity which Balboa had striven to create.

At first, such chieftains as Ponca and Comogre welcomed the "friends of Balboa," and had given them food and golden artifacts. But Ayora demanded more of everything; he took women by force, set villages on fire and introduced torture in order to obtain information about imaginary treasures. The Indians reacted with vengeance and hatred. There was no limit to Ayora's cruelty. Forgotten was the reading of the Requerimiento and the observance of the merciful and humane conduct prescribed by the king. He tortured the Indians with fire, or had them eaten alive by dogs; many of them he hanged, and others he imprisoned for slaves, first branding them for the slave market. On his return he used presents of slaves to mollify the governor and other authorities. He then complained of being ill, and arranged for a passage back to Spain on the next ship. After his departure, it was learned that he had managed to smuggle some gold aboard, gold that had cost the goodwill of all the Indians in the area.

Chieftain Pocorosa succeeded in capturing some of the Spaniards from Ayora's raid; they had tortured his people in search of treasure and raped his wife and daughters before his eyes. He had three of them tied up and clay funnels put down their throats, through which molten gold was poured as he said, "Chica oro, chica oro," that is, "Choke on gold, choke on gold."[6]

Two ships from Castile arrived at Darién in March of 1515. Among the news and orders they brought were letters from the king for Balboa, conferring upon him the titles of adelantado de la mar del sur and of governor and captain general of the provinces of Coiba and Panama. Thus royal justice was finally administered, the king having learned with great satisfaction of the discovery of the Pacific Ocean, and having decided to lend Balboa full support. Pedrarias, however, seized the letters and refused to deliver them.[7] Discovering this, Doña Isabel sent Hernando with a message to Bishop Quevedo in secret, and he in turn went to the governor to protest his action and demand a meeting of the City Council. At that meeting, Pedrarias insisted that he could not deliver the letters until Balboa's trial of residency was over, to which the bishop responded that his retaining the titles constituted grave disobedience and disloyalty to the king. However, not all of the members of the council supported the bishop's position, and the session ended in deadlock.

Undeterred, the bishop delivered a vehement sermon from the pulpit next morning, when almost all the Spaniards and many Indians were present.

"We are free men," he said, "who have come here to serve our king. We will do nothing contrary to the service of God or the will of the king. To intercept letters from him to his subjects is to deprive both of their freedom! Let us remember the great service Balboa rendered to the Crown of Castile in discovering the Southern Sea. No one could oppose the king's decision to reward one of his best servants."[8]

Murmurs of approval echoed through the church, where everybody was aware of what had happened to the letters and titles. A meeting of the council was called at once. Bishop Quevedo was severe and indignant, and reiterated his former statement.

"Pedrarias, you are committing a crime and a felony. The king will not forgive you, and you will also be responsible to God for it," announced the prelate, to the governor's astonishment. He did not wish to have the Church against him, and he also recalled the arguments put forward by his wife. Finally he yielded.

"Very well! It's almost night now. You, Morales, ask Balboa to come and see me tomorrow morning. We will deliver the title deeds to him and will also entrust him with a mission, so that he may show how well he deserves them.''[9]

Morales had started to use Hernando for special assignments so it was he who was sent to alert Balboa. He found Balboa outside his hut, smoking tobacco, a strange habit he had acquired from the local people of this new land. Hernando told Balboa that Pedrarias would hand over the title deeds and appointments.

Pedrarias saw Balboa the next morning and gave him his reasons for delaying the delivery of the titles and letters. Then, as the council had decided, he handed them over in accordance with the king's orders.

Balboa now felt that new perspectives for action were open to him, and again declared his loyalty to the Crown and the governor. He then went to thank the bishop and Doña Isabel, who were with de Soto and a group of friends.

One of the exploratory parties sent by the governor was under the command of Enciso and his nephew, also called Pedrarias. He went to the region of Cenú,[10] and attempted to gain the confidence of the Indians by goodwill and legal procedures. His first act was to comply with the reading of the Requerimiento through an interpreter. The native warriors were silent as they listened to the translation, and heard about the basis of the Christian faith and the divine inspiration of the papal bull which had given the king of Spain authority to rule over the peoples of the Indies. The scene was often repeated in those days: on one side were the Spaniards sweating under the blazing sun with their armor, helmets, lances and harquebuses; on the other were the Indians adorned in red paint and feathers, with bows and poisoned arrows. At last their chief spoke, slowly and with great dignity, as the interpreter translated.

"We agree with you that there is only one God; this we have always believed. But that the pope rules the universe and can give away our lands to your king—we think he must have been drunk when he did it! Giving away lands that are not his—let him come and take them! His head will end up on a stake just like the ones we have here."[11]

At a signal from the chieftain, some of the braves disappeared into the jungle and returned with six stakes, on which were impaled the smoked dried heads of former Indian enemies. The scribe was keeping a record on a parchment of this exchange. The chief added calmly, "As you will observe, we rule over this land as our fathers and grandfathers did before us, and we have no need of another lord."

"I beg you to try and understand our reasons," returned Enciso. "If you submit willingly, you will be protected by the Crown of Castile. Otherwise I shall have to make war on you, your lands will be taken by force, and you will all be made slaves."

"Rather, we shall have your head on a stake along with the rest of our collection!" cried the chieftain, raising his bow as a signal for his men to attack.[12]

The fighting along the beach was fierce at first, but soon the harquebuses proved more convincing than the points of the Requerimiento. The Indians escaped to the jungle, leaving three casualties among the Spaniards, men who were to die that night from the poisoned arrows.

Enciso continued his explorations along the coast of Cartagena, doing violence to those in the villages as he tried to glean information about the gold mines of Nocri. By the time he returned to Darién he had accumulated much booty, and handed over both gold and slaves to the governor.

When Pedrarias heard of the difficulties and dangers of the enterprise, he conceived the idea of sending Balboa on a mission so arduous that the Indians or disease would be the end of him. The region he decided upon was Dabaybe, in the Gulf of Urabá, and as further insurance for his plan he chose the two hundred least capable men in the settlement to be Balboa's companions. This old trick would enable him to accuse Balboa of inefficiency, or of being incapable of delegating responsibility to his team. As expected, Balboa accepted the task, though regretting that he was not to go to the Pacific Ocean zones, where he had authority and knew his ground. His party set out in twenty canoes.

The assigned area was most inhospitable, plagued with mosquitoes and alligators in an atmosphere of suffocating heat and humidity. At one point along the river, the group was ambushed by a large party of Indians. Balboa managed to hold them off, and finally made a landing on the riverbank, but many of his men were drowned, unable to swim, while others were killed in battle. One of the dead was Pedrarias's man Luis Carrillo, the second-in-command, and Balboa himself was wounded. In this his first defeat, he lost over half his men, barely managing to get them into canoes and rafts to return to Santa María la Antigua.

The news of Balboa's defeat incensed the governor.[13] He also learned that even as the man from Extremadura was recovering from his wounds, he was planning an expedition to the Pacific with a friend named Garavito and several men from Cuba. The idea of Balboa's winning fame and glory on the other side of the country while he remained behind in the regions afflicted by insects and diseases was intolerable to Pedrarias. He had his adversary locked up in a wooden cage until the council could decide whether he should be executed or sent back to Spain. Once again Doña Isabel appealed to the bishop for help, using de Soto as a messenger. Quevedo hurried to the governor and urged him to release Balboa immediately, threatening to report the entire matter to the king either in a dispatch or possibly even in person. Pedrarias realized that such a course would be extremely detrimental to his position, and had Balboa released from the cage and put in prison.

Bishop Quevedo was not satisfied with such half-measures and, with Doña Isabel's approval, he urged Pedrarias to effect a complete reconciliation in the interest of good government, such as giving Balboa the hand in marriage of one of his daughters still in Spain. Only thus could there be convincing evidence of a reconciliation between Pedrarias and Balboa.

De Soto realized what was going on. For hours at a time Pedrarias and his wife conversed in private. Hernando was certain that the plan had been shaped by Doña Isabel, who was clearly fond of Balboa.[14] The next morning, Morales was given orders to release Balboa and take him to the bishop for a conference. Hernando was glad to be one of the halberdiers in the escort, noting that those present at the meeting were the governor, Bishop Quevedo and Doña Isabel.

The bishop announced the marriage in church to silence the tongues of Balboa's enemies. The banns stated that Doña María Peñalosa, second daughter of Pedrarias, presently living in Segovia, was to marry the adelantado de la mar del sur, a nobleman from a distinguished house in Jerez de los Caballeros. Doña Isabel brought the ceremony to a close by giving a luncheon for the bishop, the captains and the senior officers, and peace and cordiality appeared restored. De Soto was seated at a table with the other young people, relieved that he could at last be open about his friendship with Balboa, his countryman and hero. Pedrarias presided over the main table, severe but courteous, his long beard giving him a biblical appearance. Toasts were proposed to the king and to the affianced couple, of whom only one was present.

De Soto later accompanied Balboa to his hut to collect his belongings and move them to quarters more appropriate for the governor's son-in-law. Only Leoncico was waiting for them at the hut; Anayansi had disappeared.

Having placated the bishop, the governor returned to his old schemes. While urging Balboa to prepare his next expedition to the lands near the Southern Sea, he was also arranging for Gaspar de Morales to undertake a mission to the same area with 150 men. Morales summoned de Soto.

This would be de Soto's first real military mission. Although he was the youngest member of the party, he had already gained some prestige as a fencer, halberdier and horseman. Doña Isabel and the girls showered him with advice and warnings, and Balboa too wished him well.[15]

Hernando left his copy of *Amadís of Gaul* with Doña Isabel.

As in that book of adventures, the protagonist sought companions-in-arms with whom to share the coming dangers; he soon found two who were to be his friends for many years, Hernan Ponce de León and Francisco Campañón. The three undoubtedly were the youngest and liveliest group of the expedition.

The column made its way toward the Pacific Ocean and crossed the isthmus over swampy ground infested with mosquitoes and other dangers. With the help of two big dogs and some Indian guides, they finally reached the other side of Chieftain Tutibra's territory. He met them peacefully. Morales told him that they wished to explore the islands for pearls, and the generous Indian provided them with four canoes. Half the men came on the canoe expedition, including Pizarro and de Soto and his friends.

They reached the lands of Chieftain Tunaca, who lived not far from the pearl islands. He received them cordially and gave a banquet in their honor, at which he suggested that they should rest before continuing their trip. Morales was adamant, however, and they set off in a westerly direction at daybreak. They soon realized that this was a mistake, as a forty-knot gale started up from a northeasterly direction. They were threatened by huge waves all that day, and spent an exhausting night in the canoes before reaching land. At sunset they landed on the island, giving thanks that they were all together and safe. It appeared that the island was inhabited. Soon a large group of Indian women appeared and the soldiers captured them at once. The Indian warriors arrived uttering their battle cries, and a fierce fight ensued; Hernando used his lance as best he could. The Spaniards won, thanks to their superior weapons and to the Indians' terror of their trained dogs, which attacked on command.

Having made this demonstration of strength, Morales tried to gain his ends by friendly means. He had some Indians in his party serve as interpreters, and they explained to the natives that they would be well advised to make peace with the white men, since they were far stronger, and follow the example of the chieftains on the mainland. Finally the chief of the island gave in and accepted the gifts Pizarro was offering. He invited the newcomers to his house for a feast, where he was told in detail what they were seeking. He acted with the lavishness of a prince: calling for a basket of pearls, he gave it to Morales, pointing out one of them in particular. Pear-shaped and the size of a nut, it was the largest pearl the Spaniards had ever seen—thirty-one carats and exquisitely beautiful.

Though Balboa was supposed to have jurisdiction over this area, Pedrarias had instructed Morales to take possession of the land on his behalf. He gave it the name of Isla de las Flores, and also took possession of the Southern Sea, though some veterans such as Pizarro, who had accompanied Balboa in the same ceremony three years earlier, kept quiet and looked the other way. Lastly, Morales explained the Christian doctrine to the chieftain, inviting him to be baptized and to send a present of pearls to the king of Spain.

In a dignified manner, the Indian replied that he would submit to the ceremony to please his guests, agreed to the name "Pedrarias," and allowed Morales to act as god-father. He then invited a group of them, including Morales, Pizarro, Ponce and de Soto, to climb a nearby hill from which they could see the mainland. He told them that to the south lay the kingdoms of Birú and there gold was to be found in abundance.

This was the first the Spaniards heard of Peru.

Pizarro, too, was from Extremadura and he made friends with young de Soto and took him hunting. He confided to de Soto the information he had been gathering about the region called *Birú* and he expressed the hope that one day an expedition might be mounted to explore this new country.

With the rich booty of pearls and some gold safely in hand, Morales decided to return to the mainland. The rest of his soldiers had been left under the command of one of his men, Peñalosa, who had caused great resentment among the natives in Morales's absence by staging raids in several of the neighboring villages. So the Indians were in a vindictive frame of mind when the canoe party returned. They imprisoned ten of Morales's men in the jungle, and mustered a thousand warriors to attack the Spaniards.

Morales's only chance of survival was to take the initiative; he gave command of half his force to Pizarro, and led the other half in an attempt to encircle the Indian camp. At daybreak they attacked with dogs and harquebuses, taking the Indians by surprise. The natives defended themselves valiantly, but the whole affair was an absolute massacre, which left seven hundred Indians dead or wounded, as the rest fled into the jungle. Morales demonstrated his cruelty when he ordered nineteen chiefs to be beheaded, together with several women and children, "to inspire fear all over these lands,"[16] as he said. De Soto had fought bravely, and was proud to have fought at the side of such an experienced soldier as Pizarro, but he felt only nausea and disgust mingled with shame at the execution of defenseless prisoners; yet, as a subordinate, he had to keep silent.[17]

The party's return to the Atlantic coast was troubled by one skirmish after another, as word of the atrocities spread, turning almost all the tribes and villages against them. They marched for nine days under almost continuous combat conditions across flooded lands so that they had to fight waist-high in water or in swamps infested by alligators and snakes, with swarms of mosquitoes around their heads. At last, the survivors reached Chieftain Careta's territories by the Northern Sea, and as he was a staunch friend and ally of Balboa, he helped them, letting them eat and rest before they went on to Darién.

Morales had lost over half his soldiers. However, he had succeeded in transporting his entire treasure of gold and pearls, and had much information about the lands on the other side of the isthmus. Pizarro told him of Hernando's manly and courageous deportment throughout the expedition. Morales promoted Hernando to captain of lancers.[18]

He was certainly on the way to greater adventures: he had seen others return with pearls and pots of gold. And he had been promoted to a rank far exceeding that befitting his age. He was only seventeen.

THE TRIUMPH OF THE GODS

VI

O miserable man
What wouldst thou?
Wilt thou dare
The all-hallow'd to profane?
No mortal-born
May lift the veil
Till I myself shall raise.[1]

Schiller

Gaspar de Morales knew that de Soto was privileged in Pedrarias's house. He was certain that this promotion would be welcomed by the governor and his wife. Moreover, he was bringing a large quantity of pearls, including the fabled pear-shaped specimen he had received as a tribute from the chief at the Island of Flowers. He hoped that all this would offset the outrages committed in his name, which might already be known in Darién. Doña Isabel and her daughters were indeed much impressed by the pearl, and pleased at the promotion of the young captain. The pearl, which they nicknamed "the Orphan," was later to be presented by Doña Isabel to Empress Isabel of Portugal, and mentioned by Cervantes and Lope de Vega.

Unfortunately for Balboa and for most members of the colony, Bishop Quevedo decided to return to Spain, assuming that after Balboa's marriage all would be peaceful in Darién. Thus comforted, the bishop boarded the ship and left the colony forever.

Whenever Pedrarias had available men, he continued to send exploratory parties out on missions. One such party, led by Gonzalo de Badajoz, was to explore the coast and seek a passage to the Southern Sea. The governor knew that the main concern of the Court was to find such a route, without which neither the discoveries of Columbus nor the voyages of Vespucci would be complete. Portugal was progressing with its explorations and conducting trade in the Moluccas and the spice islands of India, while the Spanish ships could not find a passage to reach the same areas.

Badajoz started out with 130 men from a place called Nombre de Dios near the narrowest part of the isthmus; here lay the bones of the men from Nicuesa's expedition, whitened by the sun, next to the crosses which commemorated the tragedy. De Soto went with the party as Badajoz' lieutenant, and saw how he handled the men's fear at this sight. He ordered the ship to return to Darién, and gave the men an encouraging talk before leading them up the mountains of Capira. From there they proceeded to the lands of Chieftains Totanangua, Tataracherubi and Nata, the last of which was adjacent to the Southern Sea. In all these places Badajoz used a plan of action which seemed to him the most profitable; he would kidnap the Indian chief and release him later upon payment of a ransom in gold and a promise of allegiance to the Crown of Spain. In this way he extorted 6000 gold pesos from the first tribe, and 10,000 and 15,000 respectively from the second and third. A peso or castellano would be worth 290 U.S. dollars (in 1985 currency).

Gonzalo de Badajoz showered these people with his usual gifts: glass beads, axes, mirrors and colored cloth caps, all of which they traded for gold, pearls and precious stones. What especially impressed the Spaniards were the huge gold nuggets, some of which would weigh two castellanos. Having amassed over eighty thousand pesos in ransom money, spoils and gifts, Badajoz decided to stay in the salutary lands of Chief Nata through the rainy season.

When the worst of the winter was over, they proceeded westward, capturing and holding for ransom several more Indian chiefs. One of these, Panriba, whom the Spaniards named "Paris," tried to outwit Badajoz by sending a man to him who told him that he knew some villages where plenty of gold could be found. Badajoz sent a party of forty men to explore but they found only a few abandoned shacks. In the meantime Paris charged Badajoz' remaining men with some four thousand warriors, causing many casualties among the Spaniards. Those who were left rallied in the center of the village in square formation, protecting themselves with their shields and swords. Badajoz ordered de Soto to try to break through the Indian ranks, while he, too, led a charge, and managed to bring eighty men out of the village, all wounded, including one who had been struck by a lance eleven times. Seventy dead Spaniards were left behind in the village, as well as the ill-gotten booty of gold, artifacts and clothing. Finally the devastated remnants of the party came to a halt in order to rest and attempt to cure some of the wounded with primitive methods such as applying hot irons or boiling fat taken from Indian corpses. The most desperate cases were then placed in canoes, while Badajoz led the others by land. The march was a somber one, and the already wounded men sustained new attacks by the Indians. Nevertheless, Badajoz managed to attack several villages and gather more booty. On one of the nearby islands they were welcomed by the chief, Chame, but Badajoz resorted to his old trick of kidnapping him and holding him for ransom. The Spaniards returned to the mainland by way of a cove called the Bay of Clams and the island of Taboga where they stayed for a month, performing the usual attacks and looting. Once back on the mainland in Chepo the Indians retaliated again, killing the cruel and much-hated Pérez de la Rua, an assistant to Badajoz. With less than fifty men remaining, Badajoz ordered a return to Darién, crossing the isthmus through a region of ever-increasing hostility. In the space of a few years the newcomers had destroyed all that Balboa had achieved through his intelligent policy of patience, peace and alliance with the Indians.

Pedrarias was not in Darién when Badajoz returned. He had set out with three hundred men in an attempt to overthrow Chief Pocorosa and other leaders. He landed in the port of Acla where he built a fortress of logs and mud. But the old man's will was stronger than his health, and he was obliged to return to Darién, leaving Captain Gabriel Rojas in charge. In Darién, he met Badajoz and de Soto. He accused Gonzalo de Badajoz of incompetence for having lost the gold during Paris's assault, aside from some four hundred slaves he should have taken.[2] He ordered his assistant, Espinosa, to make ready another expedition to bring back the gold and chastise Paris for his resistance.

Pedrarias ruled as a dictator in Darién. Instead of having the officers freely elected, he himself appointed *regidores,* or aldermen, from among his trusted men. This and other excesses of authority had already been reported to the Court by many, among them Fernández de Oviedo, who brought gold from Darién to King Fernando. Spain in general had an unfavorable impression of Pedrarias, but his family connections and long history of military service were of significance to the Crown. Nevertheless, the king promised Oviedo that he would take the matter up as soon as he arrived in Seville. This he never did, for in the little village of Madrigalejos in Extremadura, the Catholic king, who had presided over the beginning of an era of greatness for Spain and the opening of the road to the New World, died. Until the young King Charles could arrive from Flanders, Cardinal Cisneros took over the reins of government with a firm hand.

Pedrarias heard the news months later and felt that the Regency, while it lasted, would strengthen his position. In the meantime he wanted to accelerate the discoveries under his governorship, and sent Espinosa on a journey of exploration with some 130 men, with de Soto among them. At the same time, he started planning a mission for his new son-in-law, Balboa, to arm his ships and sail to the Southern Sea. Gaspar de Espinosa was a lawyer by profession who had become an explorer only by chance. He crossed the lands of Chief Comagre, who, with Pocorosa, had managed to raise an army of three thousand braves. But Espinosa had both hunting dogs and cavalry, which terrified the Indians since they had never seen horses before. So with little difficulty the Spaniards reached Paris's territory, where an army of four thousand Indians awaited them. There ensued a series of battles without major progress in either direction, until a division commanded by Captain Valenzuela arrived as reinforcement. De Soto was in this group, and this added strength enabled them to capture three of the Indian chiefs and extract from them information about the location of the treasure Badajoz had lost as he fled. This they found in five trunks of hardened leather, and returned to their barracks in triumph with eighty thousand pesos in gold. As the rainy season had started, Espinosa decided they would stay where they were, so they built a church and arranged for the christening of some of the Indian women, with the aid and sanction of Chief Chicacotia. The Guaymies Indian women were most beautiful, and captivated the Spaniards with their slender grace. The most charming of all was a girl named Sinca, "fresh as a mountain wildflower,"[3] who fell madly in love with Espinosa, and for several days all else was forgotten as the two reveled in their newly discovered paradise. The bearded Spaniard and the passionate and exquisitely lovely Indian girl presided over banquets and festivities where the maddening rhythm of the drums and the sensual ritual *areitos* dances heightened the excitement.

But the natives were bent on revenge against the lewd and greedy foreigners. The same drums that beat the rhythm of the dances were also sending messages through the jungle to the growing band of Indians, numbering about two thousand, who were determined to do away with the Spaniards once and for all. Sinca heard about the plan and warned her lover, who finally came to his senses and prepared his four hundred men for the fight. In early July, a most bloody battle took place, and the Indians, though heroic, had to yield to the discipline and stern soldiery of the Spaniards. Many of Espinosa's men were distinguished veterans of the Italian and African campaigns; the forces consisted of companies of pikemen, shieldmen and harquebusiers, supported by a regiment of cavalry and a pack of hunting dogs. To the determined charges of the Indians, who had to overcome great fear to fight such heavily armed men who were thought to have supernatural powers, the Spaniards answered with systematically alternating gunfire and showers of arrows from the crossbows. From behind the close wall of shields which protected them from the Indians' spears came well-aimed blows with lance or sword, far deadlier than the Indians' wooden maces. Then the cavalry would charge, putting the terrified Indians to flight with hordes of ferocious dogs at their heels.

As soon as the attackers had been repelled, Espinosa, who suffered heavy losses, ordered his men to retreat to a safe place, and sent Hernán Ponce and Bartolomé Hurtado to explore some of the islands and gather booty. Such expeditions revealed strange aspects of the remote civilizations that had some small contact with the outside world. In one place they captured an athletic Indian whose beard was shaped just like a Spaniard's; somewhere else they saw what looked like a playing field for ball games, with a stone ring through which a stone ball was thrown, the procedure having become more a religious practice than a sport. When they arrived at Acla, Espinosa's party met Balboa's, which was preparing to travel to the Pacific. The discussion between the two leaders was not cordial, Balboa treating Espinosa in a cold and aloof manner.

Upon Espinosa's return to Darién, Pedrarias gave him a hero's welcome, especially since he was bringing such vast booty. One fifth was set aside for the king, and the remaining 100,000 pesos in gold—about 29 million U.S. dollars—were distributed, as were the two thousand slaves they brought to please the governor. The old man had formed the habit of gambling with the other captains, using slaves instead of money; it was said that one night he gambled away a hundred slaves at cards.

De Soto returned to Darién later, as he and his friend Hernán Ponce had been ordered by Espinosa to explore a region of Panama where the climate was thought to be more salubrious. Hernando was amazed to find there so many pearls, so much game and strange wildlife, from whales to giant lizards, up to thirty feet long and capable of attacking boats and wounding men with their fearsome tails. He also perceived a profound artistic sensibility among the Indians; this found expression in pottery work and painting as well as in their sculpture and their outstanding skill as goldsmiths. The witch doctors spoke of their mysterious god Tabira, the keeper of secrets.

By the time de Soto and his party returned to Darién, they were certain that the richest and most salutary areas of the region and the promise of greatest adventure lay not toward the Northern Sea but on the Pacific side, by the sea of Núñez de Balboa. Speaking to his old friend de Soto in Acla, Vasco Núñez must have thought that his star[4] was about to shine once more. With Pedrarias's permission, he had built the town of Puerto de Acla, where the governor himself already had a fort constructed and was about to prepare some brigantines for the exploration of the Southern Sea. With eighty men and money provided by Pedrarias, he established a municipal government and was making ready for the trip south with shipbuilding lumber. The port of San Miguel, at the mouth of the Balsas River, was twenty-two leagues away. The administration of the region was soon organized on either coast, as well as trade relations with the Indians, who started helping him with the work. He began, wisely, by planting corn and other crops, so as to have food for his men in the future.

Balboa was the adelantado of the Southern Sea, and governor of Panama and Coiba. His dream was to explore the new kingdoms which the Indians told him lay to the south, the fabulous land of Biru, or Peru, as some called it. But such an enterprise required ships, men and money, which he saw more hope of obtaining once he got away from his cruel father-in-law. Here at least he had authority and enough independence to allow him to carry his sword confidently once more. He maintained a continuous line of communication with Darién through the Indian messengers who traveled back and forth along the coastal route.

As Balboa returned to his recently completed house one afternoon, he saw a figure inside. It was Anayansi, who had followed him silently through the mountains, and was never to leave him again. Balboa regarded her as a symbol of his attachment to the lands he had discovered and served; to him she was the fusion of two worlds in a way that transcended time, distance and convention.[5]

Pedrarias, however, feared what would happen if Balboa attained excessive prosperity or complete success, and at a given time planned to take over the exploration of the Southern Sea. His own advisers finally convinced him to abandon the scheme, as by staying in Darién he would be in closer touch with news from Spain under the Regency, and the establishment of new authorities and rules for the Indies. It was said that monks of the Order of Saint Jerome were on their way with instructions from Cardinal Cisneros to establish order and justice in the affairs of the New World.

Balboa learned of this development, and in order to expedite his business, organized with some of his friends the Company of the Southern Sea, the first private enterprise ever established for the purpose of discovering kingdoms and conquering territories in the Indies. His friend Hernando de Aguilar contributed the money, and was to be Balboa's agent in Antigua del Darién; Diego Rodriguez was to be the manager, and Diego de Tobilla, Beltran de Guevara and Rogerio de Lauria the other partners. The shipbuilding operation meant trimming planks and transporting them overland, as Balboa considered the wood inferior on the Pacific coast. Everything had to be carried, with the Indians' cooperation, to the Gulf of San Miguel. There was no time to lose as Pedrarias had given him only eighteen months for the whole undertaking; the deadline was June 24, Saint John's Day, 1518, when Balboa was expected back from the unknown kingdoms over the new sea, preferably victorious and bearing a rich booty.

As a precaution, Balboa sent his friend Francisco Campañón, a nephew of Albítez, to explore the country along the Balsas River where the shipbuilding was to take place; the information was favorable. Balboa had a warehouse built in the highlands to store the materials which were starting to arrive from Acla. The lumber, already cut and numbered, was transported by hundreds of Indians and thirty black men who were among the people sent by Pedrarias. Balboa traveled back and forth, from Acla to the highland house and then to the Balsas River where he would gaze at the bottom of the clear Southern Sea, his own Pacific Ocean. All this gave him an awesome feeling of responsibility. He knew he was the first European to set eyes on it, to have broken the mystery which for thousands of years had been kept inviolate from the foreigners, as though it had been ordained by old mythological rites. All the speculations of the Middle Ages, all of Columbus's exploratory voyages had led to this end: find the promised lands and then the passage to the other sea. And it was he, Balboa, who had been granted this privilege, or was it this terrible fate of breaking the secrets of gods? The Indian witch doctors sensed it too. They regarded Balboa with sympathy and respect, and when, in their midnight rites, they addressed their god Tabira, whose golden statue evoked a being from the depths of time, they referred to Balboa as the white magician,[6] the most powerful of them all, who had seen the great sea from a mountain and who had later been followed by lesser chieftains who were destructive and evil like a curse from hell.

Balboa noted other ominous incidents. One afternoon in Acla as he was strolling across a plaza wearing his plumed helmet, a vulture swooped down, snatched the helmet in its claws and dropped it in the street. He hesitated a moment before retrieving it, a prey to old Spanish superstitions; but with a joke he dismissed his fears, setting all his friends laughing.

Before leaving for his headquarters in the Gulf of San Miguel, Balboa had another unpleasant experience. The modest Anayansi told him that his lifelong friend, Captain Francisco Garavito, had tried to take advantage of her. Enraged, Balboa summoned the offender, who, fearful of the terrible sword of the adelantado, babbled all kinds of explanations, apologies and pledges. Seeing him so contrite, Balboa decided not to impose a physical punishment, but humiliated him verbally and then forgot the whole distasteful incident, leaving Leoncico with Anayansi as a constant guard. Garavito, on the other hand, was filled with resentment and hatred, and was ever seeking an opportunity for revenge.[7]

Balboa needed all his courage and endurance to build his ships on the new ocean. He had to overcome staggering obstacles. First of all, the wood so laboriously brought from the Atlantic side was useless, as it was riddled with worms almost as soon as it arrived. Trees in the Balsas area had to be cut down and used for lumber after all; but when the boards were almost ready, there were floods which carried away a large quantity of the timber, so the shipyard was relocated to a nearby island. There was a serious shortage of food; the men barely had enough energy to work, and the adelantado himself was forced to eat roots. Finally the men managed to build a bridge over the Balsas River, and some of them were sent to the other side for supplies. Soon after, Bartolomé Hurtado arrived with sixty men sent by Pedrarias as reinforcements, and with their help Balboa was able to build two of the promised ships. While awaiting loads of sailcloth, pitch and rigging from Acla, Balboa took the two completed ships to one of the islands of pearls in search for food. He then sailed eastward, to Punta de Piñas, where his hundred men were impressed by a good number of whales.

Upon his return to San Miguel, Balboa found that the shipbuilding had slowed down. There were rumors abroad that the king had appointed a new governor to replace Pedrarias, a nobleman from Córdoba by the name of Lope de Sosa.

As a token of friendship and forgiveness, Balboa decided to send Garavito to Acla for iron, tar and other supplies, and to make inquiries about the new governor, who had, up till then, been governor of the Canary Islands. Garavito discovered nothing conclusive, but found reasons to go to Darién, where he continued his vengeance against Balboa by writing a statement accusing him of plotting against the governor and stealing his share in the spoils of the expeditions. This statement Garavito delivered to Pedrarias, adding that Balboa was holding up to mockery his sacred union with the house of Pedrarias by flaunting his relationship with Anayansi. With this condemnation he delivered Balboa's request for a one-year extension on his deadline for completion of the four ships owing to the grave difficulties encountered in the building.

Cunning as always, Pedrarias acted as surely as a cat that spots its prey in a trap. On the one hand, he handed over Garavito's accusation to be included in the trial of residency being conducted by Espinosa, now rich and proud, eager to emulate Balboa or destroy him. On the other, he spoke in defense of his son-in-law at the meeting of the council, and obtained a four-month extension of the deadline for the shipbuilding contract.

Meanwhile, thanks to Balboa's imagination and energy, things were progressing well. He had restored good relations with the Indian chiefs and was now obtaining help from them in the form of provisions and labor. His two hundred men were either working in the yard or accompanying him on expeditions. Every day he received reports of the kingdoms in the south, where, it was said, gold was used for the facades of buildings, clothing and ceremonial costumes, weapons and even domestic utensils.

He was watching a splendid sunset on Tortuga Island one evening when he remembered a Venetian astrologer, half-crazy, half-brilliant, who had accosted him some months earlier in Darién with the warning:

"Señor Adelantado, you have too much confidence in your good luck. You have discovered a great secret of the Universe, and the gods may demand their tribute. Watch your star carefully; if one day you see it too clearly, shining over your head, beware, for a great danger will threaten you. But if you manage to survive it, you will become the richest and most renowned commander in all the lands of the Indies."[8]

Balboa saw overhead a clear, bright star which he thought must be the one the astrologer had referred to. He realized he must face up to his destiny, whatever it might be.

Then he received Pedrarias's response to his request for further time on the contract. It contained an order for him to return to Acla since the governor had important, specific matters to discuss with him. Balboa considered the situation. He knew that if he were to consult his comrades-in-arms, the very consultation could be construed as rebellious. Furthermore, most of them, as his loyal friends, would advise him to disregard the governor and undertake further explorations on his own account. On the other hand, he thought that, if he obeyed, he would disprove the smears and rumors which had been directed against him; he would demonstrate his loyalty, and might perhaps obtain the additional time needed to complete the four ships, which were almost ready. Thus decided, at the end of 1518, he entrusted his command to Francisco Campañón and hastened to his headquarters before going on to Acla.

At Acla and Darién, all was in a turmoil. The rumor that a new governor might arrive, Pedrarias's summons to Balboa and the tyrannical authority they suffered had put the Spanish expedition in a state of agitation as they speculated about the fate of Balboa. Most favored him, but the few enemies he had were powerful.

Balboa arrived on the mainland almost unguarded, and was walking toward the fort at the head of the river when he was met by a group of soldiers, led by his old friend and comrade-in-arms, Francisco Pizarro.

"Surrender, Don Vasco," said he, wasting no words. "By order of the governor, I am to take you to Acla."

"What do you mean by this, Pizarro?" inquired Balboa. "You used not to greet me in this manner when you were my lieutenant."[9]

Pizarro lowered his gaze and said nothing, merely handing him the order of imprisonment, specifying that he was to be taken in chains. Balboa was too proud to discuss the matter further. He looked toward the Southern Sea, silvery gray and serene as a goddess, unaffected by the passing of time. He looked at the majestic motion of the ships, almost completed, with all their adventures before them. He looked finally at Pizarro, his erstwhile assistant and the second European to set eyes on the fabulous sea. Coldly and disdainfully he held out his arms so that the shackles could be put on by a soldier.

When the group reached Acla, the prisoner was taken

to the house of Juan de Castañeda, the pilot who had accompanied Balboa to the Pacific. Two days later Pedrarias himself arrived, attired in his most formal dress and wearing the symbols of his authority. "Do not sorrow over this imprisonment, my son," said the aging governor. "I had to do this to please de la Puente, the treasurer, and it will show your loyalty to be clearer and more brilliant than ever."

"I hope so, milord," retorted Balboa icily, "for you well know that I am innocent."[10]

The first necessity was to isolate Balboa from his friends. Pedrarias had already alienated Pizarro by having him imprison Balboa, letting him believe that he was to take Balboa's place. The others were in prison. He authorized Bartolomé Hurtado to seize the four ships, disregarding the existence of the Company of the Southern Sea. Espinosa was to conduct the entire trial, including Garavito's accusations. Pedrarias traveled to the other side of the isthmus to see the ships, the *San Cristóbal* and the *Santa María de la Buena Esperanza*, as well as the incomplete vessels.

But the trial was not proceeding as swiftly as Pedrarias wanted. Espinosa and the notary Cuadrado feared a possible revision of the case upon the arrival of the new governor, or inquiries by the Crown. So Garavito's denunciation of Balboa was rewritten to include an open accusation that the adelantado had instigated rebellion against the governor.

Pedrarias told Espinosa that the penalty for Balboa should be death.

Espinosa wrote up the order, establishing the basis of the sentence by accumulating all possible charges, including the ones from the old trial of residency which had already been settled. Here again were the death of Nicuesa, the imprisonment of Enciso, the failure of the Dabaybe expedition, the besmirching of Garavito's character and many other charges trumped up to serve Espinosa's own purposes and his master the governor's. Balboa was sentenced to death by beheading, together with his "accomplices" Argüello, Muñoz, Botello and Valderrábano. Garavito and the cleric Rodrigo Perez were acquitted.

Hernando de Soto heard the news on his return to Acla and was much grieved.[11] He knew he could do nothing, now that the bishop had left and Doña Isabel was in Darién; even she would have been powerless despite her sympathy for Balboa. Pedrarias was bitter and implacable. He had known since September of 1518 that Don Felipe de Sosa had accepted his governorship, and attributed that situation to Vasco Núñez and his friends. That afternoon de Soto obtained permission to visit the prisoner. The reunion was a moving one; they were countrymen, the veteran and the novice, the master and the fencing student, the discoverer of the Northern Sea and the son of Francisco Méndez.

When de Soto had gone, a friar arrived to hear Balboa's confession; the sentence was to be carried out the next morning.

At dawn on that 21st day of January 1519, the roosters were heralding the day and a gray cloud was looming over the mountains of Acla and its fetid jungle as the drums started their death roll. A silent crowd already filled the square, sadness and fear showing in every face. The neighboring Indians were also watching the strange ritual of these white men whom they had thought demigods, now obviously indulging in base passions and intrigue. The native drums echoed the ceremony, carrying the news to the ends of the land.

The town crier led the procession from the prison house to the plaza, shouting as he went: "This is the judgment ordered by our king and by his lieutenant Pedrarias upon this man for treachery and usurping the lands due to the Royal Crown!"

"That is a lie and a fabricated charge!" shouted Balboa

as he marched on defiantly with his head high. "I have never considered such a thing; my only wish has been to serve the king loyally and to augment his power as far as I was capable. I am an adelantado appointed by the king, and I appeal this sentence to the Crown and the Royal Council of the Indies."[12]

Espinosa was prepared for such a demand. He had already drawn up a document of appeal which the scribe Muñoz delivered to Pedrarias, who was watching the whole event from a window. He at once returned the answer that there would be no involvement of Spain, and that the sentence must be carried out as scheduled.

It was almost noon when Balboa, having received the last rites, laid his fair head on the block. When the ax fell, there was a shudder of horror in the crowd, and from the jungle was heard a desolate, almost animal cry. It was the voice of the loyal Anayansi, incapable of fathoming the perversity of the souls of Balboa's enemies.[13]

Pedrarias was to display his rancor in a truly barbaric manner. After the execution, a soldier impaled Balboa's head on a pike which was set up in a corner of the plaza. Even in death he seemed to reproach those who abused justice. The other executions followed and more pikes were lined up beside the first, but it was midafternoon when the third "accomplice" was beheaded. The superstitious crowd started to murmur that following the deaths of Valderrábano, Botello and Muñoz, God himself was intervening to save the last life by causing night to fall. Some knelt before the house where the governor was hidden, begging him to spare Argüello.

"I would sooner have judgment fall upon me!" responded Pedrarias hoarsely, and gave the order for the last execution to proceed, as the crowd wept and prayed.

In the moonlight the five impaled heads cast bizarre shadows on the plaza. Hernando de Soto came to claim Balboa's body so that it could be given a Christian burial. Anayansi was kneeling beside it, and Leoncico was licking his master's boots. Hernando and the Indian girl buried the body on a hill nearby; afterward Anayansi told de Soto that she was returning to her people in the jungle, who were certainly less savage than these men who came preaching doctrines of love and were now beheading and humiliating their best men.[14]

Sadly Hernando returned to his quarters. On a street corner he passed a man, half crazy or drunk, who was waving his arms in the air. It was the Italian astrologer, Micer Codro, who announced:

"The star, the star . . . Such has been the punishment of him who broke the secret . . . The gods have demanded their tribute . . ."[15]

THE ROMANCE OF ISABEL

VII

In all his life he never wavered from serving her; his heart always belonged to her and their love lasted as long as they lived; and in the same measure as he loved her, so did she love him, so that they never ceased loving each other for even one hour.[1]

Amadís of Gaul

Hernando de Soto could not protest to Pedrarias for the vile deed, both because nothing could result from it and because he had the soldier's sense of discipline and respect for authority. There was a further reason: he was falling in love with Isabel, the governor's daughter. Isabel was now fourteen years old. De Soto, as a squire in Pedrarias's home, had been virtually her playmate and her personal guard. Doña Isabel was decidedly fond of Hernando, admiring both his manners and his morals. She had no hesitations about entrusting her daughters to him. As for Hernando, the truth was breaking into his unwilling consciousness: he could not live or move without thinking of Isabel. He would go to church only to look at her. He could hardly utter a word when her governess invited him to visit them, and fell silent ever more frequently, even though, in the years that followed that first sea voyage, he had acquired a reputation as an articulate, witty and entertaining conversationalist.

He was experiencing an anguish which was new to him, but amply described in the pages of his chivalry books. He realized, too, that his company pleased Isabel, and that the attraction between them had evolved naturally and imperceptibly. At first, they had treated the whole thing very lightly, sure that they were exaggerating the depth of their feelings under the influence of their imagination and romantic literature. But the truth soon became apparent. Hernando was in exactly the same situation as his favorite hero, Amadis, and would seek understanding in his fictitious adventures, as when a friend of Oriana's says to her, "My lady, he is the one you want, for he is yours and is dying of love for you, and suffers as no knight has ever suffered before," or when Amadis says to Oriana, "Madam, I am yours for you to command, ready to do whatever you order me to."

Hernando's world was expanding. He was becoming a fully fledged knight. He had his lance, his sword, horse and armor, as well as the rank of captain. He must have felt that, now that he had his lady to fill his dreams, everything was transformed. By becoming close to Isabel, he could respect her father, Pedrarias, without being troubled by his excesses. He was attached to her mother, who had been almost a mother to him and had shown him the refined and courtly side of life.[2] Without ever visiting Segovia, Isabel's hometown, he loved it; and he loved Darién, hot, humid and unhealthy, because she was there. Gradually, he must have realized that she was his whole reason for living, and that perhaps she was to share his destiny. She had awakened a new kind of feeling in him, one which he had not understood when he had read about it in *Amadis*—emotional suffering. Until then, he had thought that life was a gay succession of days, sometimes filled with great deeds of heroism, sometimes with glory and satisfaction. He used to quote a verse from one of the popular romantic comedies of the day by Juan de Encina:

> *Let us always seek pleasure,*
> *for sorrow*
> *will come unsought.*[3]

Isabel was not only the daughter of a governor who was an old knight and a courtier, the hero of a hundred battles, the brother of Count de Puñonrostro, son of the legendary Pedro Arias Dávila—she was also the daughter of one of the most prominent women in Spain, Doña Isabel de Bobadilla y Peñalosa, who had presided over a small court even before coming to Darién, and was a person of note, both in Segovia and Seville. She was the niece of the marchioness of Moya, the illustrious Beatriz de Bobadilla, friend and companion to Queen Isabel the Catholic, who had played a decisive role in the history of Spain.

Understandably, therefore, strong and opposing feelings were at war in Hernando's mind, his love and his pride. He saw the only solution as being the road of knight-errantry, Amadis's road—although the "Youth from the Sea" was the son of a king. The road to Isabel must be the hard one of struggle and triumph, for only after winning a name, glory and riches could he talk to her on equal terms. Driven by his character to challenge life, he gradually came to accept the idea of a destiny to which there were few alternatives. Either he was to live with and for Isabel, at the end of a path full of hardships and obstacles in the New World, or he would die for her in the process of reaching this goal. Amadis's example was encouraging, but difficult; yet, to a brave and lovesick Hernando, even the book's most fantastic adventures and absurd challenges looked possible. Amadis and Oriana knew the kind of love children enjoy, but before winning her for his own, Amadis had to overcome the opposition of her father, by proving the strength of his arm, the nobility and courage of his heart and the depth of his love.[4]

Hernando asked no more, but would not settle for less. The book was a reflection of the chivalrous spirit of the times, in particular in the house of Isabel de Bobadilla, where both she and her daughters had read it. She would hold soirees during which poems and romances were recited to express the heroic and romantic spirit of the century. People still spoke of the wars against the Moors, especially of the Granada campaign, in which Pedrarias had fought, when Hernán Pérez del Pulgar had crossed the enemy lines and nailed a Hail Mary on the walls of the mosque, as though the city had already been conquered.

From Isabel's point of view, Hernando was almost a demigod. Five years had already passed since they had arrived together in Panama. Hernando was nineteen and strong for his age. To Isabel he was the handsomest, wittiest, strongest and most courageous knight who had ever existed. He was her paladin. But to protect this very love, which she now understood clearly, she must keep it an absolute secret, or Hernando would fall victim to the fury of the governor. For no other reason than envy for Balboa's popularity and fame, so her mother had told her, Pedrarias had had him beheaded, though Balboa was his son-in-law. What might he not do to a nameless young man who dared to raise his eyes to his favorite daughter? So she began to pretend indifference in Hernando's presence.[5] Although Hernando was engaged in the same pretense, he was hurt by her apparent coldness and would meditate on the changing nature of women, similar to his changing fortunes in Darién.

While Isabel may have convinced Hernando, her mother guessed at once the reason for the feigned indifference; knowing her daughters inside out, she was quick to recognize the symptoms of love. For most of her life she had suffered from the terrible will of Pedrarias in proud silence, abandoning the comforts of Spain for life in an unknown wilderness and bringing two of her daughters to sweeten the harshness of his character. This last had had little effect on his rage, vindictiveness and cruelty, which had spread terror rather than respect through the new lands. The execution of Balboa had been the severest blow to her feelings as a loyal, honest and delicate woman, and she was starting to feel that if she were to remain near her husband for much longer, she would grow to hate him. So she would talk of their house in Segovia which contained all that they had abandoned, and the four boys and two girls they had left there, one of them, María, already the widow of the adelantado de la mar del sur. Suspicions of Isabel's infatuation for Hernando strengthened her resolve to return to Spain.[6] She liked de Soto; in a way, she felt responsible for his career and the formation of his character, and realized that it would be impossible to prevent such kindred spirits as his and her daughter's from falling in love. Setting aside what might develop in the future, she concluded that the wisest thing would be to put some distance between the two lovers, which should cool things down and spare Hernando from the fury of Pedrarias, more terrible than any of the perils of Darién. With this plan in mind, she felt fortified to support her husband in her customary, dutiful manner through the next trials which assailed Darién.

At the time, Pedrarias was organizing an expedition to the Southern Sea, Balboa's ships now having been put in Espinosa's charge. Doña Isabel suggested that de Soto might use the opportunity to further his career, and he was included without difficulty.

Gaspar de Espinosa set sail for Acla, proceeding by the shortest route to the other side of the isthmus and the southern coast. At the site Pedrarias had settled, he founded the city of Panama, meaning "abundance of fish," on the left bank of the little river Algarrobo. The date was August 15, 1519. With all the other men of the party, de Soto was present at the traditional ceremony of marking the trees and honoring the flag of Castile. Espinosa set up municipal authorities for the city, the first to be founded on the Pacific coast. As his lieutenant, he left Captain Gonzalo de Badajoz, and then took possession of Balboa's ships and sailed south to Chief Paris's territory, where he seized forty thousand pesos worth of gold, burying half in Panama and sending the other half back to Darién.

The most valuable result of this expedition was the more systematic exploration of the Panamanian coast to the north and the west. The explorers reached the Punta de Chame, which faces Otoque Island, and proceeded along the coast in a southwesterly direction to Punta de Guera; then on through the Gulf of Paris, the rich chief from whom the Spaniards had extracted so much gold. They continued toward what is now the Gulf of Montijo and stopped at Cebaco Island, where the astrologer Micer Codro died and was buried. From there, they traveled to Punta Burica, at the end of what is now the Gulf of Chiriquí, and explored the lands we know as Costa Rica. Visiting the Gulf of Nicoya area, they were fascinated by the sharks, swordfish and barracudas; several times when they landed they bartered for gold. Finally they decided to return to Darién and report to the governor. De Soto was a good friend of Juan de Castañeda, the navigator, and his nautical interests were reawakened by this area so full of promise, with its excellent climate and possibilities for agriculture and mining.

In Darién, meanwhile, Doña Isabel had persuaded Pedrarias to send her back to Spain; he realized the advantages of having her near the Crown at a time when his position was in danger and there was a possibility of a trial of residency which might prove unfavorable. It was expedient, therefore, to send many gifts back to Spain and to have powerful friends at Court.

As everyone in Darién knew, King Fernando had died in 1516, having designated Cardinal Cisneros as Regent until the arrival of the heir, Prince Don Carlos, grandson of the Catholic kings, who came surrounded by Flemish courtiers.

"You are a mercenary, a servant of the people," the attorney from Burgos had told the king on behalf of the Spanish Court, "and that is why the people give you a part of their income."[7] The members of parliament demanded that the king's mother, Doña Juana, be considered Queen of Spain until the new king married and had children. They also demanded that Spaniards be appointed ambassadors and religious dignitaries, and above all, that King Charles learn Spanish.

Charles had to accept all the conditions established by his vassals before being recognized as king of Castile, Aragón and Barcelona. In addition to the Spanish domain, he had inherited from Philip the Handsome, his father, the whole of Flanders, Artois, Luxembourg, Franche-Comté, Charolais and the Low Countries. Upon the death of his grandfather, Emperor Maximilian of Germany, in 1519, the Imperial Crown of Germany was also bestowed on him. So in May of 1520 he had to go to Germany, leaving the Royal Council to administer justice and appointing Cardinal Adrian of Utrecht governor of Castile. Immediately all of Spain was in turmoil and villages prepared for revolt; the result was a *Junta Santa,* or holy meeting, at Ávila in July, under Juan de Padilla.

All this activity pushed the affairs of the Indies into the background, where the Council of the Indies handled them in its own good time. The young king had not time for them as he confronted the more immediate problems of loyalty in Spain, his own coronation at Aachen, the religious reform spreading across Germany and the warlike maneuvers for controlling positions in Europe, especially from his competitors in England and France. Before his arrival in Spain, the overseer from Darién had traveled to Flanders to bring him news of the new lands and report Pedrarias's outrages against him, hoping as well to promote an outcry within the Court at Balboa's murder. But Charles knew little of the Indies, and Fernández de Oviedo y Valdés had been sent to report to one uninterested authority after another, finally returning to speak to the king himself in 1519. This time, in deference to the memory of Balboa, it was agreed that Pedrarias should be replaced and, as expected, Lope de Sosa, still living in the Canaries, was named the new governor. On the king's orders, Oviedo y Valdés departed to collect the property of those who had been beheaded at Acla.

But there was a most unexpected turn of events. While de Soto was away with Espinosa exploring the Costa Rican coastlands, Pedrarias, who had heard rumors about a new governor, arranged his wife's return to Spain. Despite all the hurry, however, the new governor was going to arrive before Doña Isabel's departure, so she decided to face with her husband whatever might occur. At the appointed time Pedrarias and his wife were ready on the shore, he dressed in his official uniform, she by his side. On board the approaching ship, Lope de Sosa was preparing himself for the landing and instructing his assistants on every detail of the ceremony, when he fell dead of a heart attack. So the formal welcoming party became a funeral ceremony, and the new governor took possession only of a tomb in Bishop Quevedo's church.

Born courtiers, Pedrarias and Doña Isabel guided the ceremonies, hinting to the distressed settlers of Darién that this was a clear sign that Pedrarias should continue as governor. He treated Sosa's companions with every consideration, particularly his son Juan Alonso de Sosa, and the lawyer Juan Rodríguez de Alarconcillo, who had been told he would be mayor of Darién. With his habitual political cunning, Pedrarias confirmed the appointment in the absence of Espinosa, and rather than opposing the trial of residency, urged him to proceed. Under the new circumstances there was nobody to accuse the old man, so in thirty days the governor was cleared of all charges, and this verdict was sent to Spain on the same ship as Doña Isabel and her daughters in June of 1520. The ship was to stop in Santo Domingo. She was carrying a cargo of pearls and gold as gifts for the new king.

Only a week later Espinosa returned to Darién with a large booty of gold. De Soto, who had been waiting eagerly to see Isabel, heard the news of her departure even before they reached the town. He was wearing her cross next to his heart under his armor, and carried the fine kerchief which was the traditional token that a damsel gave to her knight. Suddenly there was nothing for him to look forward to in Darién.

Two days after his return, there was a knock at his door. It was Señora Estete, the lieutenant governor's wife, who had been one of young Isabel's ladies-in-waiting, her teacher and friend. She gave Hernando a Book of Hours with a mother-of-pearl binding that Isabel had left for him. Placing a finger over her lips as a warning, the good woman departed; she well knew how long and vindictive the governor's arm could be when anyone offended him.

Hernando felt that hope was renewed for him as he studied the phrase written in uneven characters on the flyleaf of the book. It read: "I will wait for you all my life, darling."

THE SCOURGE OF GOD

VIII

We thank God that Pedrarias never came to these lands, for he was like a flame which blazed up and consumed many provinces, which is why we used to call him Furor Domini.[1]

Friar Bartolomé de las Casas

Left in Darién without his
family, Pedrarias had two immediate concerns: to see his
authority restored at the Spanish Court, which Doña Isabel would take care of, and to transfer the seat of his
government to Panama because of the unhealthy conditions in Darién, not to mention the bad memories it held
for him. Used to juggling with human destinies, he began
to deal more gently with everyone, particularly those he
knew were his bitter enemies. Later on he would take
care of them, one by one, indulging in his favorite activity:
the execution of vengeance.

A strange mixture of merits and defects shaped the
spirit of this most unique man. Throughout his long lifetime he had been all that a knight could aspire to in a
century of martial glory. Favored by kings and by women,
he had earned names such as the Gallant, the Jouster and
the Brave. Around his reputation as a terrible tyrant hung
dozens of legends and tales, some of them positively ma-
cabre. But the outstanding feature was his family's tradition of loyalty to the king, backed up by heroic deeds
in Granada, Oran and Bugía.

His reputation as a cold and intractable man had reached
Darién before him. Even de Soto, who had been near him
for six years, was unable to fathom his commander's complex nature. To him he was first and foremost Isabel's

father, and then a representative of the king, so Hernando was unquestioningly loyal. At the same time he was frequently horrified at the callous decisions the man made, from the day San Martín had been hanged as they arrived in the New World to the execution of the noble hero Balboa. Although he would never tolerate talk against Pedrarias in his presence, he could not avoid hearing the rumors that circulated in the colony and doubtless contained a good deal of truth.

One story was that while at a tournament in Portugal he had won a tray of gold coins which he had immediately distributed among the ladies of the Court there. Others held that he was greedy and avaricious, that he owed his post and position in the Indies to Bishop Fonseca, who had received a shady favor in return. It was whispered that he was immortal since he had outlived so many perils and was the oldest man in the colony; men said that when he was in his fifties he had suffered a stroke and been pronounced dead. His relatives were at the wake in the church of Torrejón de Velasco, when at midnight, to the horror of the mourners, the "corpse" started to move and came out of what had been catalepsy. He got up and started to curse those present when he understood what had happened. This was the origin of his custom of taking the casket in which the "miracle" had occurred wherever he went, and on the anniversary of the event, lying in it and having a friar read the funeral services over him. Some people called him "the Disinterred" and regarded him with the superstitious terror due to one who has glimpsed the mysteries of the next world.

The impressive fact among all the superstitious legends was that events always seemed to favor his cause, the sudden death of Sosa on his arrival in Darién being a striking case in point. This was when people began to call him "el furor Domini," the Scourge of God. Women and children would not utter his name without crossing themselves in fear.

Pedrarias had written the king recommending the transfer of government to Panama both because of healthier conditions and because it was near to the path between the two seas: he planned to build the cathedral in Panama, and the closest port in the Northern Sea would be Nombre de Dios. Pedrarias was right from the geographical point of view, but he also had other reasons which were contested by the settlers, who were understandably reluctant to abandon their cultivated lands and the homes they had established through many years of work. He was sure that Panama could easily be separated from Darién, so he could retain governorship of the former while the latter would be available for any successor of Sosa's. Panamá would be an ideal point of departure for expeditions to the legendary Peru, whose virtues were frequently extolled by the priest and teacher Hernando de Luque as he described his exploratory missions to his friend Francisco Pizarro.

Without difficulty Pedrarias received authorization from Spain to transfer the seat of government and the cathedral to Panama. He had also been confirmed as governor, but knew that there was little time to be lost before extending his territories, so that he could effect a division upon the arrival of a new governor.

Fernández de Oviedo had brought royal orders from Spain that were intended to be implemented by Governor Sosa, and was most disappointed by the state of affairs he found. Pedrarias thought it would be useful to have the influential overseer and chronicler on his side, so he began to praise him for all he had done for Darién and encourage him to collect a tenth of the gold from the king's mines as well as royalties from the mint. Oviedo had sided with the group of settlers who opposed the transfer to Panama, so the old governor cunningly appointed him alderman of Darién, thus pleasing him and ridding himself of the overseer's company, since he was already spending most of his time in Panama. Oviedo did not fare well in his new position. His wife and daughter died of tropical diseases; his orders to introduce discipline and morality into Darién were instantly unpopular, demanding as they did punishment of those who cursed in public places, separation of unwed couples and abolition of card games. To publicize the fact, he staged a bonfire of playing cards in the plaza.

Hernando de Soto accompanied Pedrarias to the Panama settlement. The new town was progressing well, and in 1521 received the full title of city from Emperor Charles V. Eager to succeed, de Soto drove himself hard on whatever mission fell to him. He started to save for the future from his salary as captain (about two thousand maravedis[2] per month) and from his share in any booty that was taken on the expeditions. Fame and wealth were essential if he was to fulfill his dream of attaining his beloved. His ambition was spurred, too, by the constant stream of news about the exploits of other captains in the Indies. Outstanding among these was the story of the man from Extremadura, Hernán Cortés, who had explored north of Pedrarias's domain and found the vast empire of the Aztecs and its capital city Tenochtitlán, one of the largest in the world. All the soldiers in Panama were discussing the Spaniards' entry into the Mexican capital, which was supposed to have shining walls of silver which were reflected in the canals as in a mirror. They talked enviously of the huge gifts of gold given to Cortés by Montezuma, of the delicacies at the tables of the great palaces, the strange temples, the rituals, the splendid ceremonial robes and the orders of chivalry that had been discovered among the Aztecs. Equally talked about were Cortés's differences with his former superiors[3] in Cuba and his final exoneration with the fall of Tenochtitlán in the autumn of 1521. It was rumored that some of Cortés's captains, Alvarado, Sandoval, Olid and Montejo, were seeking new lands to the south, and that they must soon reach the Panama

territory. All shared Pedrarias's concern, as well as his
hope of finding other kingdoms in order to match Cortés's
fame and glory for his achievements in the north.

They were also well aware of the voyages of an enig-
matic Portuguese navigator sailing under the Spanish flag.
He had promised the king that he would find a passage
to the Southern Sea and gain the Moluccas by sailing to
the west; Ferdinand Magellan had set out from Seville in
September of 1519 with five ships, three hundred men
and the title of admiral. Nothing had yet been heard about
his trip, but it was hoped that he would find fabulous
kingdoms; at the very least, his voyage would affect all
Spanish possessions in the Indies, especially those along
the coast of the Southern Sea.

With all this in mind, Pedrarias decided to expedite
the exploration of the Pacific Ocean. Following Espinosa's
mission there was much discussion as to what should be
the final destiny of Balboa's ships. About that time a
navigator named Andres Niño and his partner Gil González Dávila, who was a royal accountant of the city of
Santo Domingo, obtained a license from Spain to undertake an expedition to the Southern Sea; they also had an
order for Pedrarias to hand Balboa's four ships over to
them. Pedrarias raised objection after objection until finally they offered him a share in the profits; but delivery
of the ships seemed impossible, so they decided on the
arduous task of building others.[4] Gil González Dávila had
to overcome enormous obstacles, and several of his men
were killed or wounded, but he succeeded in completing
three warships and two brigantines and set out for the
nearby Island of Pearls with eighty men. Within twenty
days his ships suffered the fate of Balboa's: termites had
destroyed the wood from which they were built. González
Dávila was a remarkable man; undeterred, he returned
to Panama and obtained the reluctant help of Pedrarias
to rebuild the warships and one of the brigantines, which
involved a further year of work at the Island of Pearls. In

January 1522 he sailed south with a hundred men despite all obstacles. He reached Nicaragua and discovered the great lake, "another sweetwater lake with tides." He had christened thousands of the friendly Indians, and carried out profitable transactions with them. Returning to San Vicente, he rejoined Niño, who had been touring the Gulf of Nicoya and found several islands with civilizations similar to that of the Aztecs, where he obtained a good quantity of gold and pearls. In June of 1523, González Dávila returned to Panamá and crossed the isthmus to return to Santo Domingo, where he started organizing another expedition, much to the envy and chagrin of Pedrarias.

The old governor was still set on depleting Darién to benefit Panama. With de Soto he went to welcome the new bishop, Friar Vicente Peraza, a Dominican monk who had been appointed to succeed Bishop Quevedo, and despite Oviedo's efforts to the contrary, easily persuaded the bishop to proceed to Panama. But friendship between Pedrarias and the new bishop was short-lived; difficulties arose not only about priorities but about interest and even gambling. But once again Pedrarias's luck held: soon after the rift, the bishop took ill and died, sending another wave of superstitious gossip through Panama.

Hernando left Panama to accompany Espinosa on his next expedition, together with his countryman Francisco Pizarro, who had become even more taciturn since Balboa's death. They were to explore the coast of Veragua, in the Pacific, near the island of Cebaco. Pizarro was accompanied by de Soto on land, while Espinosa explored by sea. Chief Urraca and his men were watching from the jungle and tried to ambush them several times. There were three horses in Pizarro's party, for himself, de Soto and his friend Campañón; they attacked several villages but were strongly resisted. Espinosa wrote Pedrarias that the Veragua area seemed very suitable for the establishment of a settlement despite the resistance of Urraca. Pedrarias's answer was enthusiastic, but he said he wanted to undertake the enterprise in person and instructed Espinosa to return to Panama. Campañón was left behind with fifty men and two horses; among the men were de Soto and the navigator Pedro Miguel. Becoming aware of the great and ever-increasing strength of Urraca and his supporters, Campañón grew seriously worried and asked de Soto to try to ride to Panama for reinforcements. De Soto did not flinch at the strenuous trip; overcoming its many hardships, he reached Panama and persuaded Pedrarias to send immediate assistance in the form of forty men and a ship under the command of another of de Soto's friends, Hernán Ponce de León. They arrived just in time: Urraca's men had surrounded Campañón's, but at the sight of the ship retreated into the mountains, fearing the arrival of further troops.

Pedrarias's party consisted of 160 men, including de Soto and Pizarro, and two horses. Soon after the Spaniards had joined forces, Urraca's men descended in strength and the fight which ensued lasted the whole day, with the Indians displaying great courage. Pedrarias finally had to resort to the use of small cannons, or falconets, which drove them away in terror, but they continued to attack in the days that followed, along the whole Atrato River area, receiving reinforcements from friendly chiefs on both sides of the isthmus. There followed a succession of marches and ambushes. The forty-man vanguard Pedrarias sent under Diego de Albítez had been surrounded by Urraca's men and captured. Pedrarias marched to free them, but was met by Indian forces stronger than his own and had to fight his way through a narrow passage with his bare hands, with de Soto at his side trying to protect him. They finally succeeded in routing the Indians, and the various chiefs who had come to join Urraca's resistance effort were beaten into retreat. Pedrarias sent punitive troops through the neighboring villages, spreading death and destruction everywhere. By way of compensation, he founded a new town called Natá, and persuaded some of the terrified Indians to settle there in exchange for "protection" from the Spaniards. Albítez was left in charge of the settlement, but the mortal enmity between Urraca and Pedrarias was to continue for almost nine years of suffering and cruelty, particularly in the way the Spanish treated Indian prisoners when interrogating them about hidden treasure. Later, Campañón took over Albítez' command and continued the tradition of inhumanity, sending some of his Indian prisoners to Panama in chains. Such behavior further antagonized Urraca and goaded him to further efforts in the all-out war he was waging against the foreign invaders. Thus did Pedrarias, "the Scourge of God," interpret the solemn instructions the king had given him at the time of his appointment, which read: "You must try by all means possible to attract the Indians through good works, so that they become Christians in love and friendship." As though under some curse, Pedrarias had achieved the opposite result: he had unified the feelings of the Indians against the Spaniards who in their turn had become divided into opposing factions that weakened each other. The shadow of Pedrarias was to darken these lands for several years to come.

THE ENTERPRISE
OF DREAMS

IX

*To those who shall read these present,
Greetings. Know ye by this letter that I,
Captain Hernán Ponce de León, the party
of the first part, and I, Captain Hernando
de Soto, the party of the second part, do
both grant, acknowledge and state that
whereas we have been comrades for eighteen
or nineteen years and have shared in all
we have won or acquired in any manner so
that everything belonged to both of us
and we shared it as brothers . . . we now
renew the said association.*[1]

Deed of ratification of the
De Soto–Ponce de León Company,
La Habana, 1539

Hernando de Soto was determined to save all that he could in order to return to Spain and try to win Isabel. Whenever he could put a coin in his purse he felt it was another step toward his happiness. Pedrarias, in the meantime, had grown more sour than ever. He was upset when he heard that Gil González Dávila, already a knowledgeable explorer of the region, was undertaking another expedition to Nicaragua from Santo Domingo, with the support of Bishop Fonseca. Pedrarias decided to beat Dávila to Nicaragua and organized a group under Francisco Fernández de Córdoba, a captain of halberdiers; the group also included Captains de Soto—Fernández' close friend—Campañón, Sebastián de Benalcázar, Rojas, Garavito and a few others.

They explored the areas of the great Lake Nicaragua, "the Sweetwater Sea," going so far as to disassemble one of their brigantines, carry it to the lake, reassemble it and sail around the lake. What they discovered was of great significance: there was a more highly developed culture among the native population here than in other areas already explored, somewhat closer to that of Mexico. Fine work was done in cotton, with rich embroidery of birds and flowers, as well as feathers where the gorgeous plumage of tropical birds was used to colorful effect. They painted codices on tree barks; they built houses of stone and, in the lofty pyramids which were their temples, offered ritual sacrifices to their gods. The area abounded with rare scented woods, a huge variety of flowers and delicious fruits, amid mild enjoyable weather. It was important to give Dávila to understand that the lands were already under the jurisidiction of Pedrarias and, once the settlement had been made in the field, to report it to Spain as a fait accompli.

Both de Soto and Fernández had a full understanding of the situation, though de Soto had the added advantage of knowing the terrain better, since his earlier expedition with Espinosa. They started by founding the village of Bruselas, in the existing Indian town of Orotina; later on, in the province of Chief Nequecheri, they formally founded Granada in honor of the Andalusian city which symbolized the victory of the Catholic kings over the Arabs. With willing help from the Indians they built a fort and a temple dedicated to Saint Francis of Assisi. Then Fernández sent de Soto out in the brigantine to explore the lake, especially to search for a river or channel which might be a link between the seas, which was the main concern of the Council of the Indies in Spain. De Soto sailed across Lake Nicaragua and reached the San Juan or Desaguadero Rivers, which does in fact connect the lake to the Northern Sea. It was hard to navigate through the currents and rocks in the lake, so de Soto dropped anchor and explored the San Juan River area by land, finding several villages. But disturbing news reached him that some Spaniards had arrived from the Guaymura area of the northern coast and were coming up the Olancho valley toward the lake, seeking a route to the Southern Sea.

De Soto's party at once returned to Fernández' headquarters to report these developments, which were passed on to Pedrarias in Panama, and de Soto was sent with forty men to confront González Dávila, the leader of the other expedition.

This was the first mission which was truly distasteful to de Soto; he had to oppose one of his own countrymen. He decided to seek information first, and with his men advanced cautiously in the direction of the outsiders, setting up camp in the village of Toreba. Their rest was disturbed around midnight when the sentry warned that armed men were approaching. Then voices were heard shouting: "Saint Giles! Death to the traitors!"[2]

Hernando had taken every precaution. There had been night watch and the men had been ordered to sleep with their weapons at the ready. He himself was in full armor with his lance and horse nearby, so that he could mount and lead his men at the first alarm. In fully organized formation they charged the attackers and a confused and violent battle was fought in the darkness. With his lance, de Soto opened a circle around himself, as his men charged courageously, soon routing the intruders and winning a clear victory for de Soto. Then González Dávila's voice was heard saying, "Señor Capitán, peace, peace, in the emperor's name."

Hernando looked inquiringly at his friend Ponce de León, who said, "Do not trust them, Hernando. It is probably a trick; let's finish them."[3]

But Hernando was still the Youth from the Sea, with his bookish notions of chivalry. He answered sharply, "I shall never let it be said that I have attacked a defeated enemy or questioned a gentleman's word. Stop the fighting!"

The order was carried out, and the opposing forces returned to their camps. De Soto counted his men and checked for wounded soldiers, waiting for the defeated side to arrive. But nobody came; the attackers seemed to have vanished in the dark. De Soto tried to find an explanation: "They must be looking for their wounded. We know it's Gil González; let us send a messenger to alert Fernández."

To de Soto's astonishment, as his men were resting some three hours after the first attack, they were charged by a larger column of Spanish troops. These were the reinforcements for which González had been waiting, and he had taken advantage of de Soto's chivalry to enlarge his forces; he now had almost three times as many men as before. The fresh troops overwhelmed them, quickly surrounding the scattered men. A group of them managed to escape, but de Soto, though fighting with his sword, and thus wounding several soldiers, could not avoid capture; he was imprisoned and taken to González Dávila.

Hernando was deeply disappointed. He was plunged into the shame of his first defeat, having just tasted the pleasure of his first victory. He felt contempt for his opponent who had violated the code of honor, but determined in the future to take all possible precautions, rather than follow the rules of chivalry as described in his books. Impassively, he watched his own camp being looted and saw his purse handed to González Dávila with his entire fortune in it, about 134,000 pesos.

Hernando informed his captor that a powerful army was on its way under the command of Captain Fernández de Córdoba, and an even stronger corps would be arriving under the governor's command.

González then retorted that Hernán Cortés also believed he had claim to these lands and had therefore sent his lieutenant Cristóbal de Olid in the same direction.

He took de Soto's sword from him, but did not have him shackled. Three days later, he reached a decision: to return to his ship in the Northern Sea and confront the troops of Olid. He gave Hernando back his sword. De Soto would never forget the experience.

Fernández de Córdoba greeted him cordially and laughed at his gullibility and capture. He proceeded immediately to the Imabita region, north of Lake Managua, where the weather was mild, and the vegetation and landscape beautiful. There, under the imposing volcano Momotombo, he founded the city of León. During a fight with some Indians they noticed a group whose bodies were covered by human skins for costumes. They learned that it was a tradition based on the belief that the wearer would take on the strength of the skin's former owner, and the Indians naively hoped that in this way they would terrify and defeat the Spanish cavalry. All this was to no avail against the advanced weapons and military experience of Fernández' soldiers.

De Soto and his old friends Campañón and Ponce de León were always a merry team, and the Toreba adventure was soon forgotten, except when someone wished to make sport of Hernando. He set out on another mission, this time to search for the Olancho gold mines. He was successful, and brought back a handsome loot for the king, Pedrarias and himself. They had smaller ships this time, and were able to go downstream along the San Juan River, realizing that in this way they could reach the Northern Sea. With great joy he returned to Granada with the news, eager to see Fernández de Córdoba.

As soon as he arrived, he noticed that the atmosphere had changed. Exploration continued, and villages were founded, but no mention was made now of Pedrarias or the Panama possession; all was done in the name of the king himself and Fernández as a "Conquering Captain." De Soto realized that the soldiers were split into two factions as to their loyalties, some to Pedrarias and others encouraging Fernández to break away from the old governor. A few days later there was a public session of the Granada City Council at which Fernández claimed that he was yielding to the will of the majority and was ready to "sacrifice" himself and assume the governorship. He intended to send petitions for support to Hernán Cortés in Mexico, and to the king via the governor of Santo Domingo.

A few of the captains present at the meeting were in support of Fernández' plan, but when confronted, Hernando refused to be drawn into an act of treason, and Fernández had him imprisoned in a newly built fortress.

The whole army was shocked at this deed. De Soto was popular and had a reputation for courage and fairness. Campañón and Ponce were especially incensed and made plans, with a group of loyal soldiers, to free their friend at night. Thirty men went to the fortress and scaled the ramparts. They overcame the guards without difficulty and freed de Soto, giving him a horse and weapons. Some of them decided to stay in Granada, but a dozen of them, including Ponce and Campañón, left with de Soto to alert Pedrarias to the proposed treachery. After two hours they noticed that some soldiers were galloping in their pursuit, and Hernando ordered his men to stop and get ready for battle. His old friend Fernández was among the pursuers.

Campañón and Ponce stood by de Soto with their lances, and the rest of the men were determined to fight bitterly to the death. Fernández hesitated; de Soto was considered to be the best lancer in the area and the fight might prove fatal for Fernández. The two men faced each other under the bright sun; behind them the volcano Momotombo sent spirals of black smoke into the sky. Fernández backed down.

Hernando and his men started the long journey to Panama, leaving behind them the rich and beautiful land of Nicaragua, which had become a hotbed of ambition, conspiracies and greed among the Spaniards.

In the north, too, there had been struggles and conflicts. González Dávila had fought Olid and been taken prisoner, and Olid in his turn had revolted against the authority of Cortés and been beheaded. González then traveled to Mexico to report to Cortés, but he was away exploring Honduras with three hundred of his men, and he was about to enter Nicaragua when he heard of the turmoil in Mexico and had to return.

The journey from Granada to Panama was an arduous one for de Soto and his friends. They soon had to abandon their horses, which lost their shoes along the rugged paths and were totally exhausted. The men struggled on through unexplored regions in a continuous battle with the elements. One day they were rewarded with an unforgettable sight from the hill of Talamanca: the Northern and the Southern seas—that is, the Caribbean Sea, as part of the Atlantic, and the Pacific Ocean—stretching on either side of them. They were newly convinced of the urgency of finding a passage between the seas, and understood more fully why the Council of the Indies had given it such high priority.

The twelve men were hungry, barefoot and fatigued when they met one of Pedrarias's commanders, Hurtado, as they entered Fonseca in Panama. They were taken by canoe to Río Chico and on to Río Grande until they reached Natá, which was familiar to de Soto and Campañón from earlier expeditions. There were some settlers in the area, so de Soto was able to send a letter to Pedrarias explaining events in detail and announcing his imminent arrival.

Pedrarias's fury knew no bounds when he read about Fernández's treason. When the weary travelers arrived at Panama City he embraced de Soto and Campañón as though they were his own sons. He told them that preparations for his expedition to Nicaragua were almost complete and he was going to lead it himself, despite his eighty years. He had a compelling reason for doing this, for besides having to discipline Fernández de Córdoba, he had received the chilling news that a new governor, Don Pedro de los Ríos, had been appointed to Castilla del Oro and was due to arrive any day. Pedrarias needed to have his authority firmly established elsewhere before this occurred. But he was not yet through with Panama.

Before setting out again, de Soto, Campañón and Ponce de León had a long conversation. They made a sort of inventory of their possessions and tried to analyze the purpose of their adventurous lives. De Soto and Ponce had their own reasons for wanting to return to Spain, but there was also the alternative of finding a quiet valley where they could live and bring an end to their exhausting travels. In either case, they all needed economic prosperity and realized that it would have to be arranged systematically; they must protect themselves against losses, theft, accidents and persecution by the shifting authorities. The case of Hernando, who had lost his fortune to González Dávila, underlined the need for precautionary measures. His release from prison by his friends demonstrated the benefits of a group which could take joint action. On the basis of these lessons they decided to organize a corporation which would give shape to all their ventures. Each of the three partners would contribute the total sum of his assets, and if one of them should die his wealth would be inherited by the others unless he had provided otherwise in his will. With this capital, they planned to finance two or more ships and, if necessary, could finance their part in the explorations of other captains. If they were able to enter into mining or agricultural ventures they would reinvest their profits in the corporation. First they would go to Nicaragua, both to support Pedrarias and to look for a good agricultural area. Whenever possible, Ponce de León would travel in search of new ventures. Any assets would belong to all three of them, and all of them would fulfill the agreement in every detail.

When this was done, they took a brief rest and then had to take up their weapons again and accompany Pedrarias on his march to Nicaragua. The very name of the awesome governor was enough to restore discipline: when they arrived in Granada, Fernández de Córdoba reported to him in person and was at once put in prison. Pedrarias then entered the fortress while the captains and troops waited outside in the plaza. They assumed that there would be a trial, but Pedrarias's justice was even more expeditious. A few minutes later, a soldier came out carrying a pike on which was impaled the head of Fernández, who had been Pedrarias's captain of halberdiers, founder of cities and major explorer of Nicaragua.

The judgment of Pedrarias was prompt and terrible. Isabel's father was still, and above all, "el furor Domini."

THE NEW KINGDOM OF LEON

And I arrived and saw, in the clouds, the prestigious head of that peak of ages, that volcano of legend, standing before me—a true revelation. Lord of the heights, emperor of the waters; at its feet, the divine lake of Managua, with islands filled with light and song.[1]

Rubén Darío

While, in the city of León, Pedrarias was busy setting up the administration of Nicaragua, his captains were, in various places, fighting Hernán Cortés's officers or the Indian rebels. The board of Santo Domingo had appointed Diego López de Salcedo governor of Honduras. Salcedo had come to the country in 1526 and had forced Cortés's men to obey him, including Hernando de Saavedra, to whom he entrusted the governorship of Honduras, although he had just thrown him into prison. Salcedo was very stern in his dealings with the Indians and he treated them with extreme cruelty: this increased their resentment against the Spaniards whom they had at first welcomed in a most hospitable manner and with a great show of friendship. Driven by his ambition, Salcedo immediately clashed with Pedrarias by announcing that he was naming the territory of Nicaragua, which was under his authority, the new kingdom of León.

Pedrarias learned of this without flinching. He already had several problems on his hands, and acting as the good politician that he was, he attended first to the most urgent, which certainly was not the matter of Salcedo's ambition. The truth was that a new governor of Castilla del Oro had arrived in Panama, a certain Don Pedro de los Ríos, who brought with him Licentiate Juan de Salmerón, an auditor of stewardship, who came with the title of senior magistrate and would certainly review Pedrarias's stewardship. He also knew that his old enemy, Overseer Gonzalo Fernández de Oviedo, was back and that measures against him had already been taken, the first of which was the seizure of all his property and servants in Panama. The old governor did not for one moment hesitate to set about defending his administration and his interests: he appointed a triumvirate of captains to govern Nicaragua in his absence and to keep Salcedo in line; they were Gabriel de Rojas, Diego Alvarez and Andrés de Garavito—sinister memories of the tragedy at Acla. It was 1527 when he reached Panama.

The presence of Governor de los Ríos in Castilla del Oro essentially reflected a wish on the part of the king and the Council of the Indies to initiate a political reform in the new possessions. The impassioned pleas voiced by Father Las Casas and several other Dominicans and Franciscans in defense of the Indians had caused deep concern. Pedrarias was accused of bringing about the depopulation and destruction of extensive regions and of being responsible for the death of nearly two million Indians since his arrival in Darién in 1514. New laws applying to all possessions in the Indies required that all promises made to the native population be scrupulously kept in all cases, that their women be treated with respect, that houses and places of worship be built for them and that schools be set up for their instruction. To avoid more violence and bloodshed, Governor Pedro de los Ríos was expressly forbidden to engage upon new journeys of exploration and discovery, so that he might focus on the well-being of the conquered provinces, and bring them peace and attract settlers.

Pedrarias arrived in Panama, met the new governor and gradually became his friend and adviser. He cleverly persuaded de los Ríos to go to Nicaragua, to make sure the land was arable and also to attend to the sale and

exchange of the many goods[2] he had brought from Spain—
a fact that had not escaped Pedrarias's notice. This served
several purposes: it delayed the holding of the trial of
residency, while giving Pedrarias a chance to turn it to
his advantage; it turned over to de los Ríos the many
problems of Nicaragua while giving him the opportunity
of gaining firsthand knowledge of tribal problems and
internal strife; it showed that, in the long run, the settlers
of Nicaragua would be better off with their own governorship, rather than answering to Cortés, Cuba or Panama; and it also made it clear, while Pedrarias was away,
how valuable his orderly and well-disciplined rule could
be, however harsh and feared his name might be.

Events proved the old jouster to have been right. De
los Ríos's expedition in Nicaragua was disastrous, while
Pedrarias remained quietly in Panama. Leaving Honduras, López de Salcedo made for León, where he met de
los Ríos, in a country in great turmoil. Everywhere, Pedrarias's men were constantly fighting Salcedo's; the tyranny Salcedo exerted over the Indians had caused them
to rise against him, while in their settlements, especially
in the valley of Olancho, hundreds of their people had
been killed, massacred or taken into slavery by the soldiers who took or were given the Indians' property. Such
was their despair that their chiefs made the men swear
to refrain from procreating, to avoid providing the invaders with more slaves. Even the most peace-loving tribes
had taken up arms and were looking for a chance to tangle
with the white man. Salcedo had first jailed, then dispatched to Cuba the aldermen of the city of León, Diego
de Albítez and Sebastián de Benalcázar, as well as the
registrar, Juan de Espinosa, all appointed by Pedrarias.
In Honduras, all the Indian settlements had taken up
arms, the inhabitants having been sickened by the trail
of hangings and atrocities Pedrarias left behind him. The
Indians had surrounded the city of León and were threatening to destroy it when Hernando de Soto and his friend

Campañón arrived. They had until then been engaged in running their mines. De Soto and Campañón defeated the assailants; however, neither of the captains could countenance the abusive, inhuman ways of Salcedo and they treated him with aloofness. Keeping him at arm's length for the moment, they waited for Pedrarias to return and put things in order. Meanwhile, Salcedo, fearing that the recently founded city of Bruselas might become a subject of dispute with Panama as to who held jurisdiction over it, ordered it destroyed stone by stone, entrusting the zealous Garavito with this pointless mission.

When Pedro de los Ríos arrived in León, Salcedo gave him a cool reception, and the haggling and arguing over jurisdiction started immediately. Some maintained that the land should be governed from Panama, others held out for Honduras, while others yet thought the matter warranted the creation of a new governorship and that Pedrarias should return to fill the post. Since de los Ríos had, on the advice of Pedrarias, brought a great deal of merchandise with him, pressed by his wife who "was fond of receiving money," he was given three days by Salcedo to sell his goods, with instructions to leave the city of León thereafter under penalty of a fine for noncompliance. All this considerably reduced de los Ríos's authority, though by no means preventing him from making a comfortable profit. Convinced that he was better off leaving such troubled regions, de los Ríos returned to Panama. Meanwhile, de Soto and a few of his friends addressed dispatches to the king, over the signature of many residents of the country surrounding the city of León, stressing the advisability of granting self-rule to the land.

Events turned out as Pedrarias had hoped they would. The Crown had been convinced that only a man with an iron fist could restore order, and appointed Pedrarias governor of Nicaragua, separating it from Panama, and ordering Salcedo to remain within the territory of Honduras and to refrain from intervening in any way in Nicaragua. The king also showed his regard for Pedrarias by sending him an authorization to claim for the return of his personal property and to appear by proxy at the trial of residency so that he might lose no time in taking over his governorship in Nicaragua.

The partnership of Hernando de Soto, Ponce and Campañón was prospering and the mining operation yielding good profits, to such an extent that the three friends were numbered among the richest citizens of León. Such was the situation when the ever faithful Hernando, satisfied with the good progress of his plans, was among the first to welcome Pedrarias.

Meanwhile, the devious Garavito had busied himself with fomenting a veritable palace revolution, seizing Diego López de Salcedo as well as Gabriel de Rojas, who had not cared to declare himself openly for Pedrarias. The old governor brought them to trial and brought his usual cunning and severity to bear on them, exacting ample revenge from Salcedo, whom he suspected of giving orders to prevent his coming ashore.[3] He started by making him pay damages for all the outrages committed, including the destruction of the city of Bruselas. After seven months' imprisonment, he set Salcedo free and allowed him to return to his governorship of Honduras after obtaining from him repeated promises and assurances that he would not meddle in the affairs of Nicaragua.

Hernando de Soto, who had been lukewarm in assisting Salcedo, was able, once again, to attend to the task of running the mines of Nueva Segovia, where his partner Campañón spent most of his time, and to scouting the various parts of the country in peaceful exploration and in search of trading and farming possibilities. In November 1527 or thereabouts, he journeyed to Panama, to help Pedrarias by testifying as a prime witness at the trial of residency brought against the governor to inquire into the reasons for the Córdoba executions. It ended with Pedrarias's exoneration and the return of his property, including the opulent trusteeship of the Island of Pearls.

At this time, life was being kind to Hernando. The excursions he undertook in the company of his two partners to the various tribes in the back country were happy adventures, devoid of any violence. Once in a while, he took part in tournaments with the most famous captains and Hernando, always a winner, was the favorite of all the ladies, be they proud or humble, Spanish, mestizas or natives. One young girl, the daughter of an old soldier, María by name, who was taken with Hernando, approached him at the end of one such joust where he had distinguished himself, and tied the Victory Ribbon around his arm. There ensued a passionate idyll which ended in the birth of a little girl who was given the name of María de Soto, whom Hernando was to remember in his will.

The brave and chivalrous Francisco Campañón, Hernando's friend and partner and a veritable brother to him, described as "a most manly man" by Fernández de Oviedo y Valdés, was at that time struck with an illness, in the city of León. He died suddenly in the arms of his comrade, whom he made his heir, together with Hernán Ponce. This legacy undoubtedly made of Hernando and Ponce the richest Spaniards in the town, but it was nevertheless for the man from Jerez a very deep and painful loss. Francisco had been his friend and confidant, had often saved his life and won back his freedom; he had been a merry companion on festive occasions and a stalwart comrade-in-arms. De Soto would never forget him.

A peaceful life offered itself now to the young and vigorous captain. He could think of returning to Spain and laying his fortune at Isabel's feet who, as he learned from the messages he received from her once in a while, still waited for him, ever faithful and proud. Yet, for that very reason, he felt in some way that he had a duty to remain at Pedrarias's side in the difficult days of his governorship. There was also another attraction that appealed to his adventurous spirit; the journeys of his old companions-in-arms were much talked about. Leaving Panama, they went in search of the kingdoms of Peru. Three people that Hernando knew well had formed a company in Panama to explore those regions: they were friends of his and veterans of the first days in Darién—Francisco Pizarro, Diego de Almagro and the schoolmaster and chaplain Hernando de Luque, whose whimsical and unexpected sayings he well remembered. The man of the cloth brought the cash, Pizarro contributed his experience as an old explorer and conquistador, Almagro his tenacity, his strength and his knowledge of men. At first, Pedrarias, too, had been a partner, but he subsequently withdrew from the company, against payment of one thousand pesos that Almagro had to pay to obtain permission to leave again for the south.

In November 1524, Pizarro set off with 114 companions. They endured months of hardships; one third of the men died of starvation and exposure in the course of various landing incidents. On one of his foraging sorties, Almagro lost an eye in a skirmish. Yet they had gathered information, found some gold and seen warrior chiefs covered with gold and emeralds. Back in Panama, Pizarro delivered a few presents to Pedrarias and then, imperturbably, renewed his undertaking. The persistent Luque agreed to contribute twenty thousand pesos which, rumor had it, came from Espinosa, "for the discovery and conquest of the kingdom of Peru, for profit or for loss"; he also agreed to share everything that might be gained, among himself, Pizarro and Almagro, in three equal parts. A new document was executed in March of 1526 and, shortly afterward, the two captains embarked on a new expedition. They reached the San Juan River, on the coast of Colombia, where they obtained gold and silver in barter exchanges with the Indians, to a value of fifteen thousand pesos. Almagro returned to Panama to carry the good news to their partner and to the authorities, while Pizarro continued on his way south. Keeping to the river San

Juan, he ordered his pilot, Bartolomé Ruiz, to explore
what is now the coast of Ecuador; Ruiz managed to cross
the equator, on a sea all at once of jade, turquoise and
emerald. He had actually landed in a place later called
The Emeralds, because of the number of such gems which
the amenable natives wore in their headdress. On another
occasion, they reached the region of Manabí and came
across sailing rafts manned by skillful Indians from the
south who, without any trace of fear, boarded Ruiz' ship
and spoke to him of a great empire which extended along
all the lands along the coast and reached very high up in
the mountains, some of which could be seen on a clear
morning marked with diadems of snow that sparkled in
the sun. Learning this, Pizarro decided to stay and he
settled with a few companions on the island of Gallo, in
the Gulf of Tumaco, while Almagro grudgingly returned
to Panama, once more in quest of men and supplies. It
was also learned that among the things sent back by the
soldiers who reluctantly stayed with Pizarro was a ball of
finely spun cotton obtained from the Indians and sent to
Governor de los Ríos's wife by a soldier named Saravia.
The ball of cotton contained a few rhymes denouncing
the cruelty and stubbornness of the commanders who led
so many men to their deaths in a senseless adventure.
Referring to Pizarro and Almagro, one of the strophes ran
as follows:

> *Look out, Señor Governor,*
> *For the drover while he's near,*
> *Since he goes home to get the sheep*
> *For the butcher who stays here.*[4]

The governor of Panama finally dispatched a boat under
the command of one Juan Tafur of Córdoba, with an order
calling all the explorers home. The soldiers greeted Tafur's
arrival with great enthusiasm and there was much rejoicing at the sight of the instructions for their return. It was
then that the taciturn Pizarro made a gesture that was to

be remembered in history as the occasion of the birth of the group of the "Thirteen Men of Fame." He had also received the news, in private letters from his partners Luque and Almagro, who urged him to resist the order at all costs, and to stay where he was until help arrived. With his sword, he drew a line on the ground and challenged his soldiers to choose sides, saying, "You may return to Panama and live in poverty, or follow me to Peru and become rich. Let the true Castilians choose what they would rather be . . ."[5] Thirteen men crossed the line and followed Pizarro; among them were Bartolomé Ruiz and Pedro de Candía, the Greek. With the scant help they received, they roamed the country near Puná and Tumbez, picking up stories about a huge empire, ruled by Indians called Incas, who lived in the mountains and who seemed to be the powerful heirs of an ancient civilization, judging by their lordly bearing, their wealth of gold, their fine textiles and their delicate pottery. Toward the end of 1527, Pizarro carried back these stories to Panama and tried to get help setting up a new, larger expedition, but, lacking the governor's support, he had to go to Spain to try to win over the Court.

News of all this had reached the Spaniards of Nicaragua and had set Hernando de Soto dreaming of new journeys of discovery, of finding a great kingdom and becoming famous, laying his name at the feet of his lady fair. Pedrarias, by contrast, stubbornly maintained that Pizarro was bound to fail in his venture, and that only a man of his own temper could carry it off, despite his great age and his many ailments: he had to be carried in a chair, sometimes even in a litter.

Yet, Pedrarias never relaxed the military discipline with which he ruled. He had brought peace to the land and stepped up production in the mines: he intended to maintain this climate of peace and prosperity. He could muster approximately one thousand gentlemen-at-arms whenever he wanted to "show the flag," parade the troops or just bring them together for the many jousts and tour-

naments he directed from a high seat of honor. This is
how they celebrated the great exploits of the Spanish King
Charles, who was drawing ever closer to realizing his
imperial ideal with every day that passed.

To Hernando de Soto, the remote monarch was like
a star, guiding his own on a parallel course, their fates
sharing things in common: they were both born in the
same year and the lady of Hernando's dreams bore the
same first name and was also born during the same year
as Isabel of Portugal, the dazzling beauty of the age, whom
King Charles married in 1526. Once again, the old ideals
of chivalry were firing Spaniards' imaginations at the news
of events in Europe. At the battle of Pavía in 1525, following a charge by the Spanish captains to mark the king's
birthday, young Charles had beaten and taken the Knight-
King of France, Francis I, whom he led off to Spain and
held prisoner until the Treaty of Madrid was signed in
1526; he then released Francis on his own pledge, the
conditions of which were not subsequently kept. Isabel
and Charles also rejoiced in 1527 at the birth of their first
child, Felipe II. It was during that same year that the
Spanish troops, with their Italian and German allies, attacked Rome and compelled Pope Clement VII, Giulio de'
Medici, to take refuge in Fort Sant'Angelo, exacting a
ransom for his release. King Charles had condemned the
looting and gone into mourning for the excesses committed at the time. France and Spain finally made peace,
thereby settling the root cause of the problem. Charles
met the pope in Bologna in an atmosphere of cordiality
and he reached the pinnacle of his power when, in February 1530, on his thirtieth birthday, the pope placed on
his head the Crown of Emperor of the West, together
with the Roman Crown and the Iron Crown, at a ceremony in the church of Saint Petronio.

Pedrarias celebrated this remarkable event, which made
the king the most powerful monarch on earth, with festivities and tournaments lasting several days. At the same

time the old man was secretly inquiring of Hernando about the possibility of his setting off, on his own account, on an expedition to Peru with his friend Ponce. This would foil the plans of Almagro's emissaries, Nicolás de Ribera and the pilot Bartolomé Ruiz, who were in Nicaragua looking for people for their own venture. These men, however, also dealt directly with de Soto, cleverly painting a dazzling picture of the tempting lands they had seen. About that time, Pedrarias asked the Crown, yet once again, to grant him leave to see his family, visit his old haunts in Segovia and reassert his authority by personal visits to the new rulers in power: when he had left Court, it was to Fernando the Catholic he had paid homage. The long-awaited authorization finally came, whereupon he set about making preparations for the voyage, intending not only to go to Spain with his son Arias Gonzalo, the only remaining son,[6] but also to return to his governorship, as though he were a young blade in the best of health. He was fond of inspiring awe and giving the impression he was immortal.

He never managed to undertake the longed-for voyage. Early in 1531, his ailments grew worse and he took to his bed; there he remained for a number of months, with Hernando de Soto keeping solicitous watch by his side. Difficult though it was for him to speak, Pedrarias nevertheless liked to talk to his protégé, his faithful captain, about the years spent in the Indies. He boasted of having upheld the king's authority above all else and he pointed out that, with hostile Indian and willful Spaniard alike, all quarrelsome and brave, only one method would serve: the hand of iron meting out exemplary punishment. While reviewing the faults of each of his men, including those who had disobeyed him and incurred his wrath, he would say that he had succeeded in training and shaping them for the formidable task of extending the empire of Spain. He would reel off the names of all those who had served under him since the Darién days, for the glory of his country, Spain, now mistress of the world. De Soto nodded in agreement at the remarks of this man who had truly been his protector and his teacher in the arts of war; watching him, he thought of Isabel, whom he imagined he represented at this moment, most of all when Pedrarias talked with misty eyes of his wife and children.[7]

Pedrarias died on March 6, 1531. He was ninety-one years old. He was an extraordinary, paradoxical man; a typical Spaniard of his day; a mixture of sturdy qualities of the Middle Ages and of the vices and violent emotions of the Renaissance. Through a strange coincidence, the old and proud Indian Chief Urraca, the only man to have steadfastly stood up to Pedrarias, died near Panama in that same year. With Arias Gonzalo and other captains, Hernando de Soto stood by the bier, that old, legendary casket, at the lavish ceremony in the Cathedral of León and he carried it to the burial grounds in the Monastery of La Merced.

On the casket were draped the flags of Castile and León and the Moorish standards he had taken during his campaign years, which always went with him. While the Gregorian chant of the Franciscans, Dominicans and Brothers of Charity filled the church, Hernando felt the silver cross given to him twelve long years before by a tearful, beautiful girl who had promised to wait for him always.

Before the altar and the casket, he renewed his knight's oath:[8] all his undertakings would be inspired by Isabel and they would all lead back to her, whatever the cost, the time or the obstacles to be overcome. His duty to the father of his loved one was now done. There still lay before him the conquest of fame before he could return to Isabel's side.

THE FASCINATION OF THE SOUTH

XI

To describe all the admirable things that were, and are to be found in this kingdom of Peru would require the skill of a Livy or a Valerian, or one of the world's great writers and even then, the task would be found difficult.[1]

Pedro de Cieza de León

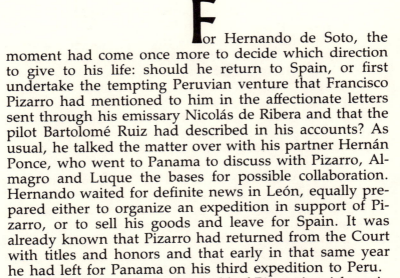

For Hernando de Soto, the moment had come once more to decide which direction to give to his life: should he return to Spain, or first undertake the tempting Peruvian venture that Francisco Pizarro had mentioned to him in the affectionate letters sent through his emissary Nicolás de Ribera and that the pilot Bartolomé Ruiz had described in his accounts? As usual, he talked the matter over with his partner Hernán Ponce, who went to Panama to discuss with Pizarro, Almagro and Luque the bases for possible collaboration. Hernando waited for definite news in León, equally prepared either to organize an expedition in support of Pizarro, or to sell his goods and leave for Spain. It was already known that Pizarro had returned from the Court with titles and honors and that early in that same year he had left for Panama on his third expedition to Peru.

Ponce's letters to de Soto told of Pizarro's mishaps in Spain, which would most certainly interest Hernando.[2] Pizarro had arrived in Seville in the summer of 1528, only to be sued shortly afterward for old debts by the implacable attorney Enciso, and be thrown into prison. But news of Pizarro's arrival had reached the Court, either through the efforts of his companion, Pedro de Candía, the Greek, or because he had brought with him a group of Indians, clothed in typical Peruvian dress, and carried samples of gold, silver, cloth and pottery. The Crown ordered him set free and requested his appearance before the king in Toledo. Charles V listened with attention[3] and sympathy to the story of the quiet man from Trujillo whose impressive bearing marked him as a man of resolve who had known great suffering. He came close to tears at hearing of the great exploits and incredible hardships of the first two exploratory expeditions and learning the facts about the opulence and the organization of the Inca empire. Spain's sun was at its zenith. Hernán Cortés, who was at the Court at that time and who was a kinsman of Pizarro's and an old friend from the days of Santo Domingo, had described in detail the splendid grandeur of a huge empire the size of Europe. Pizarro now brought a plan for acquiring, quite easily it would seem, yet another empire that appeared to be even richer. The king, who was about to leave for his imperial coronation in Bologna, left instructions that the man from Trujillo be given all necessary titles and other requirements. He even suggested that a troop of 500 men be levied, only to hear with great surprise that a bare 150 would be sufficient, given the nature of the land and of the people of Peru.

The beautiful and wise Empress Isabel of Portugal signed the commission, appointing Pizarro governor and captain general of New Castile, the name given to the land known as Peru to the explorers, also conferring on him the Order of Santiago and naming him adelantado and high constable, although in Panama he had promised to obtain these titles for Almagro. For the latter, Pizarro obtained the titles of marshal, warden of the fortress of Tumbez and gentleman. Hernando de Luque was made bishop of Tumbez and protector general of the Indians, with an income of a thousand ducats; to Bartolomé Ruíz went the title of first pilot of the Southern Sea and to Pedro de Candía, that of captain of artillery.

The low-born Francisco Pizarro of Trujillo, endowed with titles and money, proudly returned to the town where he was born, to seek out his brothers[4] and give them the opportunity of joining him on his ventures. These brothers quickly agreed, for they were as proud as they were poor and as short of substance as they were desirous of acquiring it.

Pizarro was unable to organize the expedition exactly as it had been stipulated, and had to leave Seville secretly in January 1530. His brothers followed in other ships; all told, five ships met in Gomera. Bitter quarrels, due to displeasure over the arrangements made and the titles obtained, detained Pizarro and his partners Luque and Almagro in Panama, but, when their common covetousness united them again, the expedition left Panama in January 1531 on three ships, with 183 men and 37 horses on board.

After giving him this news, Hernán Ponce's concrete proposal to Hernando de Soto was that Pizarro offered him the post of lieutenant general, that is to say second-in-command of the expedition in recognition of his good tactical judgment, his experience in Indian affairs, his skill as a lancer and good horsemanship. Ponce suggested that Hernando muster the greatest possible number of men and horses, as the people he brought with him from Spain had fallen ill or had not wished to go any further once they had reached Panama. Hernán Ponce suggested he get the expedition ready as soon as possible and set off to rejoin Pizarro in the south, while he remained in Panama to negotiate with Almagro and Luque and went on representing the company for the two of them.

Hernando made his decision quickly. A good number of his friends and veterans wanted to go with him. He had nothing else to do in Nicaragua and he therefore sold his property, bought two boats and made for Panama with a hundred men. There, he attended to the last details, bought fifty horses, victuals, arms and tools, took leave of his friend Ponce and headed south to meet Pizarro. He was, in fact, bringing reinforcements that were more than half what the tough native of Extremadura had managed to assemble. He also brought his youth, his daring and his experience: he was about to take part, in his own right, in an extraordinary adventure. Among his personal belongings he had packed a token of his past dreams, his old copy of *Amadís*, carefully concealed in wrappings, since a royal decree at that time prohibited "such worldly books as *Amadís*," for fear they would bring discredit on the authenticity of the Holy Scriptures. But for Hernando, the book had all the reality of a caress, for its lines had once carried the gaze of Isabel's beautiful black eyes. He had entrusted to Ponce, in Panama, a passionate letter which Ponce was to forward to her, in which he explained his decision, and said that he would shortly go to see her and keep his promise, since he sustained himself on the trust that Isabel would also keep hers.

Pizarro traveled through places already familiar to the pilot Bartolomé Ruíz. He stopped in Coaque, and on the Ecuadorean coast, in the district of Emeralds. The soldiers obtained from the amenable and generous natives a number of such gems, but hammered them to dust, in the mistaken belief that the real gems withstood such treatment. He later stopped at the village of Puerto Viejo in Manabí, and there suffered a food shortage, but at last a ship sent by Almagro arrived, carrying Sebastián de Benalcázar, the overseers and the royal treasurer. Continuing on his way south, to the Gulf of Guayaquil, and landing on the rich, large island of Puná, he entertained peaceful dealings with the natives, and stilled their fears about his intentions. Through the intrigues of two native interpreters, Felipillo and Martinillo, whom Pizarro had kept with him since his earlier journeys, he decided to take prisoner several of the Puná chiefs, as a protection against a supposed conspiracy. The Indians resisted, became aggressive, then frequently attacked the Spanish encampment. Moreover the climate was weakening the

Europeans, unaccustomed to the tropics, and discontent was rife. At the other end of the gulf, near Tumbez, the Indians, who were enemies of the natives of Puná, had invited Pizarro to bring his forces to the continent; but he could not bring himself to do so for fear of exposing the few men he had to new dangers. Several of them had already died of wounds and sickness; his brother Hernando had been wounded by a spear that had pierced his leg.

Pizarro's expedition was in bad shape. No news of help came from Panama. Almagro's resentment was said to be the cause of this silence; dispirited men spent their days gazing at the horizon, hoping to catch sight of a ship. One afternoon the miracle occurred: two sails were spotted on the sea, making for the gulf; they were Hernando de Soto's ships with the hundred men and fifty horses. They were greeted with cries of jubilation by the men of the expedition. Pizarro embraced Hernando as an old comrade, despite the difference in their ages, and, telling him of his plans, said that he would immediately cross over to the continent, and would make Tumbez the starting point of their march on the fabulous empire of the Incas.

De Soto was able to conceal the great disappointment he felt on his arrival. The terrain seemed difficult, Pizarro's soldiers could not be in worse spirits and, above all, the post of lieutenant general that Pizarro had offered him was already taken by his brother Hernando Pizarro, an arrogant man, "tall and fat, with a gross tongue and full lips, the tip of his nose overladen with flesh and highly colored."[5] The wisdom and calm which de Soto displayed and the prestige his name enjoyed among the soldiers made him popular and, as Francisco Pizarro himself acknowledged, he was in fact the second-in-command of the expedition.

The landing at Tumbez was difficult. The natives, who had pledged their goodwill and assistance, fell upon the first expeditionaries to land while men and horses were still crossing from Puná on boats and rafts. Pizarro reached Tumbez after three attempts and he found the people very different from those Pedro de Candía and Alonso de Medina saw when they came to gauge their prosperity: the country was torn by civil war and the population had suffered from it.

With his usual cautiousness, Hernando organized a column to pacify the surrounding district and managed to rout a band of Indians who had fought the landings and were preparing for further attacks. The horses, harquebuses and lances spread terror among the inhabitants of Tumbez. Many were taken prisoner by de Soto, who then sent for Chief Chilimisa through interpreters, reproaching him for his treason, offering his friendship and promising friendly treatment in the future. Hernando greeted with courtesy a mistrustful Chilimisa who appeared before him with his chieftains. De Soto advised the chief to order the villagers home in the interests of the prosperity of his dominion. Chilimisa agreed to the terms and ordered his bands to lay down their arms and to return to Tumbez; he then went back with de Soto to Pizarro's camp. Pizarro confirmed Hernando's terms and congratulated him on his firm and appropriate action, which certainly enhanced his prestige.

Chilimisa gave long accounts of the empire to Pizarro, to de Soto and the other captains who listened in astonishment to the interpreters telling them how best they could set about penetrating this kingdom that lay before them, with the huge mountains of the Andean range looming in the distance, as a barrier that reached to the clouds.

The Incas called their Empire Tahuantin-suyo, meaning the "Four Corners of the World." Rumors reaching Panama had led to naming it Peru, after the river Birú, south of the isthmus: it was really Tahuantin-suyo. Its four corners included Chincha-suyo to the north, extending up to Quito and over to the land south of Colombia as well as to the warm lands along the coast; Anti-suyo, the mountainous eastern region of the Peruvian highlands and Bolivia; Conti-suyo to the west along the Peruvian coast and Colla-suyo to the south, reaching down to Chile and Argentina, the most temperate region. Before the Spaniards' arrival, this enormous empire had had two capitals: Quito in the north and Cuzco in the south. Quito was the main city of the kingdom of Quito and seemed to have been founded in the ninth century; Cuzco was somewhat more recent and was the seat of the Inca Court. One Inca, or lord, called Manco Capac had founded a great dynasty. Coming down from the north and reaching Lake Titicaca, he had declared himself to be the Son of the Sun-his-Father and asserted that his god Viracocha had entrusted his lineage with the mission of saving the world. To this end he had chosen the valley of Cuzco, 10,200 feet above the sea, to be the center of this world and from there his sons, all proud, intelligent and active men, had moved across the map of America, extending their possessions and organizing the kingdom into a highly centralized and unified entity. They bound its people together by means of the melodious Quechua language, "the language of men,"[6] unifying all regions and displacing the Aymara language of the old Tiahuanaco empire, which had prospered in Bolivia in earlier centuries. In the fifteenth century, or thereabouts, the Inca Tupac-Yupanqui, "the Resplendent," had made great conquests: leading fifty thousand soldiers through the ravine of Humahuaca, he had reached Tucumán, in Argentina, and Bío-bío in Chile. He gained the population's obedience by levying tributes, posting garrisons, imposing an austere military discipline, building solid roads and strongholds, setting up posthouses and relay services, the graceful llamas carrying the mails in parcels weighing up to fifty pounds. Later, at the head of an even greater army, he invaded the kingdom of Quito, where he succeeded in overpowering the old *Schyris* kings. Though opposed by many tribes, he imposed his authority and built strongholds before returning south. About 1450, in the district of Tomebamba (Cuenca), he had a son who became known as Huayna Capac, the Inca who consolidated the empire. Huayna Capac was educated in Cuzco, which means the "Navel of the World," and after following his father on new warlike expeditions, while still young, he took over the government of the empire, wearing on his forehead the wool tassel, the *llautu*[7] that was the symbol of imperial dignity. Huayna Capac was a generous Inca, but he was also a strict soldier "with good features and a very stern countenance; he was a man of few words but many deeds and he rigorously applied the law, showing no restraint in punishment."[8] Among other chastisements he imposed on whole regions, he would remove large groups of people to other areas; such displaced Indians were known as *mitimaes*. Huayna Capac consolidated the conquest of Quito by marrying its Schyri queen, Paccha. The clear, fresh air of Quito, the luminous green of the mountains around the volcano, Pichincha, the gentleness of the people, all this fascinated the Inca, who visited Cuzco ever less frequently and spent more than twenty-five years of his life in Quito. He maintained the peace and built a wide road from Quito to Cuzco; he was the Son of the Sun, the supreme priest in his theocratic state and he had delved into the prophecies with the soothsayers, and found strange similarities with those relating to Quetzalcoatl, the god of the Aztecs, in the north. Among the Incas, the talk was of Viracocha, a white, bearded god who was to come one day to help his people in times of crisis. When Huayna Capac, the formidable warrior, felt the approach of death, he faced the problem of having to decide which of his two principal sons (he had more than one hundred) should inherit his empire: Atahualpa, his favorite, the son of the queen of Quito, who had followed him on his journeys

and had been at his side during his campaigns, or Huáscar, son of a *ñusta*, or princess, Rahuar Ocllo, of Cuzco,
favored by the Court of Cuzco. When he finally died in
1526, in Tomebamba, on the way to Cuzco, he had already
heard the first reports of the Spanish explorations along
his coast and, having related this to the disturbing prophecies of Viracocha, he had decided to split the empire
between the two capitals, the north going to Atahualpa
with his kingdom of Quito, the south to Huáscar with his
Cuzco Court.

Huayna Capac's funeral was impressive; by his own
last wish, his heart remained in Quito and his embalmed
body was slowly carried over the enormous roads to Cuzco,
where it was laid in the temple of Cori-Cancha dedicated
to the Sun. After the funeral, the brothers lived in peace
for a few years, or rather in peaceful coexistence, since
they hardly entertained cordial relations with each other.
This state of affairs lasted for nearly five years, when
Huáscar chose to send a strong army to help the Cañaris
Indians of Tomebamba who had rebelled against his
brother. Thus he started a fratricidal war. Under the circumstances, and for lack of more experienced generals,
Atahualpa took personal command of his army, which
had already suffered a few setbacks at the hands of the
Cuzco troops. He won three successive victories, at Am-
bato, Jauja and finally at Quipaipan, where he met the
last enemy army headed by Huáscar himself; there, General Quizquiz of Quito respectfully took Huáscar prisoner,
and kept him under lock and key in a stronghold.

Atahualpa was triumphant; his troops consolidated
his authority in Cuzco. He was just thirty years old and
he wore on his head both the *llautu* of the Incas and the
emerald of the *Schyris* kings of Quito. Tired by his battles
and recovering from a wound, he retired to rest in the
district of Cajamarca, when news reached him of the arrival of white men in large floating houses, with rods of

thunder and monstrous animals that seemed to join and separate while carrying strange beings covered with shining metal.

Hernando de Soto marveled at learning of all this. The advanced political and cultural state of this vast empire was immediately apparent to the Spaniards: the living standards of the Tumbez Indians, the delicate art of their beautiful, many-colored pottery, the most varied and refined ways they had of preparing their food, the skill they brought to the weaving of their variously tinted cloths of cotton or vicuña wool, out of which they made fine clothes and noble mantles, the profusion of gold that every important person wore as part of his apparel.

The Spaniards were also impressed by the state of the roads which, though not intended for carriage traffic, were yet wide and well built, solidly compacted, often paved with stone, and always very clean. They ran over substantial bridges, defying the broken terrain; at intervals were found *tambos*, or shelters, where road maintenance crews and imperial agents alike could find rest, or which served as relay stations for the *chasquis*, those swift couriers who carried the news and the Inca mail, strangely recorded on variously knotted cords, called *quipos*, which also served as accounting documents and calendars.

Their agriculture was also to be marveled at. As the explorers penetrated the mountain areas, they saw how the Indians fought land erosion by practicing terrace cultivation, and in the villages, which were supervised by the Inca's representatives, they saw the great stores of Indian corn and other provisions for the community's use, since everything belonged to everyone, such being the Inca's wish.

Nevertheless, the soldiers were in very low spirits and with their typically Spanish talent for venting their ill-humor, they indulged in reproaches and recriminations against Pedro de Candía, who was responsible for giving the most glowing accounts of the riches of the region, in order to persuade those who, in Panama, were still wavering. Pizarro understood that he could not allow the morale of his men to deteriorate any further and he therefore prepared to take action. He decided to leave a small group with the sick in Tumbez under the command of Riquelme, the royal treasurer and the inspectors. He then set about organizing his own expedition, to explore the land, gathering more information before devising a final plan of action. He would lead a column one hundred men strong to explore the lowlands, while de Soto at the head of a second column of seventy riders would head for the highlands, possibly going as far as the Royal Highway of the Inca.

Hernando set off immediately and went as far as the Cajas area, close to the mountain district of what is now the province of Loja. He then reached the impressive Royal Highway, built by order of Huayna Capac, and led his riders and round-shield bearers over it without any difficulty. He came across large buildings, strongholds and temples, as well as flocks of llamas, whose graceful and delicate elegance seemed to lend a peaceful note to the landscape, forever dominated by the towering mass of the mountains in the background. Driven by their curiosity and their friendly disposition, the local inhabitants came out to gaze at these strange expeditionaries, whose fame had already spread far and wide. They would gape at their beards and a few giggling women would ask them to bare their chests, to see how white they were.

They gave the travelers ample supplies of food they grew or made, cakes of Indian corn and delicate fruit, such as pineapples and mangoes, which eased their weariness and quenched their thirst. They also provided roasted meat of small rodents, called *cobayos* (a variety of guinea pig) which proved to be delicious. Several Spaniards exchanged the cloth and glass they brought with them for gold plate. Nonetheless the Indians wondered at the apparent foolishness of these bearded people who, by splitting into several columns, exposed themselves to attack, and it was not long before they set a trap, hoping to overcome them. But Hernando had not for one moment dropped his guard, and when the attack came at dusk, he was ready for it and retaliated with a strong and orderly repulse; with his horses, lances and a few volleys from his harquebuses, he soon broke up the enemy ranks and took a few prisoners to lead back to Pizarro's camp on the following day.

As for Pizarro, he had scouted the country along the coast. He found it to be arid and inhospitable. He was therefore delighted to hear de Soto's good news and accept the small booty. He was coming to rely more and more on de Soto, whose outstanding military talent he greatly appreciated. He ordered those who remained in Tumbez and were able to travel to come down and join him and then set off for the south, marching until they reached a river that flowed into what was known as the Valley of Tangarala. There, he thought that the climate and the closeness to the sea made this the ideal spot to found a city, the first of his expedition. So it was that, on May 16, 1532, the city of San Miguel de Piura came into being in the province of Chila, some thirty leagues south of Tumbez, near a spit of land known as Payta. Later, a port on the Southern Sea would be built there. He made de Soto commander of Tumbez and also gave him the thirty leagues of land extending to San Miguel. By awarding de Soto such a high mark of distinction, Pizarro meant to soothe Hernando's tacit resentment at not being chosen to be lieutenant general. De Soto accepted the favor with dignity, reflecting on the irony of fate. He now had the assets of a knight: he had a horse, a sword and a fief to lay at the feet of the lady of his dreams. Yet he was not to enjoy such things. She was in a distant land and his lot was to leave, always to leave in search of new adventures, such as the fabulous expedition he was now engaged upon. In San Miguel, Pizarro deputized Purser Antonio de Navarro, charging him, together with other officials of the king and soldiers unfit to join the expedition, with the responsibility of building the city. Meantime, news came from Panama that, because the titular bishop, Friar Hernando de Luque, was too ill to travel, Friar Reginald de Pedraza was being appointed protector of the Indians by the new governor, Licentiate de la Gama. That night, there was much rejoicing in the camp and, for the first time, the wine flowed and Spanish guitars sounded under the deft fingers of two Andalusian soldiers.

Pizarro then decided to take 160 men and make for Cajamarca where the Inca Atahualpa was said to be resting after unifying his empire. He sent de Soto ahead with a dozen riders to find out what he could about the movements of the Inca's troops. Hernando went as far as the Royal Highway and was able to determine that there was indeed a considerable number of men on the move, most probably going to join Atahualpa in his camp. On the highway, Hernando was met by a magnificent deputation from the Inca, headed by an Indian who belonged to their nobility and whom the Spaniards called "Long Ears"[9] because of his enormous earlobes that were pulled out of shape by the fist-sized gold earrings he wore.

Speaking in deliberate utterances, the haughty Indian expressed himself through interpreters in precise and measured terms, but the Spaniards' attention was far more directed to his amazing headgear and gold jewelry than to his message. A beautiful mantle of many colors fell down his back. It was made of wool and cotton and each of the two faces of the cloth carried a different design, fancifully colored in shades of yellow, pink, and red, intermingled with touches of ocher for contrast. Figures were fashioned on it, and although the same shapes were repeated, the color of the threads changed. It must have taken many months to weave. He wore a gold diadem

that kept his hair in place and, hanging from his nose
was a gold ornament in the shape of a half-moon, covering
his mouth and edged with a most delicate fringe that hung
from its lower side. A gold pectoral showed a miniature
reproduction of his own face, complete with nose ornament and earrings. On his wrists were large gold cuffs
and on his ankles, wide bands of gold. Round his neck
hung a beautifully made ornament of turquoise beads,
with pieces of red shells and quartz and jade of various
hues, from the darkest to the most limpid. Wound round
his waist was a beautiful waistband of vicuña wool, embellished with symbolic designs in red, white, blue, dark
purple and pink; from it hung a woolen bag or pouch,
dyed with vegetable dyes in yellow and dark tones of
coffee and black, decorated with a jaguar-head pattern.

The Spaniards had been through a great deal. Their
lively imagination was now aroused at the sight of this
messenger, for if such was the emissary, what must the
master be like? Their attitude suddenly changed from jaded
disaffection and cynicism to the greatest possible elation,
a mood much more in keeping with their temperament.
Long Ears asked de Soto to give Pizarro the gifts he brought
from the Inca: several finely wrought stone vessels and
some aromatic dried powder which the great of the Inca
empire seemed to use as a scent. Hernando elected to
lead Long Ears to Pizarro's camp. Pizarro greeted him
with consummate courtesy, though he seemed to be bearing rather modest gifts from so great a king. Perhaps he
was more interested in ascertaining the Spaniards' strength.
Be that as it may, Long Ears arranged for Pizarro to meet
Atahualpa in Cajamarca.

Pizarro gave orders that the emissary and his followers
be provided with food and lodgings for as long as they
might wish to stay. But when they said they had to leave
immediately, Pizarro gave instructions that Long Ears be
given a linen shirt, a red cap, knives, scissors and glass

beads, all of which seemed very much to the Indian's liking.

Pizarro sought de Soto's counsel and came to the conclusion that the road to Cajamarca had to lie over the high mountains. This would heavily tax the strength of people accustomed to living at far lower altitudes, or even at sea level. The horses, too, would suffer during the climb over steep mountain paths. Yet it was worthwhile taking them along, since horses were an invaluable if not a decisive element in the task of bringing peace to the country.

Methodically, de Soto set about preparing for the ascent of the Andes. He briefed his men, reviewed the equipment and had ropes made, as well as special bridles, to help the horses up the steep slopes. He felt he was at the start of a new chapter of his odyssey. He was about to enter a new world, the world of the mountains, where the clouds, stark white against the intensely blue sky, sometimes floated by below the paths they would tread; where the air was purer and more rarefied; where tall peaks pierced the sky along the snow-capped crests, seeming to guard the mystery of the heir to the Sun.[10]

THE CHILD OF THE SUN

XII

Hernando de Soto was truly chivalrous and he may have been the only noble mind among the one hundred and seventy Spaniards who took the Child of the Sun prisoner.[1]

Ricardo Palma

The march to the Andes was the first difficulty that the 170 Spaniards had to overcome; with a few dozen servants, they were breaking into the great Inca empire. Pizarro knew that he was approaching the quarters of a stern and triumphant ruler who was surrounded by a very great army. He also had no choice but to keep marching forward, trusting in luck and in the boldness of his enterprise. He had already waited long enough; he could entertain no further hope of help from his resentful associates Almagro and Luque. Were he even to lead twice the number of men, his column would still only be a diminutive force by comparison with the Inca's legions. He trusted in Providence and maintained a calm and even jovial appearance before his men.

Francisco Pizarro also knew that this was the biggest gamble of his lifetime. He was weary of the hardships and the sacrifices that attended his life in the Indies. He realized that his own men were grumbling behind his back[2] and deriding him for assuming airs of nobility, when everyone knew his humble origins: he was the little swineherd from Trujillo. Only after learning of the titles and deeds he carried everywhere with him in a great leather chest did his own half brothers, especially the arrogant Hernando, deign to show him some consideration. Yet the heaviest burden this sad and silent man had to bear was the thought of the long existence of sacrifice he had led, with success always out of reach. Memories crowded in on him:[3] his life from Hispaniola to Darién, the first explorations of the unfortunate Nicuesa, the bad business with Balboa, whom he had accompanied on his discovery of the Southern Sea and whose death he witnessed in Acla. All this he would rather forget. Moreover, he had always had the junior role, been given the most difficult job, left out when the time came to share the spoils. Today, all-powerful and trusted, he had but one way to go; there was an empire to be had at the end of his sword and an example to guide him, that of his distant kinsman Cortés, whom he had always envied. He would either succeed, or die in the attempt.

Greed bound the other Pizarro brothers to Francisco. Hernando never lost an opportunity of reminding the others of his position as the elder brother, playing on his title of nobility; though Francisco had only recently met him for the first time, he nevertheless treated him with respect and even deference. Hernando was, admittedly, well practiced in courtly skills: his repartee was witty or cutting, as occasion demanded, his manner haughty, as befitted an impoverished gentleman, and his temper quick; he was prompt to draw his sword and his moods were sudden and extreme. He took a liking to Hernando de Soto despite their relative positions which must necessarily place both men in competition, since they both were in effect the governor's lieutenants. But he harbored an open hatred and contempt for Almagro, whom he had publicly insulted in Panama. This was the reason for the absence of reinforcements. There were also rumors that Almagro was setting up another expedition on his account. Be that as it may, the Pizarro clan respected the opinions of the elder brother, Hernando, who was always listened to, and always given the place of honor whenever the family met.

As for Gonzalo, who was the youngest and the most impetuous, ambition was his mainspring; it drove him in all his undertakings, though he managed to save his energy for action. He was above all the paladin, with a reputation for being the best lance in Italy and a determination to remain undisputedly so. For the time being, he had pledged his loyalty to Francisco and, under his direction, he would give his best. Later, he would seek success on his own, for his ambition relied on the strength of his arm. He was on friendly terms with de Soto, as befitted companions-in-arms; they were both of the same age and they both shared a liking for the skills of war. Gonzalo Pizarro would admit that de Soto was the second-best lance in the Indies, the only one worthy to challenge him. On the other hand, the soldiers knew that de Soto was the best horseman of the expedition and that practically no man could match his swordsmanship. De Soto had gained his experience in Panama and Nicaragua where he had trained under the formidable Pedrarias. Gonzalo's experience came from the Italian wars, under the banners of the Great Captain and of Navarro.

The other Pizarros were more modest and reserved. Juan was a model of loyalty and good judgment, though just as brave as the others. Martín de Alcántara, Francisco's half brother on his mother's side, always present when needed, seemed to hide and vanish when the time came for making merry and dividing the spoils. Nephew Pedro served as a page boy, quietly observing, privy to all secrets and taking notes for his chronicles whereby he was to pass on his impressions to posterity.

De Soto felt he was an honorary member of the clan. He enjoyed Francisco's preference and always kept his favor. He was always given the most difficult tasks and he knew that, for that very reason, it would be fatal for him to make the slightest mistake that might incur the displeasure of the Pizarros. Apart from his natural tact, his experience and his prestige, two factors aided him: he had joined the expedition with one hundred men and fifty horses, provided for out of his own pocket; then there was the immoderate price of the Pizarros, each believing he was entitled to a coronet, who would have thought it unbecoming to confide in an outsider. Beyond this, de Soto had only a passing interest in the venture. He would share in its success and would then leave. Other, more spiritual and nobler reasons beckoned him to Spain and it was that devotion and that ideal that directed his efforts.

As the Spanish columns moved up the Andean slopes, they found the air was beginning to cool. They had to climb to the high ground to reach the Inca highway and make for Cajamarca. In the span of a few hours, the landscape changed completely. The mild air of the coast, the rustling, humid tropical vegetation, were quite left behind. Great rocks now stood in their way and new kinds of vegetation, of a different green, surrounded them. Freshwater streams ran in the open spaces between the rocks and seeped into the ground, making it slippery and unsafe for the horses. The climb was turning into an ever more hazardous operation. Gradually the men shed their armor, their helmets, their padded cotton jerkins and gave them to their Indian servants to carry. But the horses were the main problem. The men sometimes had to spend hours tying the beasts, head and tail, to help them up a steep passage. The soldiers were beginning to complain of the cold, but the horses were panting with exhaustion. Men and horses were used to lower ground. The soldiers felt their hearts pounding, while their ears buzzed with the unusual atmospheric pressure of the heights.

Hernando watched the Indians of his column with great interest. They moved with an easy, steady lope, betraying no feeling of any kind, their faces as stone, as if resigned to their fate: they were meant to accompany these white foreign invaders and conquer those mountains of which they seemed to be a part. Indeed they appeared to be made of the same black rock as the Andean spurs: hard, indifferent, mysterious. They, in turn, looked upon him with friendly feelings;[4] they had sensed the true kindness and the honest nature of the young captain. They felt he was treating them better than other Spanish officers, hearing them out, heeding their opinions. When Hernando, exhausted by the strain and the altitude, showed signs of fatigue, some would approach him and offer him mountain garlic which would reinvigorate him with its strong flavor, while effectively checking, albeit for a while, the dangerous mountain sickness they called the *soroche*.

The friars chanted their breviary in nasal tones, each intoning a versicle in turn, partly to keep the mind occupied, partly to give the enterprise an air of solemnity, since everyone seemed obsessed with the feeling they were penetrating a veritable fortress and could be heading straight to their own destruction.

Francisco Pizarro, Hernando de Soto and forty men went ahead, while the rest of the column, under the command of Hernando Pizarro, followed more slowly and awaited instructions. The first party was blazing the trail and easing the path for the others. They sometimes had to lay timbers across the ravines, and were delayed by such tasks. Even the Indian paths, which they sometimes encountered, were inadequate. The llamas, with their light, almost ethereal tread, could follow such precarious tracks; but not the horses. Moreover, the way lay through awe-inspiring gorges that seemed to have been carved out of the mountains. They occasionally spotted Indian lookouts high above them on the escarpments and the sight filled the Spaniards with apprehension. Were they heading for a trap? Taught by their soldiering experience, Pizarro and de Soto realized that a handful of defenders, armed only with stones, could wipe out their column in any of the narrow passes. But the Indians appeared to be obeying orders from a higher authority to refrain from resorting to violence. The Spaniards felt that they would be let through. Out of friendship? Out of fear? Perhaps out of curiosity? Or was it only the better to destroy them later? Whatever fate awaited them, the struggle to conquer the cordillera made the men of the expeditionary force realize their own puny strength. They were ever contrasting their small force with the enormous empire they were taking on.

The vegetation had changed. As they climbed, they noticed the thinner shrubs, making way for the rushes in the frozen marshes. Accustomed as they had been for years to living in the tropical heat of Panama and Nicaragua, the men felt the considerable altitude and the cold, which were becoming unbearable for man and beast alike. Yet they were determined to push forward: Pizarro and de Soto with the vanguard, Hernando with the rearguard. One night they bivouacked in an abandoned fortress, where the thick walls, built of enormous blocks of stone laid together without mortar, but cut with admirable precision, filled the Spaniards with amazement. Once they had crossed the crest line of the Andes and started down the eastern slopes, another of Atahualpa's emissaries came to them with presents, including some llamas that trotted beside him with their graceful, jogging gait. The envoy said he was the Inca's brother; he had with him several servants who proffered fermented corn milk, or *chicha*, in richly ornamented gold cups that drew the covetous stares of the Spaniards. Pizarro treated the envoy with courtesy and gave him a few presents for the Inca, reaffirming his peaceful intentions and telling him he would soon pay a visit and bring the salutations of the pope and of the king of Spain. The Spaniards continued their descent and seven days later came into view of the valley of Cajamarca, which appeared very green, with its luxuriant vegetation and an abundance of carefully tilled parcels of land. They met groups of local inhabitants, moving swiftly with easy movements, dressed in dark clothing relieved by red embroidery. They were trying not to look straight at the white men, pretending to be absorbed in the task of tending their flocks of llamas trotting beside them, the animals' necks straight up, gazing into the distance with all the intentness their enormous eyes could muster. On one side lay the city with its white houses lined up in rows, the main square in the center. At the other end of the valley, swirls of vapor rose from the hot springs, the famous thermal baths of the region, and farther down the slope, the breathtaking spectacle of thousands upon thousands of white cotton field-tents, lined up with mathematical precision; this was the camp of the Inca and of his victorious army. De Soto and Pizarro were afraid that their men would panic at the sight of the thousands of tents.

To their surprise, the city was empty; everything seemed to fit a pattern: no guards in the gorges, no garrisons in the fortress and now, no one in the city, yet there was the army bivouacking close by. Things were ever less to Pizarro's liking—a gloomy, suspicious man by nature— and his concern showed in his bearing. It was the 15th of November 1532 when they entered the city and took up their quarters in the buildings in the main square.

Pizarro was uneasy and did not want to lose a minute. It was already late in the day. He nevertheless resolved to send a deputation to Atahualpa, and for this mission he chose de Soto, who thus would be the first European to look into the eyes of the Child of the Sun. Pizarro ordered de Soto to take fifteen riders, convey Pizarro's salutations to the Inca and invite him to Cajamarca to talk about Spain.

Hernando chose his men. He allowed the mounts a few minutes' rest while he dressed in full armor and donned the splendid suit he had brought with him from Nicaragua. When all were ready, he briefly inspected them; he then led them in a charge, at full gallop, down a fairly good road, into the Inca's camp, which stood about a league away. A standard-bearer carried the banner of Spain and next to him rode a trumpeter blowing shrill notes into the wind. By Hernando rode Felipillo the interpreter, the Indian who had been with Pizarro since the second expedition, years ago. He came from the province of Poceos and did nothing to conceal his aversion for Atahualpa. He was in fact a liar and an intriguer and de Soto intensely disliked him.

When they reached the camp of the Inca, rain and hail started to fall, but this in no way detracted from the dash and glitter of the cavalcade, nor did it dull the attention of the Indians, who were gazing at the foreigners they had heard so much about. Rather, the distant thunder and the dark sky cast a fantastic and mysterious glow on these bearded, awe-inspiring envoys of a remote king, these riders of huge animals that had never before been seen in these lands. In front of each tent stood clusters of spears, driven into the ground. A small brook protected the inner circle of the camp and a small bridge made of boards gave access to the center. Disdainfully ignoring the bridge, de Soto led his men straight through the water where the horses' hooves splashed up a fine spray that glistened and sparkled as it caught the light; with his retinue of riders, he made his arrival as dramatic as he could. The Indian guards, lined up along the way, stood motionless and expressionless at their posts, so that it was easy for Hernando to find the place that marked the center of the Inca's quarters. It was a large mansion, brightly painted white and decorated with variegated colors; in front was a raised terrace and a pool that was fed by converging streams of steaming hot and cold water. Gardens could be seen on the sides and behind. About then the rain stopped and the sky began to clear, with the atmosphere taking on that typical transparency of an Andean evening. On the stairways flanking the house, on either side of the portico and on the lower terrace behind the pool, the most powerful men of Atahualpa's Court stood in a line. They wore rich clothes, resplendent with gold, and displayed a magnificence that marked them as noblemen. In the middle, in the space under the portico, occupying a low stool that allowed him to cross his legs on the ground, sat, with the same quiet majesty as his own mountains, Atahualpa the priest, the serene one, the king of Quito, lord of Tahuantin-suyo, the Child of the Sun.

Hernando thundered on with his men, sweeping in amid a clatter of horses' hooves and the blare of the trumpet, to the very edge of the first row of noblemen that surrounded the Inca. There, he checked his lively mare and dismounted. Taking off his plumed helmet and tossing his head back, he advanced with deliberate calm and solemnity until he stood before the Inca. Felipillo was at his side with two other soldiers, one of whom was the standard-bearer. Atahualpa was in the fullness of youth and his presence was impressive. He was about thirty-six years of age. His gaze was stern and bright. He wore a high crown of gold on his head and on his forehead hung the tassel of red wool, plaited with threads of gold, the imperial *llautu* of the Indian Incas, which he had just won from his brother, after a triumphant campaign. It was said that he still held his brother prisoner in an inland fortress.

"Greetings, my lord," said de Soto, "I bring you the salutation of my governor, Don Francisco Pizarro, who earnestly wishes to pay his respects to you in person, in the name of our lord, the king of Spain."

Atahualpa gave no answer and pretended not to see the young captain, although, of course, not a single detail had escaped his notice: the monstrous horses, the metal suits of armor, the strange lances which, rumor had it, the white soldiers spent the whole day cleaning with seemingly nothing else to do, the round shields and the gauntlets. De Soto was the first European he had seen. Tall, bearded, of dark complexion, De Soto reminded him of the words of his father Huayna Capac, the prophecy telling of the arrival of the emissaries of Viracocha. But he had been given wrong information.[5] His governors on the coast had told him these soldiers were weak; they had also told him of their outrageous behavior, of their violence in the villages of the gulf. Pondering all this, he remained silent, not deigning to look at de Soto. A heavy silence hung over the assembly of six hundred noblemen gathered round their master. Then, one of the men close to Atahualpa said:

"It is well."[6]

Silence fell once more at this first encounter of the men from Europe with the powerful ruler of America. De Soto then became aware of a familiar noise. It was the clatter of armor along the same road his own horsemen had taken, signaling the arrival of another column of twenty men on horseback, led by a figure de Soto immediately recognized: it was the well-known, corpulent, pompous Hernando Pizarro. The governor had probably thought that de Soto's fifteen horsemen might have been running too great a risk among such a large army and he must therefore have decided to send Hernando after him with more men as reinforcement. De Soto said:

"And here, my lord, comes the brother of our governor, who will repeat the invitation."

Pizarro came forward on his horse, alone, before the Inca. Without dismounting, he bowed and, taking off his hat, he said:

"My lord, I have come to inform you of our arrival in Cajamarca and to thank you for your hospitality, in the name of my brother the governor. We have been sent from across the seas by a great prince who has heard of your victories. We are here to offer our services and inform you of our religion, the only true religion. I bring you an invitation from my brother to visit us in our quarters."

Atahualpa did not move a muscle and went on staring blankly, pretending to be unaware of what he heard through the interpreter. The long-eared nobleman who stood at his side of a row of women servants said once more:

"It is well."

Hernando Pizarro waited a few minutes; he knew that this was an interview in which he simply had to get results. He therefore went on:

"I ask you, my lord, to give us a reply yourself."[7]

There was a moment of tension in the audience when Felipillo translated the sentence, since everyone understood that the affront to the visitor would be manifest if the Inca did not speak.

Eyeing Felipillo with contempt, but without even glancing at the Spaniards, Atahualpa gave the following reply:

"Tell your captain that I am keeping a fast that will end tomorrow. I will go and visit him with my captains; meanwhile he may repair to the buildings on the square and wait there until I arrive and ordain what should be done next."[8]

Atahualpa raised his eyes and looked at de Soto's mare which was champing at the bit and pawing the ground. Its rider understood the Inca's natural curiosity and, promptly jumping into the saddle, he spurred his horse and gave a demonstration of his great skill. He first went into a gallop across the flat ground and returned after putting his admirable mount through its paces with extraordinary grace and precision. Now to the left, now to the right, he had her trotting in half circles, all the while brandishing his lance and dropping the reins on the neck so that all could see that she obeyed her master by responding to a mere pressure of the knees. He then changed the pace and made her rear and take a few paces on her hind legs. Finally taking her over a fence in one spectacular jump, he led her at full gallop toward the imperial group and checked her brutally just in front of Atahualpa himself, so close that some froth from her mouth fell on the hem of the Inca's mantle. The Inca remained imperturbable, showing both courage and majesty before the caprioles of an animal he had never seen before. Some of his men, however, were unable to conceal their fright and took a few steps back, whereupon the monarch glowered at them. It was later learned that he had sentenced to death that very night those who had allowed their fear to show in front of the foreigners.

Atahualpa then said:

"Maizabilica, my chieftain on the River Ruricarami, has told me that you ill-treated my governors and that you threw them in chains. He sent me a sample of the chains. He also told me that he killed three of your soldiers as well as one of those great sheep you ride."

"Maizabilica is a prevaricator," Pizarro retorted haughtily; "he is incapable of killing one of our soldiers; he is an old hen. Neither the governor nor ourselves treated the chieftains badly when they did not want war. When we help you against your enemies, you will see how Maizabilica has lied."

"There is a chieftain who has refused to obey me," replied Atahualpa. "I'll send you with a few of my soldiers to wage war on him."

"For one chieftain, however many men he may have," bragged Pizarro, "there is no need for your people to come. Ten Christians on horseback will destroy him."[9]

For the first time, Atahualpa dropped his hostile attitude and smiled at the Spaniard's swagger. He made a gesture and several richly dressed women promptly approached them bearing *chicha* in gold cups. Atahualpa looked at the women, silently ordering them to return with more cups, also made of gold, this time larger and more finely wrought.

At first, Pizarro said that they, too, were fasting, for he did not trust the native beverage, but when the Inca looked at him in surprise and de Soto nudged him, he accepted the drink and dismounted, whereupon all his companions followed suit. Night was closing in on the camp and Pizarro as well as de Soto took their leave of the monarch, bowing ceremoniously; they then mounted and took the road back to the city.

The captains rode back to headquarters in Cajamarca greatly impressed by what they had seen. They dwelt on the majesty of the Inca, his obvious intelligence, his serenity and courage, but most of all, they wondered at the enormous force that surrounded him and at the extraordinary discipline he seemed to have instilled into his garrison troops. Moreover, they learned from Felipillo that these were only raw recruits, and that the veterans, under the command of the Quito generals Rumiñahui, Quizquiz and Calicuchima, were still some distance away, expected to join the rest of the troops shortly. They reckoned that Atahualpa was surrounded by thirty thousand men, in a camp that extended over practically one full league, nearly 3.5 miles.

When they reported the results of their first meeting to the governor, the latter showed obvious concern and ordered double sentries to be posted. He then told them to be ready for the events of the following day, which was to be Saturday the 16th of November 1532.

Having taken those precautions for the night to be spent uncomfortably close to such a large army, Pizarro called a council of his captains. They were his brothers, with Hernando de Soto, Sebastián de Benalcázar, Captain of the Artillery Pedro de Candía and two of the friars. In his usual cool, calculating and decisive way, Pizarro quickly reviewed the situation. They were in the heart of the Inca empire, next to the Inca's victorious army, obviously quite hemmed in. Reinforcements had been expected from Almagro, who had not sent them. If they were to conquer a kingdom, it had to be done with the 170 men of the expeditionary force alone, with no alternative offered: they had to succeed. Only by a bold strike could they gain control of the whole country in the name of Spain. They had to seize Atahualpa himself. He, Pizarro, now knew exactly how Hernán Cortés felt, when in the Aztec empire he had also come to realize that it was the only way; and he had pulled it off, since he had governed the country for several months through his prisoner Montezuma. That was before Alvarado had rashly upset the balance and triggered an outbreak of violence. But then, Pizarro could not call upon friendly indigenous troops, as Cortés had been able to do with his forty thousand Tlaxcaltecas. True enough, Pizarro had learned from Felipillo that there were Indian parties hostile to Atahualpa, mainly at the Court of Cuzco, but all were now under the heel of the armies of the Quito generals. There was therefore only one card left to play: a surprise move when the Inca came to the city of Cajamarca. They must be prepared to act the very next day.

When Pizarro asked his captains for their opinion, each and every one agreed to his suggestion, except de Soto, who spoke up when his turn came:

"Certainly we are surrounded by an army, but it would be better if we acted openly and attacked the Inca in his headquarters, rather than invite him to our camp in order to seize him here; it would be more fitting behavior for Castilians. However, if there is no other way, then at least let not History point an accusing finger at us: we must undertake to do two things. Firstly we must merely take the Inca prisoner, making sure that no harm comes to him, and secondly, we must, when he arrives, tell him of our designs and read him the Entreaty, or Requerimiento, as prescribed by royal decree, inviting him to acknowledge the king of Spain."

"You are right, Hernando," said Pizarro, unmoved, but suppressing a faint smile, "and both requirements you mentioned shall be met. I shall personally see to it that the Inca is safe, that no harm, not even a scratch, be done to him. As for the Entreaty, I think Friar Vicente Valverde should read it to him, and let the interpreter summarize the main points for him. If the Inca submits of his own volition, so much the better. In any case, the cavalry will be posted in three troops in the buildings at the corners of the square, where they will hold themselves ready to intervene; you, de Soto, will lead the first troop; you, Hernando, my elder brother and lieutenant general, will lead the second, and you, Benalcázar, the third. The foot soldiers will be under your command, Juan Pizarro, except for twenty men who will follow me, and the artillery with ten men and its two pieces of ordnance, the falconets, will be in the fortress with you, Pedro de Candía. Everything hangs on our discipline and timing when we make our move."[10]

At dawn, Hernando Pizarro inspected all formations, checking the armor of both men and horses. He even suggested that bells be hung on some of them to make more noise and create a greater impression. The ecclesiastics, who had spent the night in prayer, said Mass and exhorted the men to victory. Pizarro himself delivered "a most Christian homily."[11]

Nothing happened in the morning and it seemed that preparations for the visit were being made with great calm in the Inca's camp. However, a messenger arrived to say that Atahualpa would come with armed warriors, as Hernando Pizarro and de Soto had done the day before.

Toward midday, the Indian army slowly moved off along the road. First came several groups of dancing girls and musicians, the men armed with slings and more men bearing copper maces; after them came by the thousands the bearers of *sillos*, a kind of spear fitted with a slipknot, used for capturing men and game. Several hundred servants swept the road clean of every leaf or stone on the passage of the Inca. He came last, surrounded by several hundred long-eared noblemen, covered with gold that glittered in the sun. The noblemen of the Court, dressed in a sort of blue livery, carried Atahualpa on a litter decked with parrot and toucan feathers of the brightest hues, and richly overlaid with gold plate. On a small seat of solid gold sat the Inca, with his luxurious mantle draped behind his back; on his head, he wore a gold crown from which hung the wide red tassel which practically covered his forehead and enhanced his imposing appearance. He also had a necklace of emeralds round his throat. Two other Long Ears of the royal household were being carried on smaller litters and, although they displayed equal composure and majesty, they kept a respectful distance behind Atahualpa. One was his uncle and the other the governor of Cajamarca. Finally came several hundred women, preceded by the "Virgins of the Sun," who were the servants and concubines of the Inca.

Atahualpa was thinking about the coming encounter[12] and recalling the prophecies and traditional tales handed down by his ancestors.[13] The theocratic society he lived in had taught him to accept the lofty notion that he was the head of his people. He was the State and the State was absolute master of all individuals. Their land, life, harvest, their joys and sorrows were his to hold by right of inheritance from his Father, the Sun, the Inti, who looked after his children. The mountains, the rivers, the vast sea, the animals and the plants, all belonged to him. That is why he distributed his gifts so generously among his chiefs, his loyal servants or the enemies he could win over to his service. He believed he had eradicated all poverty and sloth from his kingdom; everyone had his share of happiness. As his ancestors had done before him, he tried to make everyone's lot uniformly happy.

These were the notions that had fashioned his conscience, had formed his idea of the world; yet now, doubts assailed him.

He changed his mind when he was only a short distance from the square; he ordered one of his courtiers to tell Pizarro that it was too late, that he would pitch camp where he stood and would visit him the following day.

The soldiers started to set up the tents, ready for the night.

Pizarro had spent the day under great strain. Cavalry and foot soldiers, fully armed, were packed in the houses where they had been posted, grumbling and trembling with fear. Hardly anyone hoped to live through this desperate affair in which they were embroiled with no other choice than victory. As the hours went by, the Castilians' initial courage had worn off and the old, familiar waves of discontent came over them once more, reviving criticism of Pizarro, who had deliberately led them into this death trap. When Atahualpa's emissary arrived to talk of delay, Pizarro knew he must insist:

"Tell your master that I ask him to come all the same, right now, before nightfall. I have prepared a meal for him and I will not sit down at table until he comes."

Atahualpa was barely half a league away; he quickly thought the matter over and decided to go after all. He sent his messenger back to Pizarro, to say:

"My master is coming and he orders that you prepare for him the House of the Serpent in the middle of the square; he will spend the night there. Moreover," the long-eared nobleman added contemptuously, "he orders me to tell you that his people will come unarmed; the army will bivouac outside the city."[14]

A guard of five thousand men went along with Atahualpa to the main square of Cajamarca. Six hundred noblemen surrounded his litter. Evening was drawing near and the sun over the Inca's land had become an enormous red disk that bathed the horizon in fiery hues of gold and red. Atahualpa saw that the square was deserted and he asked:

"Where are the whites? I see no one. Are they hiding?"[15]

Thereupon, Friar Vicente Valverde came out of one of the buildings. He was tall and thin and his deep-set eyes

glowed like embers. He was dressed in his black and
white habit and carried a crucifix aloft in his right hand,
a Bible in the other. Oviedo depicts him as a "troubled,
unstable, and lewd cleric," but he acted his part very
conscientiously and regarded himself as the spokesman
of the true Faith, come to enlighten this South American
monarch. As he slowly drew nearer the litter in the ex-
pectant silence that had fallen upon the square, the men
of the Spanish column, exhausted by the strain of spending the whole day lying in wait, watched him through
the openings of the doors left ajar. Next to Valverde walked
Felipillo, the wily interpreter who saw his chance of taking
his revenge of the hated Inca of Quito. The friar bowed
slightly and started his address:

"I am the servant of God and I teach the Spaniards
about the things of God. I have now come to tell you
about those things before you meet my governor. God in
One and Three Persons created the World for Adam and
Eve. Their descendants sinned and God sent His Son,
Jesus Christ, to redeem them. But people rose against
Him and nailed Him to a cross, like the one you see here.
He named Saint Peter his representative on earth and the
popes are his successors. The present pope has given our
king, Charles the Fifth of Spain and Germany, dominion
over the lands of the New World, where yours are situ-
ated. I therefore entreat you, in the name of the God of
the Christians, to befriend the Spaniards, for they will
bring you nothing but good."

Atahualpa listened patiently to the friar, looking at the
crucifix with curiosity. When the interpreter finished, his
interest turned to distrust and, half closing his eyes in
anger, he asked:

"How can I tell that what you say is true?"

"It is the Word of God," replied the friar, "and the
Word is in this Book."

Atahualpa took the Bible from Valverde's hand and
looked it over. When the cleric made a gesture to help

Atahualpa open the Book, the Inca brushed him away contemptuously and continued his examination, finally carrying the Bible to his ear. His eyes blazing with anger and annoyance, he cried:

"This tells me nothing . . ." and he indignantly threw the Bible to the ground, adding, "My captains have informed me of your depredations, of the arson, the plunder and the latest outrage you have committed; you will now have to return everything you have taken before I go back. You must be evil people, since you told me yourself, speaking in the name of God, that your own people put your God to death. I will have nothing to do with this. My god is my Father, the Sun, who is up there, going to hide now, but who looks after his own at all times. He is a living god, a giver of life and warmth to his kingdom; it is thanks to him that we grow our plants and keep gathering plentiful harvests for all of us. My kingdom and all my possessions were earned by my father Huayna Capac and by my ancestors. I admit your king must be great to have sent you from such a great distance, but I too am a king and I owe obedience to no other. As for the pope you speak of, he must be of unsound mind to think he can give away kingdoms that do not belong to him. I have shown you enough patience and now you will pay dearly for all your wantonness."[16]

Valverde turned pale and flinched when the Inca threw down the Bible. For a brief moment, he imagined himself striking a pose before History and saving Atahualpa's life; but then he thought of Pizarro and his companions, itching with anticipation, and of the prepared plan. Therefore, with great theatrical gesturing, he bent over to pick up the Bible and cried aloud:

"Blasphemy! Blasphemy! Charge. I absolve you."[17]

Pizarro leaped forward and, standing in front of the house where he had been hiding, he drew a kerchief from his pocket and, waving it aloft, cried:

"Santiago! Charge!"

A tremendous noise filled the square as the three cavalry detachments sallied forth and fell upon the Indians round the Inca. Meantime Pizarro rushed forward, followed by his twenty men, with drawn swords; they attacked the litter of the Inca who, taken by surprise, could not believe what was happening. Surely, this brash handful of foreigners could not possibly have the sacrilegious impudence of using violence against his person. The horsemen were spreading alarm among the unarmed Indians, belaboring them with lance and broadsword. Pedro de Candía's falconets and harquebuses were showering a thunderous hail of death on the unarmed and terrified guards around Atahualpa, who also could not believe that an attempt was being made on his sacred person. By trying to protect him, they only gained a sure death for themselves. The remainder of the crowd fled in utter panic, but was stopped by the accumulated dead and wounded at the four corners of the square. So great was the pressure of the crowd of four or five thousand in the square that one of the thick sidewalls finally gave way, releasing all those who could scramble through the aperture. Pizarro, now standing close to Atahualpa, tried to protect the Inca with his own body, and shouted:

"Let no one harm the Inca, under penalty of death!"[18]

Several soldiers were already attacking Atahualpa and one named Estete had just managed to pull the tassel off his forehead, when Pizarro, raising his sword, opened a path among the Spaniards and, grasping the Inca first by his long mantle, then by the arm, dragged him off the litter and took him, under the protection of four soldiers, into one of the houses; Pizarro, however, suffered a hand wound in the fray.

It all happened in slightly under half an hour. The Inca's sun was sinking below the horizon and the evening shadows were falling over the mountain ridges. The cries of the fugitives could be heard in the distance, mingled with the rumble of galloping horses; a few isolated harquebus shots told of the continuing massacre. By nightfall, over two thousand dead lay in the square and nearby. Several hundred had been taken prisoner. The governor of Cajamarca and all the noblemen who carried the litter had lost their lives.

In the house, with Pizarro, Atahualpa showed nothing but haughty indifference. He let fall a remark in the presence of Hernando Pizarro who, as befitted the courtier that he was, stood by his side, looking solemn and ceremonious:

"Maizabilica lied."

He was referring to the message from the coastal chieftain, that the Spaniards were cowards, fearing for their lives and that eliminating them would be an easy matter.

Hernando Pizarro responded that the Spaniards had no choice but to take him prisoner for his own safety and to comply with the orders of their king, Charles the Fifth. They were a strong race, great fighters, and Atahualpa should feel no humiliation at being taken prisoner. Atahualpa looked at him serenely and replied dryly:

"It is the practice in war to conquer or be conquered."[19]

De Soto arrived then, back from his cavalry reconnaissance mission, which had ended with a few notes on the trumpet to indicate that the Inca's army had retreated. Of the Spaniards, no one except Pizarro had been wounded. De Soto bowed gravely before Atahualpa, whose frankness and gravity he had liked from the first. Francisco Pizarro made all the necessary arrangements to install the Inca in the room next to his and sent word to ask Atahualpa to dine with him. Atahualpa grandly accepted; he would eat and drink the food of his enemies. His spirit knew no fear and as a prisoner or a free man, he remained the emperor. Hernando Pizarro who, with de Soto, attended the dinner, had previously arranged that the terrified Indian girls attached to the Inca's service, who were weeping loudly outside, should come into the house and minister to their royal master, take care of his apartment and attend to his needs, as they would in his palaces. That day, the 16th of November 1532, the sun of the Incas had set. A new era was about to dawn for the American people.

On the following morning, Pizarro sent Benalcázar to ransack Atahualpa's camp and collect more spoils. The Spaniards returned with enormous quantities of field tents, furniture, clothing and arms. Above all, they had collected gold and silver, fashioned into enormous vessels, dishes, pitchers, pots, fire baskets, seats and facing panels for buildings, all of which, Atahualpa explained later on, were part of his private plate. There were so many llamas that the Spaniards turned most of them loose, since feeding them would have posed a problem. They kept just enough for their needs, to be able to eat fresh meat every day. In Cajamarca, they also found an enormous amount of clothing for soldiers' use, as well as arms. They had probably chanced upon the military supplies used to equip the army during the recent campaign.

Hernando de Soto refrained from engaging in the looting, which he found distasteful, preferring, like Hernando Pizarro, to cultivate Atahualpa's friendship. He even set himself the task of teaching Atahualpa Spanish. Gradually the Inca grew to trust de Soto and started to converse with him. They fell into the habit of exchanging impressions, sometimes for days at a time. Hernando would talk to him of King Charles the Fifth, the customs of Spain and the European wars, the other conquests in America and even his own personal experiences. The stories of the Aztec empire and of Cortés's exploits greatly impressed the Inca who in turn gave de Soto a description of the main features of the Inca empire, the system of tributes, the educational program, the army, the means of communication. He also mentioned his father Huayna Capac and the marvels of Quito. Finally he recounted his rivalry with his brother Huáscar.[20]

Days, weeks and months went by and Atahualpa remained a prisoner. The sentries, whom Pizarro posted to watch him, had grown to like him. Hernando de Soto assumed responsibility for the illustrious prisoner. Atahualpa gradually came to notice the difference between his conquerors. He realized that some could read. One day, he asked de Soto to spell "Dios" for him and bade him write it with a pen on his nail. Afterward, he would ask anyone coming into the room to repeat the word on his nail and he thus found out who could read. When Francisco Pizarro looked away and pretended not to hear his question, he smiled contemptuously and understood that the Spaniards' governor even lacked that basic skill.

Pizarro sent his brother Hernando to reconnoiter the country and find out if any conspiracy was brewing. Hernando returned with an enormous amount of booty. No conspiracy was afoot; only shock, distress and despair prevailed everywhere. Once the head of this great theocratic empire had been severed, no leader could be found to lead a revolt, at least for the time being. Hernando had, however, managed to speak to Calicuchima, the great Quito chief of the army of the south and Atahualpa's uncle on his mother's side, who still ruled the land around Cuzco and was preparing to return to Quito. After much elusive talk, he agreed to meet Pizarro, hoping to see Atahualpa. When the veteran warrior set off, he was carried in a litter by native servants, with nearly as much pomp as the Inca himself.

The meeting of the two leaders was extremely moving. Despite his dignity, his rank and his age, Calicuchima took one of the native servant's load from his back and shifted it to his own shoulders before entering Atahualpa's apartment, as a courtly sign of respect. The old servant of Huayna Capac appeared in the presence of Atahualpa with his eyes downcast, filling with tears.

"My lord, those men in Cajamarca could not defend you; if I had been with you, with my army of Caranquis and Puruahes, this would never have happened!"

Atahualpa smiled at him affectionately.[21]

Atahualpa realized that the Spaniards were essentially attracted to one thing only, gold, the metal the Incas treated with contempt, so great was their store of it. He resolved to buy his freedom and asked to see Francisco Pizarro.

"I'll give you enough gold to cover the floor of this room."

"I find that hard to believe," Pizarro replied, while the two or three captains who were with him also smirked in disbelief.

"I'll do more than that. I'll give you enough gold to fill this room up to this row of stones," he said, as he straightened up to his full height and raised his arm; with his hand, he reached up to a ledge of stone blocks along the wall of his room. "Within two months, it will be full of cups, ewers, pots and plates of gold. I will also fill the next room twice over with silver. You will then keep your word and immediately set me free."[22]

Pizarro was astounded. He could hardly believe what he had just heard. Pacing the room with long strides, he found it to be twenty feet long by seventeen wide. The stone ledge was nine feet above the ground. Never had any monarch been able to bring together so much gold at one time. All his life, he had doubted the word of others; he had always taken orders from others and kept his ambition concealed. Now he had just heard with his own ears the most extraordinary proposal a prisoner had ever made. For such riches, Atahualpa would be set free.

GOLD, CRIME AND TREACHERY

XIII

And they fell to bringing charges against him, in a badly contrived and worse-written document, devised by a facetious and unprincipled priest, a clumsy notary without a conscience, and others of the like stamp, who were all concerned in this villainy.[1]

Fernández de Oviedo y Valdés

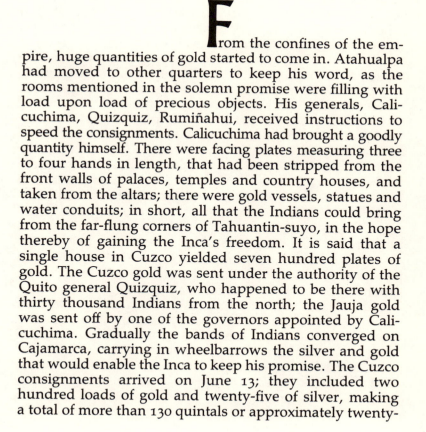

From the confines of the empire, huge quantities of gold started to come in. Atahualpa had moved to other quarters to keep his word, as the rooms mentioned in the solemn promise were filling with load upon load of precious objects. His generals, Calicuchima, Quizquiz, Rumiñahui, received instructions to speed the consignments. Calicuchima had brought a goodly quantity himself. There were facing plates measuring three to four hands in length, that had been stripped from the front walls of palaces, temples and country houses, and taken from the altars; there were gold vessels, statues and water conduits; in short, all that the Indians could bring from the far-flung corners of Tahuantin-suyo, in the hope thereby of gaining the Inca's freedom. It is said that a single house in Cuzco yielded seven hundred plates of gold. The Cuzco gold was sent under the authority of the Quito general Quizquiz, who happened to be there with thirty thousand Indians from the north; the Jauja gold was sent off by one of the governors appointed by Calicuchima. Gradually the bands of Indians converged on Cajamarca, carrying in wheelbarrows the silver and gold that would enable the Inca to keep his promise. The Cuzco consignments arrived on June 13; they included two hundred loads of gold and twenty-five of silver, making a total of more than 130 quintals or approximately twenty-nine thousand pounds. Pizarro, who could hardly believe his eyes, would go daily to look at the room filling with its mass of precious gold objects, rising ever closer to the appointed line.

In order to speed the collection of the gold ransom, Hernando Pizarro was sent, on Atahualpa's own advice, to Pachácamac, the holy city in the south, near the city now called Lima, where the cult of Pachácamac held equal sway with that of the Sun; it was also the site of the famous oracle of the empire. Hernando de Soto went to Cuzco, the old capital city, to hurry the dispatch of gold and thus hasten the monarch's release from captivity. Near Jauja, he met an escort leading Atahualpa's brother Huáscar in chains. From the conversation he had, de Soto learned that Huáscar, while still a prisoner of the generals loyal to Atahualpa, was making plans to use the Spaniards against his brother and throw the district into turmoil. De Soto preferred not to get involved in the affairs of succession to the throne, but, out of consideration for his friend Atahualpa, he immediately reported to Pizarro that he found that all was peaceful in the territories, and that the Indians were in a kind of stupor, lamenting the loss of freedom of their venerated chief, but imbued with a fatalistic resignation to the spell of the white invaders, bearers of thunder.

On his way, Hernando Pizarro met another of Atahualpa's brothers, the Inca Illescas, or Quilliscacha, carrying three hundred thousand pesos of gold and a great quantity of silver for the ransom. During the ride, Hernando Pizarro and his twenty horsemen found that their mounts' shoes had worn out and, since they had no iron, they thought the best solution was "to fashion shoes and nails for their horses out of silver, which the hundred Indians cast most admirably, as many as they required, and the shoes lasted two months." In this manner they returned to Cajamarca.

Atahualpa's guards were divided into two parties: those in his favor included Hernando de Soto, Hernando Pizarro, Pedro de Candía, Blas de Atienza, the interpreter Martinillo and a few captains and soldiers of a chivalrous disposition. But Treasurer Riquelme, Friar Valverde and, above all, the artful interpreter Felipillo were forever conspiring against the noble prisoner. Using the rumors that the Cuzco Indians and their abettors were spreading, they constantly assailed Pizarro with tales of the plots Atahualpa was supposed to be framing for the capture and destruction of all Spaniards, in order to regain his freedom. Pizarro was just as interested in the growing heap of gold as he was in the rumors and intrigues around him.

The reports Hernando Pizarro and de Soto brought back from the provinces confirmed the fact that these districts were at peace and gave credence to the Inca's promise to maintain peace. But Felipillo conspired with ever greater fervor, having now become infatuated with one of the Inca's concubines and knowing there was no way of satisfying his passion other than through the Inca's death.

Pizarro, who could see the day approaching when the terms of the pact would be fulfilled, the agreed amount being nearly assembled, started to pay more attention to the rumors Felipillo brought to him about Huáscar's promises. The Inca's brother was reported to have said that, if it were only a matter of gold, he could give the whites an even greater quantity; but in Cuzco now, those same whites were being called the messengers of Viracocha, sent to deliver them from Atahualpa's tyranny. Pizarro chose to take advantage of this situation and let it be known that it would be beneficial to bring Atahualpa's brother to him, so that he might set up a court of inquiry and refer to the king of Spain the matter of deciding who was the rightful heir to the throne. The matter soon came

to be known by the chiefs who were still loyal to Atahualpa; they in turn started forming a plan to dispose of
Huáscar. They felt his presence weakened Atahualpa's
position, particularly now that the time was drawing near
when they would have to ask Pizarro to keep his side of
the bargain.

Almagro's arrival at this juncture aggravated the Inca's
situation. The old and stubborn marshal had heard of
Pizarro's success and, in a vague way, of the Inca empire.
Although he was ailing, in Panama he had organized an
expedition of 153 men and obtained from Hernando de
Soto's partner Hernán Ponce the two boats that brought
his men to join Pizarro's expedition. Sailing with the nav-
igational help of Bartolomé Ruiz, he followed Pizarro's
route down the coast of Ecuador, enduring starvation and
great hardship, until, near Tumbez, he heard of the Spanish settlements and of the success of his associate. In San
Miguel de Piura, he was met by a friendly deputation
from Pizarro who assured him once more of his friendly
feelings and asked him to join him as soon as possible in
Cajamarca. Almagro then learned that his secretary, Rodrigo Pérez, had secretly written to Pizarro, warning him
that Almagro intended to start a separate expedition and
get a separate governorship. Almagro acted swiftly: after
a quick trial, he had his secretary hanged before leaving
for the interior. Pizarro left Cajamarca to meet Almagro,
and the two old companions-in-arms exchanged effusive
embraces when they met just outside the town. The marshal then went to visit Atahualpa, whose hands he kissed
in the manner of the Indian generals, not forgetting, of
course, to look in at the famous treasure room where the
terms of the pact were being complied with.

Shortly after this, Hernando Pizarro returned from his
mission, followed by Hernando de Soto. On meeting Almagro, Hernando Pizarro refused to speak to him and
treated him with all the scorn he had shown him in the
past; the situation deteriorated to such an extent that Fran-

cisco Pizarro was forced to intervene to restore calm. De Soto, on the other hand, greeted his old comrade affectionately and reminisced about their peregrinations through Panama and Nicaragua.

Almagro's soldiers soon started to cause a stir, demanding that they be included in the distribution of the spoils taken from Atahualpa. This became a major cause of tension and rivalry. Pizarro realized that he would have to act promptly. He gave orders to melt down the gold into bars while they waited for the remaining portion to be brought in, since the gold from Quito and the northern cities had not yet arrived in Cajamarca. Nine Indian smelters set to work and turned into ingots all the finely wrought vessels, plates and tableware, in a process of attrition that took no account whatsoever of any aesthetic feeling or consideration for the admirable expression of the Inca goldsmiths' art.

About that time, it was learned that the generals who had remained faithful to Atahualpa had killed Huáscar; they had drowned him when crossing the Andamareta River, while transferring him from one prison to another. When Pizarro tried to blame Atahualpa for this, he protested that he had no knowledge of the deed; rather did he grieve at the sad news.

Shortly after the smelting had begun, the full ransom was delivered and Atahualpa thought it was time to demand his release. But Pizarro, though expressing his full satisfaction, told him that he first had to settle the differences with Almagro's men. He finally agreed with the marshal to let his men have the sum of one hundred thousand ducats of gold, and everyone seemed satisfied with the arrangement. The royal fifth was taken out after all the bars had been weighed on a scale and found to be worth 1,326,539 pesos for the gold and 51,610 marks for the silver.[2]

Pizarro brought great solemnity to the distribution. The ceremony took place in the same square where Atahualpa had been taken prisoner, with the troops assembled in close formation, the cavalry to one side, the infantry to the other and Almagro's men forming a third wing. The distribution started with those who had taken part in the short action that led to the Inca's capture; then came the late arrivals, for whom the sum already mentioned of one hundred thousand ducats had been set aside. The royal fifth came to the equivalent of 262,529 pesos of gold and 10,121 marks of silver. Among the gold sent to the king were the only items which, because of their beauty, had been saved from the smelter's crucible. Some objects were worth several hundred thousand ducats of gold, such as the cobs of corn made of gold, finely wrought with silver leaves, and the fountain from which a fine stream of gold seemed to spring, with birds playing in its waters, fashioned in silver, and human figures drawing water from the fountain, all admirably proportioned and of exquisite beauty. Several other items, vessels and hollowware of outstandingly fine workmanship were also kept for the king. Some articles were truly fine examples of the extraordinary development of the goldsmith's art, either in lost-wax castings, repoussé work, filigree or brazing. Various kinds of gold were used, as well as wrought platinum. There were vessels with double spouts for water or *chicha*, ornamented with animal figures and complex geometric designs. There were gold hatchets and knives with intricate hieroglyphics that may have told the story of unknown exploits; mantles and chest ornaments with exquisite work of gold thread, inlaid with turquoise, emeralds and other gems, in the most complicated arrangements, often representing human figures with enormous ear pendants or nose ornaments that covered the mouth, also fashioned in gold. All sorts of animals, flowers and fish served as models for the designs used by these most sophisticated of goldsmiths. Added to Governor Pizarro's share was the Inca's stool or seat, beautifully done in gold; it was the very throne the Inca had used on his litter the day of his capture. Also held out of the total was the smelters' share of 1 percent. Pizarro's lot came to 57,222 pesos of gold and 350 marks of silver, as well as the Inca's stool, valued at 25,000 pesos of gold. His brother Hernando received 31,080 pesos of gold and 2350 marks of silver, a share deliberately inflated as if to encourage him to leave, never to return. Hernando de Soto was given 17,740 pesos of gold and 724 marks of silver, "far below what his services or talent merited," as the chronicler has it.[3] Each of the 60 horsemen was given 8800 pesos of gold and 362 marks of silver; for various reasons, some got more, others less, than this average sum. Each of the 105 foot soldiers received 4400 pesos of gold and 180 marks of silver.

In terms of 1986 values, the fabulous ransom paid by the Quito Inca may be estimated at 1.5 billion U.S. dollars.[4] Some four years earlier, the king of France offered the king of Spain a ransom for his sons amounting to 2 million ducats, that is to say, 6.75 million U.S. dollars. Pizarro did not forget the Church: San Francisco, the first church in Peru, in Cajamarca, was allotted 2200 pesos, half a foot soldier's share. The settlers and invalids of San Miguel de Piura were granted 15,000 pesos of gold in all, to be shared among approximately thirty people.

For the Spaniards of that period, this was a dream of riches and abundance come true. Never in their wildest flights of fancy had they ever imagined anything like this. The Inca's treasure was so large, so incredibly fabulous, that current values in Spain, and even in the other possessions in the Indies, were totally changed. The immediate effect was to upset completely the relative worth of goods in the unreal atmosphere of Cajamarca. The value of gold dropped steadily and the price of goods grew apace, especially for those that had to be brought from Spain and, consequently, were more difficult to get. A horse sold for 3300 pesos of gold; hose, cloaks, swords, went for astronomical prices; a sheet of paper that Hernando de Soto bought to write to his ever-faithful beloved Isabel cost him ten pieces of gold. Gaming debts were settled with pieces of gold, valued at sight, without taking the trouble to weigh them. Some soldiers were followed by an Indian laden with gold who went with them settling debts from house to house, by means of lumps or pieces of gold recklessly appraised.

But despite the apparent reconciliation imposed by the governor, feelings still ran high among the men. Most of all, Almagro's partisans could not accept the fact that they had arrived late and were given what they considered to be a few crumbs. Pizarro thought it wise to keep his brother Hernando away; in any case no one was better qualified than he to go to Court and present the monarch with the gifts and the royal fifth, and ask for new offices and titles for his men. Almagro thought it was a splendid idea and, as a mark of reconciliation, insisted on charging Hernando with a mission himself, for which he appears to have given him some twenty thousand ducats, to ingratiate himself. In his letter to the king, Almagro asked for the governorship of the land south of Pizarro's, with the title of adelantado. Ever a suspicious man, Almagro made sure that Hernando would not fail to deliver the letter, by giving secret instructions to that effect, well paid for in gold, to two of his men, Cristóbal de Mena and Juan de Sosa, who were to go with Pizarro on the journey to Spain.

Hernando Pizarro's leave-taking of Atahualpa was very moving. He had previously had a long talk, in company with de Soto, with his brother the governor and made a reasonable and dignified case for the fate of the Inca. Now the treasure had been delivered, to Pizarro's entire satisfaction and in accordance with the Articles of Agreement, duly subscribed to before the public scrivener and publicly proclaimed through the camp as required by law. There was nothing more to be done except for the governor to keep his word and set the Inca free. Since, how-

ever, the governor had reason to believe that certain conspiracies were afoot, and since it would be hazardous to
restore the former overwhelming imbalance between the
conquerors and the conquered, the two noble captains tried
to persuade Pizarro that he should at least agree to sending
the Inca to Spain so that His Caesarean Majesty, dealing as
one king with another, might decide what should be done.
The saturnine governor was not in favor of this recommendation, although he offered to think about it.

Hernando Pizarro and de Soto went to the apartments of
Atahualpa, who greeted Pizarro with an embrace and told
him, with great emotion:
    "When you go, Captain, I am sure that your com-
panions, the fat one and the one-eyed man will have me
killed."[5]
    The two Hernandos tried to reassure him, although
they had serious misgivings themselves about what might
happen. The one-eyed Almagro was certainly the most
fervent exponent of a plan, first to do away with the Inca,
as the most serious threat to all Spaniards, then to strike
camp and undertake new explorations where his rapa-
cious men might feed their ambition. The fat one was
Riquelme, the evil treasurer and accountant who had come
out to his great personal advantage in the distribution,
with more than his share, and who ruthlessly practiced
usurers' trading terms. Then there was Felipillo, who was
secretly communicating with Atahualpa's enemies in Cuzco,
trying to bring about a tragedy that would redound to his
great benefit, as well as hand over to him the woman he
sought among Atahualpa's entourage. To this end, he
distorted at will the natives' testimonies and stopped at
nothing to spread calumny.[6]
    De Soto wrote to his mother and to Isabel enthusiastic
letters announcing his coming return. He could now see
the time drawing near. He had at last amassed an appre-
ciable fortune, what with his share of the ransom, his

earlier profits and those Ponce's astute management brought him in Panama. He really was now what one might call a rich man. Soon, he hoped to have his rank confirmed. His reputation as a prestigious captain was already made, and he hoped to be able to return to Spain. But Francisco Pizarro had most persuasively asked him to stay on a little longer. Now that his brother Hernando had gone, de Soto was to assume the duties of lieutenant general which he had previously shared. Hernando Pizarro departed via Panama and Santo Domingo, leaving a trail of admirers along his passage, won over by his tales of adventure and the display of the huge treasures he was carrying. The legend of Peru and of the fabulous land of gold spread across the whole of the Indies and started a rush of whatever covetous and idle souls lurked in the young colonies, all hurrying to rally round the standards of the Pizarros.

Hernando met with extraordinary success in Spain, where he presented himself at Court with his display of gold and his well-related tales of brave endeavor in the conquest of the Inca empire. For himself, he obtained the distinctions of Member of the Royal Household and the Order of Santiago; for his brother Francisco, the title of marquess and seventy leagues of land to be added to his governorship; for Almagro, his enemy, he chivalrously obtained the title of adelantado and the governorship of two hundred leagues of land along the coast, south of Pizarro's territory, to be known as New Toledo; for Father Valverde, he obtained the See of Cuzco. A great number of knights decided to sail back with him to Peru.

Meanwhile Atahualpa's Spanish enemies kept trying to persuade the governor to strike camp and leave Cajamarca and before doing so, to rid themselves of the Inca. Almagro, the ecclesiastics, Riquelme, Felipillo, all conspired to this end. Pizarro did not find the plan unreasonable. Nevertheless, Hernando de Soto and a few of his friends continued to watch over the Inca and to defend him before the governor, reminding him that the imprisonment of the Inca could not be justified. The ransom having been paid, the rules of chivalry demanded that he be set free. The well-informed de Soto invoked the case of the emperor Charles the Fifth who, a few years earlier, had set free the king of France, Francis the First, the captive having merely given his word of honor. Pizarro retorted that things were different in America and that one could not adduce examples of dealings between Christian kings and apply them to the solution of matters relating to infidels. The astute and crafty governor then conceived the idea of sending de Soto away; he gave him a mission to the distant region of Guamachuco, where he was to ascertain whether there really was a plot being hatched for setting Atahualpa free.

"Go, my friend," said Atahualpa. "I am sure that these wretches are about to kill me."

"Have no fear, my lord; only the king of Spain may decide your fate," answered de Soto. "My friend Juan de Herrada will stay here and he has promised to defend you."

"He will carry little weight before so many," Atahualpa said gravely; "what is more, last night I saw a sign in the sky; a red comet crossed the heavens and that is a sure sign that a great captain of our nation will die. Such a sign was seen a short time before the death of my father, the Inca Huayna Capac."[7]

The day after de Soto's departure, the trial began. The associates Pizarro and Almagro were named judges; Sancho de Cuéllar was the clerk and Juan de Herrada the defender, in deference to Hernando de Soto's recommendation. Atahualpa was charged under twelve counts by the prosecutor, who was none other than the fat and also one-eyed Treasurer Riquelme. Among the accusations brought against him were usurping the throne, assassinating Huáscar, dissipating the empire's revenues, criminal idolatry, polygamy and sundry plots against the

Spaniards. The fanatical Valverde, posing as a moralist and a crusader, made several disquisitions, cluttered with Latin verbiage and biblical quotations, in which he attacked the monarch who had made them all rich and who, from his prison, by his express orders, had kept his realms at peace. He had collaborated with the Spaniards, trusting in Pizarro, before he produced the ransom. Juan de Herrada did what he could to defend him, insisting mainly on the fact that only the king of Spain had the power to decide his fate, quite apart from any consideration touching the absolutely formal agreement previously entered into, in exchange for payment of ransom. The judges, however, turned a deaf ear to all this and Felipillo continued his work to his own base advantage. Twenty-four people were needed for a verdict of guilty. Only thirteen went against him, the eleven remaining jurors finding him innocent. These honorable captains were Francisco de Chávez, Diego de Chávez, Francisco de Fuentes, Pedro de Ayala, Francisco Moscoso, Fernando del Haro, Pedro de Mendoza, Juan de Herrada, Alfonso Dávila, Blas de Atienza and Diego de Mora.

In the end, Pizarro and Almagro sentenced Atahualpa to be burned at the stake, unless he converted to Christianity, in which case he would die by common strangulation.

Juan Pizarro personally pleaded before his brothers on behalf of Atahualpa. It is reported that Francisco Pizarro hypocritically wept when signing the sentence. He nevertheless ordered the sentence to be carried out promptly, that very night, Saturday, August 29, 1533. The intercession of a group of captains headed by Rodrigo de Chávez, a friend of de Soto's and a companion of his since the days of the Nicaragua excursions, proved of no avail: they wanted the execution put off until after de Soto's arrival which was due shortly. Pizarro expected de Soto back within two or three days and he feared he would bring to bear the full force of his prestige to oppose, by force of arms if need be, as he had intimated he would, any idea of doing away with the Inca. For greater safety, Pizarro requested a written opinion of Father Valverde; the latter reiterated his sentiment that sentence should be carried out immediately, and signed the document without a second thought.

Atahualpa met Pizarro, and the two high officials who came to read him his sentence, in a very lofty manner. He was surrounded by his *apus* and his *amautas*, the priests and wise men of his Court. He answered in reasonably clear Spanish:

"We Incas cannot lie. You, Pizarro, have lied. I kept my part of the bargain and you have shared the treasure among yourselves. You have not kept your word. You are what your compatriots call a rogue knight. By my orders, my people have shown you nothing but courtesy, and you know that not a bird flies nor a tree leaf moves in my dominions without my consent, even though I am in prison. You pay me back with a death sentence."[8]

The Spaniards had no answer to this plain talk that gave the lie to all shameful misrepresentations of the trial. Faced with this cruel fate, Atahualpa simply commended the lives of his children and his wives to the Spaniards. He then asked to be left alone with his advisers. They were weeping, as they were very much affected by all that was happening. They advised the Inca not to refuse to go through with the baptism ceremony, not for any importance that might be attached to it, but simply because the Child of the Sun could not be burned by earthly fire, since this would prevent his spirit from returning to his Father the Sun. If he died any other kind of death, his body would be secretly borne away to the vaults of his ancestors, where he would lie in peace, next to the founders of the dynasty. These reasons convinced Atahualpa and he asked that Pizarro be informed of his decision.

The governor unctuously offered to act as his godfather and thus Pizarro's name of Juan Francisco was imposed on the Lord of Tahuantin-suyo. It was already two hours past sunset when the troops formed in the fateful square of Cajamarca. An unknown, supernatural fear drove the Spaniards to consummate their ignoble act under cover of darkness. After all, millions of Indians looked upon Atahualpa as the Child of the Sun; who knows what miracle might not occur during an execution held in broad daylight, in full view of the King of the Firmament? Better do the deed by the light of torches flickering round the execution stake driven in the middle of the square. Atahualpa strode forward majestically while the lugubrious requiescat was being chanted and the soldiers, standing to attention, formed an ironic guard of honor. With his head thrown back, Atahualpa kept a proud bearing, his vicuña and gold mantle draped over his shoulders and sweeping the ground behind him. He was the emperor of the Four Corners of the World, the Inca, the king of Quito, who had trusted the word of the white man when he had set foot in this same square, almost a year earlier. The Indian men sobbed and the women and servants rent the air with their cries, as Atahualpa was tied to the stake; the infamous black hood was placed over his head to hide his agony; a roll of drums broke out and the executioner began to twist his wooden rod that tightened the rope until the young, vigorous body of Atahualpa grew limp and, slumping, came to rest with the stillness of death.

Following ancient custom, the Inca's wives took their own lives there and then, some strangling themselves with their own hair, others with ropes. Pizarro had to order his soldiers to use force in order to stop the others from following suit. The Spaniards were on their knees, crossing themselves and praying for the generous and gentle Inca whose innocence they nearly all acknowledged. The Indians, wailing dolefully, fled to the mountains and spread the terrible news throughout the empire. The Indian flutes and pipes would henceforth grieve balefully in all the Andean reaches, where an endless dirge would sound for centuries to come, as a permanent protest against the hateful, cruel deed, its stain never removed, the guilt of its authors forever retold.

All those responsible for the monstrous crime were to fall victims of the Inca's curse. Pizarro was assassinated by Almagro's partisans in his palace in Lima. Almagro was executed by Pizarro's partisans in Cuzco, after he lost the battle of Salinas. The dismal Felipillo wove his complicated web of intrigue and treachery till he met his doom, drawn and quartered by four horses to which he was tied in the very same Cajamarca square. The dreadful Dominican Valverde, having attained the dignity of bishop and grown old and ailing, was one day captured by the Indians of the island of Puná. They killed and devoured him.

But none of this lessens the tremendous guilt of Atahualpa's slayers in the eyes of posterity. The huge empire had lost its leader; the young, strong and brave man who ruled the extensive Tahuantin-suyo and had taught such telling lessons of generosity, chivalry and valor to the foreigners had his life cut short at a time when he was about to enjoy the fruits of maturity.

Spain's contact with America was a saga of violence and discord that unfolded after Atahualpa's death, when Indian chiefs and Spanish officials clashed, with cruel, pitiless oppression on the part of the whites and sullen, vengeful resistance on the part of the Indians. The result was that the nations developed slowly and painfully, missing a great deal of what destiny might have held in store for them.

THE PACIFIER OF CUZCO

XIV

This is the greatest city ever seen in the world, let alone in the Indies; and I can assure you that it has buildings as beautiful and as solidly built as one could hope to see in Spain.[1]

Letter from the Chief Justice and City Magistrate of Jauja

Two days after Atahualpa's death, Hernando de Soto returned to Cajamarca. The news had reached him on the way and, unable to contain his indignation, he went straight to Pizarro to protest.

"You have covered us all with shame by committing this felonious act," he said hotly; "you could at least have waited till I returned, since you sent me to find out whether there was a conspiracy. There was none. I could have vouched for the Inca myself, with my own life, and I could have taken him to Spain. The emperor will hold you accountable for your arbitrary decision."

"My son," answered Pizarro, who was in mourning and wore his black felt hat pulled over his eyes, "I admit that I acted with precipitation and that I was misled by Riquelme and Father Valverde. But here we are now, free to strike camp and complete the pacification of the kingdom."

"I would ask you, Mr. Governor," de Soto replied coldly, "kindly to relieve me of my duties and let me return to Spain. I have given the matter a great deal of thought."

"And I would ask you to stay with me for a little while longer. You are the only one I can rely upon to take us to the capital of the empire, Cuzco, while we prepare another expedition to Quito. Help me pacify Cuzco, and once the work is done, you may return to Spain. I know that you have powerful reasons for going back. Do this for our king; it will only be for a few months. If you listen to me, you will gain glory and riches aplenty. You will not regret it," said Pizarro, doing his best to sound convincing.[2]

Hernando decided to reconsider.

There were still many matters to be settled before he could be ready to leave for Spain. The task of pacifying Cuzco, of penetrating to the heart of the empire, the Navel of the World, as the name proclaimed the city to be, held a great deal of attraction for his incorrigibly adventurous nature. In the highlands, close to the clouds, there were temples and riches, unknown spirits and strange forces at play, let alone power and rewards to be had for those brave enough to dare. He decided it was worth staying a few months more. Pizarro made him captain general of the expedition.

Meanwhile, as news of Atahualpa's death spread, reports from the confines of the empire brought cause for alarm. Confusion reigned everywhere and a general relaxation of discipline was taking place. The civil war of the last few years between Quito and Cuzco had created an unsettled situation, and since there no longer was a clearly established line of succession to the throne, Atahualpa's generals each staked a claim to rule the regions over which they held sway: Calicuchima in the south, Quizquiz in the center and Rumiñahui in the north, in the former kingdom of Quito. Moreover, the powerful Cuzco factions wanted to proclaim another Inca. All regional commanders had given orders to stop shipments of gold to Cajamarca and to hide the treasures. It is said that in Quito in particular they managed to hide considerable quantities of gold and the hiding places are unknown to this day. In addition, the Indians were rebelling in several districts. They were the Yanaconas, Indian servants who were, for all intents and purposes, the Incas' slaves, and who were now trying to turn these dissensions to their advantage, making off with whatever riches they could, or giving vent to old resentments whenever they were in their cups. It seemed, indeed, that the whole empire was attempting to drown its sorrow at the Inca's demise. The system had been so centralized, the individual's will and initiative so controlled throughout the Inca empire, that now that the head had been lopped off, the body was incapable of recovery, paralyzed, on the verge of disintegration.

Pizarro noted this fact with concern. At times he felt that the collapse of the Inca institutional system would work in favor of his plans for the peaceful conquest and occupation of the territory. At other times, however, he realized that it would have been much easier to maintain peace by ruling through an Inca, installed by the whites and enjoying their support as long as he did as he was told.

He thus settled his choice on one of Atahualpa's siblings, the young Tupac Ullpa, or Toparca. In this manner, he gave new life to the Quito party and enlisted the support of the triumphant generals and of their scattered armies. Pizarro called together as many of Atahualpa's courtiers as possible and consulted them about the appointment. Being for the most part of the Quito party, they gave their assent. Thus it happened that the coronation ceremony was held in the very city of Cajamarca, though it was on a much more modest scale than it would have been in Cuzco. The high priest sacrificed a spotless young llama. After a few days of ritual fasting, the young king's head was adorned with the crown of gold and the *llautu*, by the old warrior Calicuchima, who was the first to pay homage to his new lord.

Pizarro then turned to settling who was to govern the region, in order to be free to continue his journey to Cuzco. Since San Miguel de Piura and its neighboring port of Payta were key points of contact with the sea routes along which moved the expedition's supplies, Pizarro decided to entrust the lieutenancy of this city and its outlying district to Sebastián de Benalcázar, whose thoughtful judgment and deliberate manner inspired him with confidence. Having settled matters on that score, he then proceeded to organize his expedition to Cuzco, sending de Soto as usual in the lead, with a vanguard of forty horses. Almagro and Pizarro led the main body of troops, now almost five hundred strong, not counting the many Indian servants and the Court and household of the new Inca. They and Calicuchima accompanied the expedition, each borne on his own litter.

They soon reached the Royal Highway linking Quito and Cuzco. Everything about this highway, its stark perfection, its purposeful routing and its efficient services filled the Spaniards with admiration and stood as concrete proof of the Inca's power and organizational ability. It stretched over 2422 miles, a perfectly smooth road, wide enough for six horsemen to ride abreast quite comfortably. There were Inca highways along the coast and in the highlands. The coastal strip was protected against floodwaters by a flanking wall; the highland route had been cut through the redoubtable mountainous terrain of the Andes, at the cost of considerable human effort, and through the dogged determination of the Inca builders, especially Huayna Capac, the man of iron, who had most persistently wanted Quito linked to Cuzco by an efficient communications system. Wooden or suspension bridges of agave or reed ropes spanned the rivers and carried the flocks of llamas across. Occasionally there were two bridges, one for the common folk and the other for their betters, with collectors permanently posted at the entrances to collect a toll commensurate with the load. *Tambos* served as taverns, or relay stations, all along the Royal Highway; between the *tambos* ran the *chasquis*, who were the news carriers, or the teams of conveyance carriers, who bore officials in either hammocks, litters or seats slung over a man's back, according to the traveler's rank.

Marching along this highway, the expedition reached Guamachuco, then Guanuco and lastly Jauja. There it halted to establish a Spanish settlement and Pizarro asked de Soto to lead the way with his forty horses, to reconnoiter the country and repair the bridges, so that the march could continue. Hernando proceeded cautiously, since he could tell that there were enemy troops in the district, judging by the destroyed or looted buildings they had come across, and the abandoned campsites that dotted the region. All this warned of the passage of the army of Atahualpa's general Quizquiz, who had ruled over Cuzco and appeared to be retreating north. De Soto caught sight of the body of Indian troops near Vilcas; in a gorge, he fell into an ambush and lost three men. Crossing the rivers Abancay and Apurímac, near the Vilcaconga Range, he entered the mountain pass, in spite of the unmistakable signs of the presence of Indian troops on the cliffs. In the middle of a cañon, he called together his horsemen, whose mounts were reaching the point of exhaustion. He told his men that their objective was to reach the top of the mountain, in order to gain the advantage of high ground. The Castilians set off in good spirits, but the shrill sound of war cries suddenly exploded, signaling the onslaught of the Indians who appeared at the edge of the cliff. They had remained hidden, but now they started to loose rocks, which rolled down the steep slopes, frightening the horses and inflicting casualties on the small body of men. Then hundreds of Indian warriors appeared and launched an attack against the horses, which, frenzied by the noise and confusion of the affray, turned in flight, while de Soto did his best to rally his troops. Hernando saw that, unless he managed to reach the top of the slope, he and his men were lost. He then wrenched his horse free from the grip of an Indian grappling with the animal's legs to bring it down and, spurring his mount, he threw himself forward, determined to open a passage with his powerful lance in the ranks of the Indian spearmen who vainly tried to oppose him. A few soldiers, electrified by his example, imitated him; the rest followed suit and they finally reached the top. Exhausted by this extraordinary exertion, at an altitude which seemed to strain European hearts to the point of collapse, the two armies stood facing each other: forty Spaniards against hundreds of Indians, also exhausted by the efforts of the last few hours. A stream of water provided a little refreshment for the horses before Hernando once more gave the order to attack. With their primitive weapons, the brave Indians resisted with all their might against this final charge in the day's failing light. There were neither victors nor vanquished. Hernando's men were amazed at the extraordinary courage of the Indians. They must have been fighting the Inca's most experienced troops. They had inflicted many casualties on them, but de Soto had lost six men and three horses, a proportionately higher casualty list for his column.

Meanwhile, one of the messengers sent by de Soto to Pizarro the day before, to warn of the superior forces he was about to meet, reached his destination. Pizarro then gave orders to Marshal Almagro to take the rest of the cavalry and ride to de Soto's aid. When dawn broke, Almagro entered the very pass where Hernando had joined battle. Determined to make his presence known, he had his trumpeters announce the cavalry. The sound reached de Soto's camp and brought him great comfort. He immediately ordered the trumpets to answer. It was not long before the leaders of the two columns embraced, giving each other new courage. The Indians, witnessing the reunion, decided to withdraw into the Andean mists.

The resistance was headed by the Quito general Quizquiz, who seemed to be determined to avenge Atahualpa's death. When, at his Jauja headquarters, Pizarro learned of the hard battle, he grew very angry and, yielding to his sullen cruel streak, he seized upon the rumors spread by the Indians of the Cuzco party and fell to suspecting the brave Calicuchima who accompanied him. He first threatened to burn him at the stake if the Indians did not lay down their arms. Calicuchima heard the accusation and the threat with great calm and haughty composure.

"I have had neither news nor prior advice of the movements of Quizquiz's troops; since I am a prisoner, I am hardly likely to have any influence over them. You can do as you please with me."[3]

Pizarro ordered that the great general be put in chains. He, in turn, retreated into proud silence. About this time, the new Inca, Tupac Ullpa, fell ill and died without anyone being able to determine the cause of his death. He had not ceased to show his contempt for Pizarro and his great mortification at being placed in such an equivocal situation and at receiving such an affront to his imperial dignity by being turned into a mere instrument of the conqueror's designs. This new development gave the governor an opportunity to heap more blame on Calicuchima, whom he accused of giving orders that the young Inca be poisoned.

Pizarro then moved on, in the direction of Cuzco, and joined Almagro and de Soto at Jaquicaguana (also written as Xaquixaguana) in the Vilcaconga Range, five leagues from the empire's capital. There, he found large army stores of clothing and food which the Incas had used to supply their troops.

While in Jaquicaguana, Pizarro carried out his designs against Calicuchima: he pronounced sentence against him and had him burned at the stake. Once again de Soto tried to no avail to intervene with Pizarro, trying to save the old fighter who had won so many battles for Atahualpa. The ghoulish Father Valverde led Calicuchima to the stake in the town square where he was to be burned. Through his interpreter, he explained the doctrine of the

Faith and pressed him to convert. Calicuchima answered him coldly:

"Do not explain your religion to me any longer. I do not understand it. I shall die, believing in Pachácamac, the giver of life, the force of the Universe."

When the flames began to swirl round his body, the Indian must have fixed his thoughts on his distant native city of Quito, where Huayna Capac had won his friendship; it was also the city he had left to accompany his emperor and nephew, Atahualpa. Amid his cries of agony, one could still hear him invoking the name of Pachácamac.[4]

Two days after this tragic event, a splendid procession of natives reached the camp. It was the retinue of Prince Manco, brother of the late Huáscar. The prince had come to stake his claim to the Imperial Crown and express his friendship to Pizarro. Pizarro understood the political advantage to be gained from winning the support of the Cuzco party, opposed to Atahualpa, Calicuchima, Quizquiz, Rumiñahui and other northern generals. He greeted Manco with courtesy and great demonstrations of friendship and told him that he wished to restore Huáscar's dynastic line to the throne; that he would decide what should be done when he reached Cuzco, the heart of Tahuantin-suyo. He then asked Prince Manco to join him in the march, and the noble Indian agreed.

Supported by Almagro and Juan Pizarro, de Soto fought his way on to Cuzco, in a deep pass in the Jaquicaguana valley, on the way to the Eastern Range. The brave Quizquiz was determined to stop the hated invaders who had killed his countrymen, the Inca and Calicuchima. Nevertheless, the cavalry of the three experienced captains overcame the resistance of the intrepid Indians, whose only weapons were stones and copper maces. By skillful maneuvering on Almagro's and de Soto's part, the Spaniards feigned a retreat and drew their assailants into a valley, where suddenly turning about, they inflicted heavy losses upon the Indians and put them to flight. Thus the column was able to continue its march to Cuzco.

On instructions received originally from Francisco Pizarro, de Soto had to charge right up to the city limits, for the Indians who had escaped from the skirmish and those who were guarding the capital city seemed determined to set fire to their town, rather than allow the invaders to take possession of it. De Soto managed to put out the fires and he set sentries at the main buildings, later joining Pizarro, who decided to pitch camp outside the town, in order to make a ceremonial entrance on the following day. For everyone in the group, that night spent high up in the cordillera was one of great anxiety. Under the tropical roof of stars, it seemed to the adventurers that those unknown constellations held the secret of a mysterious universe.

In the cold Andean morning of November 15, 1533, the Castilians assembled in battle formation for their historic entry into the town. The center wing was under the command of Governor Pizarro himself, the right wing being led by Almagro and the left by de Soto. Their armor glistened in the sun, the horses stamped the ground[5] and the blare of the trumpets sounded loudly in the morning air, to the great confusion and trepidation of the population in the city.

The Indians saw their opposite numbers as the bearers of thunder who had won every encounter with Indian armies, who had seized the Inca and stripped the temples of the Sun. For the Spaniards, this was the heart of the huge empire, the legendary city that sheltered some two hundred thousand inhabitants, in beautiful buildings of stone and marble, still bearing their silver ornamentation, standing next to the sacred temples that made it the holy city of the Inca empire, the last resting place of the Incas of the Cuzco dynasty.

Pizarro took possession of the capital in the name of the king of Spain, with great pomp and ceremony; this was the high mark of his odyssey, of his conquest of the empire. Prince Manco observed the ceremony in silence, preparing to salvage at least a semblance of power for the time being. The main square was surrounded by substantial buildings that housed the imperial nobility. Cuzco, the center of the world, was divided into two sections, Anancuzco and Urincuzco, grouping the inherited estates of the main Inca families. From the main square, which was oriented, according to astronomical calculations, in such a way as to make it possible to use the mountain peaks to trace the course of the Sun, started the four main roads leading to the four corners of the empire: Chincha-suyo, reaching Quito and Pasto; Conti-suyo to Arequipa; Anti-suyo penetrating the Bolivian territory and mountain villages and Colla-suyo linking up with Chile and Argentina. The roads were most admirably well built, flanked by royal mansions and palaces, and the great temple to the Sun or Coricancha [the Place of Gold]. Here stood such splendor as the Europeans had not even imagined. The main square and the roads were carefully paved and were drained by gutters running down the middle. On the near side, close to the hill, stood the extraordinary fortress, built of precisely joined stones, with three semi-circular parapets and a main tower that overlooked the full extent of the huge, sparkling, verdant valley.

Huayna Capac's mansion and the Great Temple to the Sun were the main buildings in the center of the square; the Spaniards chose them for their headquarters. There were dormitory convents for the Virgins of the Sun, which still had a few silver ornaments left on their facades, the gold decorative plates having been stripped earlier. In the Temple of Coricancha, laid out in a circle, as if holding a royal conventicle, were the mummified bodies of the Incas, dressed in their burial attire, surrounded by gold, their sacred vessels and their traditional appurtenances. De Soto and his men stayed in the building called Amarocancha, a residence of the former kings.

Despite Pizarro's proclamation forbidding the Castilians to loot or take anything from the inhabitants, for fear they might flee, each soldier promptly amassed for himself a fabulous amount of booty. There was still a great deal of gold left; not only vessels and ornaments, but also life-size statues of massive gold, such as were found in a cave near Cuzco, representing women and ornamented with snakes and grasshoppers. In the imperial storehouses they found ceremonial dresses, many of which were handsomely patterned, embroiderd cloth, cotton goods, vicuña wool cloth and other woven material spangled with gold beads. In one place, they found ten silver beams, intended for the house of a noble family; they were twenty feet long, one foot wide and three inches thick.

Pizarro could not do otherwise than organize the distribution of these treasures, as he had done in Cajamarca. The total reached two thirds of the value, approximately, of Atahualpa's ransom. The royal fifth was deducted, leaving six thousand pesos of gold for each horseman and half that amount for each foot soldier among the 480 men of the expedition. Sancho, the royal notary, calculated that the total amount distributed was 580,200 pesos of gold and 215,000 marks of silver; Pizarro himself and Treasurer Riquelme both signed the audit of this account. These great riches, added to those that the soldiers brought from Cajamarca, or had acquired along the way through trade or plunder, altered the mental outlook of the men of the expedition. Many found it increased their lust for gaming. Some lost a fortune in a single day and many contracted debts that would take a lifetime to pay off. A horseman named Leguizamo received, in his share of the spoils, a gold sundial mounted on silver, which had been in the main temple. He had lost it in the course of one night's gambling, giving rise to the Spanish expression, "He gambled away the sun before it had risen."

Hernando de Soto received his own considerable share which, as a sign of Pizarro's esteem for him, amounted to a substantially greater proportion than he had been allotted in Cajamarca. Pizarro also appointed him governor of Cuzco.

Preparations for the coronation of Manco started immediately. It had been decided that he would be given the appearance of holding power, the better to use him as the head of the local government, on condition that he agree to serve as an instrument to rule the country in the name of the king of Spain. The young Inca endured the ritual fast, then proceeded to the solemn ceremony held before the Spanish garrison drawn up in Cuzco's square. Mass was celebrated by Valverde and the son of Huayna Capac received from the hands of Pizarro himself the crown of gold and the tassel of the Incas of Peru. Manco Capac Inca II was the name given to the new ruler, whose first act was to swear loyalty to the Crown of Spain and to Pizarro, sealing his pledge with *chicha* sipped from a gold vessel, while trumpets sounded and scriveners read the oath aloud, to confer even more solemnity to the event. Following tradition, the mummies of the former Incas were ceremoniously brought to the square by numerous servants, and were seated at the royal banquet table, surrounded by countless members of the nobility.

On March 24, 1534, Pizarro appointed to the government of the municipality two magistrates and eight aldermen, among whom were his brothers Gonzalo and Juan. The indomitable Quizquiz kept the flame of rebellion alive. His army daily attracted in ever greater numbers those who were unwilling to acknowledge Manco Capac's authority, and they constantly harassed the Spaniards. Quizquiz's forces were engaged in several encounters and were obliged to withdraw to the north. His troops were finally scattered in a battle near Jauja. Thereafter, Quizquiz retreated to the neighborhood of Quito to organize new battalions that might keep the Spaniards constantly at bay, until one day, in a heated argument with his own officers, whom he had accused of faintheartedness, he was wounded by a spear and died without ever bowing before the invader. He had entrusted the leadership of the Cuzco resistance to another general, Incarabayo, who continued to hound de Soto's troops.

Just then, Pizarro received news of much greater import than the Indian resistance. Don Pedro de Alvarado, who had conquered Mexico with Cortés, and was now governor of Guatemala, had finally realized his dream of coming to Peru and taking part in the conquest of this fabulous empire. He had reached the coast of Ecuador at Bahía de Caraquez with eight ships and five hundred men; from there, he started to march to the interior, hoping to reach Quito, the northern capital of the empire and birthplace of Atahualpa, whose treasures had never reached Cajamarca. When news of the Inca's death had been received, the Quito general Rumiñahui ordered the treasure returned to the fortified town that nestled on the slopes of the volcano Pichincha. Alvarado started a Homeric climb from the humid tropical plains of Manabí up to the towering heights of the Andes. It was a long succession of marches and countermarches, from swamps to torrents, fighting mosquitoes, enduring sickness and hunger, altogether a tremendous effort. When it reached the heights, the valiant expedition lost in turn its horses, its dogs and its flocks, over the edge of cliffs, or crossing the mournful frozen expanses of the Andean highlands drenched with bitterly cold rains. To save themselves from dying from exposure, a few horsemen are known to have opened the corpses of their horses and to have slept within them. Other men in the expedition had brought their wives and children from Guatemala and heartrending scenes took place, when the head of a family of stragglers unable to keep up any longer would turn back to join them and face certain death rather than leave his loved ones.

They finally ran into a rain of stones and ashes thrown up by the Cotopaxi volcano, and took this as an omen, foretelling the diminishing chances of success of the expedition. But Alvarado was a man of extraordinary mettle and insatiable ambition. He was the fighting redhead, the "Tonatiuh," the blazing sun, as the Aztec Indians had named him, who had been responsible for the Night of Sorrow at Tenochtitlán through his wild and violent behavior. With the remainder of his troops, he finally reached the top of the Andean sierra and, following the valley that opens up between the two ranges, where he found the climate slightly more temperate, he came to the plain of Riobamba. There he learned that several Spanish expeditions were moving close to him.

When Alvarado's arrival was known and when it was also learned that Rumiñahui and Quizquiz had retreated to the north, Don Sebastián de Benalcázar, governor of San Miguel, assumed the role of captain of an expedition at the head of approximately two hundred men and launched on the conquest of the kingdom of Quito. He engaged Rumiñahui in several battles, the most cruel of which was that of Tiocajas, where the brave Indian general used countless stratagems and wiles to overcome the Castilians. He had great pits dug in the ground, the bottoms of which were bristling with pointed shafts into which the enemy cavalry was supposed to fall. This battle engaged veteran Indian war leaders, such as Zopozopangui, Nina, Razo-Razo and others. It lasted from midday until nightfall and the Spanish losses were considerable; it was only thanks to the darkness that Benalcázar was able to escape with his survivors, after lighting great fires to simulate a non-existent camp. After several encounters, Benalcázar reached Quito, which he found completely destroyed by Rumiñahui, who had hidden the members of the royal family, slain the Virgins of the Sun to spare them from the Spaniards, burned or demolished all the mansions and temples and hidden their treasures. Such was Benalcázar's position when he received an urgent request from Almagro, who, on his way up from Cuzco, was about to confront Alvarado. Benalcázar met Almagro in Riobamba and was upbraided by him for acting precipitously and setting off on an expedition without prior approval from Pizarro and himself. Benalcázar made repeated protestations of loyalty and gave Alvarado's arrival as an excuse for having acted rashly.

To save time, Almagro established a Spanish settlement called Quito, near Lake Colta, trying to lay a legal basis for preempting Alvarado. Alvarado got wind of these preparations and sent Almagro a messenger to tell him that his intentions were peaceful and that he only wished to settle the lands that were not occupied by Pizarro. He also informed him that he would attend a meeting in Riobamba.

Two Spanish armies were drawn up in close order, with colors flying, when Alvarado came forward to meet Almagro. The troops fraternized immediately and, hearing tales of the fabulous treasures of the Inca empire, Alvarado's soldiers lost no time in voicing their wish to cross over to Pizarro's side. Alvarado, however, was an adroit negotiator and he reached an agreement whereby he would deliver his men to Almagro, together with his victuals and ships, against payment of one hundred thousand pesos of gold. Once the details were settled, Almagro and Alvarado set off for the south in order to meet Pizarro and obtain delivery of the agreed quantity of gold. After the meeting with Pizarro in Pachácamac, which took place amid a flourish of ceremony and pageantry, as the courtly manners of the day dictated, Pizarro sent orders to de Soto requiring him to bring gold from Cuzco, to a value of one hundred thousand pesos. Hernando complied and reached Pachácamac in the middle of a series of jousts and knightly tournaments that had been organized before Alvarado's return to Guatemala, leaving Pizarro's troops strongly reinforced by his men.

Hernando de Soto remained as governor of Cuzco. At the same time, he kept the Indian rebels under control and ensured that the Court of Manco Capac continued faithful. Sumptuously installed in Huayna Capac's palace, Hernando restored order in the city and arranged for the construction by the Spaniards of mansions and Christian temples that would gradually change the appearance of the capital. One of the most beautiful ladies of the royal household, Princess Toctochimbo Coya, a daughter of Huayna Capac, took a fancy to the young and elegant captain and there ensued a wild and passionate romance. A daughter was to be born of their love; she was named Leonor, after the Spaniard's mother.[5]

Meanwhile, Francisco Pizarro, who had sent Almagro north to stop Alvarado, took the road to the coast. In the neighborhood of Pachácamac, in the mild climate of the Rimac Valley near the sea, in a place that was easy to reach unlike remote Cuzco, Pizarro made his old dream come true by founding the new capital. On January 6, 1535, Pizarro solemnly traced on the ground the outline of the center of the City of the Kings, since January 6 was the Feast of the Epiphany. It would not be long before the Spaniards gave it the shorter name of Lima, which was the way they pronounced the Indian name of Rimac.

About this time, Almagro was arriving in Cuzco, still ruled by de Soto, clearly a supporter of the Pizarro faction. Almagro wished to take over the government of the city; Hernando refused. It was not long before opinions divided sharply, while a certain amount of trouble arose in the wake of the outrages committed by Alvarado's men. All this added to the uneasiness of the Spanish rulers. Displaying his usual tact and diplomacy, Hernando tried to separate the dissenting groups; he even managed to isolate the firebrands, confining them to certain buildings they could not leave. He immediately sent for Pizarro, explaining the urgency of the situation. The governor was engaged in founding the new Trujillo among the Yuncas; he nevertheless understood the importance of the message and left for Cuzco.

Lavish ceremonies were being prepared for the governor's arrival. De Soto tried to create an atmosphere of festivity and pageantry for the reunion of the two old friends, thereby laying the foundations for a cordial settlement. Almagro and Pizarro held lengthy talks with the courteous and active participation of de Soto, who constantly sought to find a way to reach an agreement and avoid a stalemate, which would have been fatal for both men. Almagro agreed to undertake the journey to Chile, with the help of whatever number of Spaniards and Indians was necessary, in order to extend his territory toward the south. On June 12, 1535, were signed the Heads of Agreement to which de Soto had devoted so much work and which stipulated that neither of the parties would try to malign the other when writing to the emperor and that all proceeds of future discoveries would be equally divided between the two chiefs. The document ended with an appeal to the Divine Providence.

Hernando considered that he had then reached the end of his mission in Peru. He had effected a reconciliation between his two chiefs; Cuzco was now at peace and others could take over his post of governor. He owned a considerable fortune, still untouched, as a result of his campaigns in Peru. His old partner, Hernán Ponce de León, had arrived from Panama and they both signed a new agreement of "brotherhood and company," involving all his goods and future enterprises, including his property in Nicaragua and his ships in Panama, as well as his rich domain in Tumbez, which Ponce would henceforth administer for him. He then decided to return to the City of the Kings, in company with Francisco Pizarro, who tried in vain to persuade him, for the last time, to remain by his side. There were still many lands to be discovered; the treasures of Quito had not yet been found; there was talk of a land of Canela, near the kingdom of Quito; there was also talk of Prince Dorado, and there were many kingdoms to the south, although Almagro was already marching toward the region that was known as Chile. But de Soto would not be swayed this time. He carried more than a hundred thousand pesos in gold and he earnestly wished to return to Spain to see his family, his land and above all to keep his promise as a knight and see Isabel, who, he knew, was waiting for him.

When he arrived in the City of the Kings, de Soto quickly prepared to board the next ship for Panama. The bombastic Hernando Pizarro had just returned from Spain with more land grants for his brother Francisco, as well as the title of marquess de los Atavillos and legal authorization for Almagro's enterprise in Chile. De Soto could see that in spite of everything new violent eruptions were in store between the rival captains, his chiefs and friends, and among the Indians who, led by Manco himself, no longer disguised their hatred. So far, he had managed to maintain a certain climate of understanding and harmony that reflected his own temperament, but he could discern threatening thunderclouds looming over the future of the colony. His wish to leave seemed to come at an appropriate time, and a few days later, accompanied by Pizarro, he left Lima for the coast to sail for Panamá. The governor gave the captain, whom he loved as a son and whose merit he appreciated, a splendid gift of gold. Without de Soto's contribution in men and horses at the beginning of the expedition when they were most needed, without his loyalty and clear judgment, his talent and sincerity as an arbitrator, his skill as a lancer and his adroitness at handling men, perhaps the whole enterprise would not have met with such success. Peru would not have been conquered; Pizarro acknowledged this. His grief, his gratitude and his affection went with the departing young captain. The names of both men would remain forever bound in the history of one of the greatest human endeavors.

Up there, however, in the holy mountains of the Incas, in the majestic mansion of Huayna Capac, a tearful woman remained alone, although expecting a baby who would become a sweet daughter. She was an Inca princess who had watched the departure of the cavalcade led by the two captains, on their way from Cuzco to Lima: the dashing de Soto and the old governor. For the rest of her life, the Inca princess, the Coya,[6] would remember his silhouette clad in shining armor, the proud cant of the plume he wore in his helmet; this man who had come one day on the wings of legend and prophecy and who had been the first to address the Inca and had defended him, who had gone on to dispense justice, spreading good humor and smiling all the while, displaying courage without cruelty, was leaving memories of a warm and ephemeral love in the wounded heart of the princess, the daughter of a fallen household, in an empire overthrown. She was watching the departure of her Viracocha, "the foam of the sea."

IMPERIAL KNIGHT

XV

*Some people, moved by malice and excessive
envy, have accused Spain of having bought
dominion over the whole of the New World
at no greater outlay of fortune than the
expenditure of stupid and persistent madmen.
But such malicious and envious persons fail
to consider that these same stupid and
persistent individuals were the sons of
Spain, a nation whose best fortune lies in
the men she has produced, men reared to
conquer the New World and, at the same time,
to make themselves feared by the Old.*[1]

Garcilaso de la Vega

De Soto sailed to Panama in company with the bishop—Friar Tomás de Berlanga—and several companions-in-arms who were making their way back to Spain; among them were Luis Moscoso de Alvarado, a kinsman of Don Pedro de Alvarado's, who had led the expedition to the kingdom of Quito, Nuño de Tovar and Juan Rodríguez Lobillo. They were all taking with them a good portion of their booty in gold and were hoping to make up in Spain for the privations they had endured in the New World. They also expected to find an audience ready to listen to their tales.

Friar Tomás de Berlanga was a brilliant and gallant Dominican who had become de Soto's friend during the latter's short stay in Peru. On board ship, they had long talks about their personal experiences. Friar Tomás had been the prior of his order on the island of Santo Domingo and he had become father provincial[2] in 1530. In 1516, he had brought to Hispaniola, from the Canaries, banana plants which were well known in the latter islands and which commended themselves because they were easy to grow and had a very high nutritive value. As it turned out, they multiplied in Santo Domingo and quickly spread from these to all the other kingdoms the Spaniards visited. It was enough to plant a piece of a shoot in the ground for it to grow into a healthy banana tree nine months later, at which time it already bore fruit. In 1530, Friar Tomás was made archbishop of Panama and the Royal Council of the Indies sent him on a mission to Peru; in fact the idea was to limit Pizarro's power as much as possible and also to quell the unrest fomented by Almagro's supporters. At the same time, the emperor had requested Friar Tomás to make a study of the geography and the ethnic composition of the region. His greatest adventure, however, had been his crossing from Panama to Peru in February of that same year 1535, when, carried by wind and current, his ship left Panama bound for Puertoviejo in Ecuador. He was carried out to sea and he sighted one of the islands which were full of *galápagos*, water turtles so large that "they could each easily carry a man on their back—as could the iguanas, which looked like apocalyptic monsters," while the birds and the seals were so tame that they let themselves be approached and patted. After a few days spent exploring the archipelago of the Galápagos, which he had just discovered, the bishop was able to collect sufficient water to return to the mainland, which he reached at Puertoviejo; there, he wrote his report to the king, telling him of his discovery. The prelate had spent some time with Pizarro and had ascertained that peace reigned once more between the captains, thanks to de Soto's intervention; he was now on his way back to his diocese of Castilla del Oro in Panama, where he would stay a little while longer before returning to Spain.

In Panama, de Soto settled his affairs, obtained more ready cash, as a result of his negotiations, and changed as much of his fortune as he could into gold. In current values, he now embarked with over 4.5 million dollars to take back to the mother country. He carried with him a name and a legend; fame and fortune had smiled on him; and he could lay all this at the feet of the object of his dreams, the noble daughter of Pedrarias.

In 1535, Seville was astir with news from the Indies and from the whole of Europe. It was a much livelier, busier town than he had left in 1514, more than twenty years earlier. In that year 1535, an aura of Spanish grandeur and imperial nobility surrounded the towering figure of Emperor Charles the First of Spain and the Fifth of Germany; this was accentuated by the fact that halfway through the year he gained a complete victory over Barbarossa. The imperial fleet, together with the pontifical galleys, were led by the Genoese admiral Andrea Doria and by the Castilian Alvaro de Bazán. In June, the fleet entered the Bay of Tunis, and in the span of one month, Charles the Fifth had razed the fortresses and captured eighty ships. Entering the city in July, he proceeded to free twenty thousand Christian captives, and he restored Muley Hassan to the throne of Tunis and put Barbarossa[3] to flight.

In the eyes of Spaniards, and indeed of everyone else in the world, Charles the Fifth was the embodiment of the imperial ideal. He was perhaps to be the last of such stature in the history of mankind.[4] This feeling was common to all people, those in the American kingdoms just as much as to the Europeans who were part of the empire. It was not that the Spaniards felt that they reigned supreme from one end of the empire to the other; rather did they feel neglected by their king, who was often absent and gave too much attention to the other lands, for their liking. They rather considered the American lands as an extension of Spain and—this was a typically Spanish reaction—they noted with pride that Charles the Fifth was becoming more and more Spanish, speaking Spanish to his family, French when there were many European personalities in the audience and German on rare occasions only. One day he told the pope, in Spanish: "And do not expect from me anything but Spanish, which is such a noble tongue that it deserves to be spoken and understood throughout Christendom."[5]

The Spaniards felt a certain amount of pride at the overseas exploits and victories, yet they realized that the European wars were costing the Spanish taxpayer dearly. Spain and France had fought two wars that had been marked by acts of valor and chivalry, but that had also given rise to mutual accusations. The emperor's rivalry with Francis the First, the knight-king of France and the friend of Suleyman, had revived in 1535. Francisco Sforza, duke of Milan, was married to one of Charles V's nieces, and when he died that year, Francis I invaded Savoy and occupied the duchy, after deposing the emperor's brother-in-law, Charles II. This happened at the very moment when the monarch was on his way back from his triumphant expedition to Tunis and was about to inform the consistory of cardinals of his triumph over the infidels. The young monarch, thirty-five years of age like de Soto, announced there and then his third war against Francis. The emperor's other concerns had been his struggles against the infidels on the Danube and efforts to reduce the tension caused by the Lutheran problems which had come to a head when, in 1534, an extraordinary explosion of fanaticism erupted in the Westphalian city of Münster which consisted of tragic days of orgies, violence and death. It was also in 1535 that Pope Paul the Third struck Charles the Fifth's other rival, Henry the Eighth of England, with excommunication when the willful Tudor monarch revealed that he had secretly married Anne Boleyn.

Isabel of Portugal, as ever the sweet, beautiful, serene and respected empress, acted as the lieutenant governor of the kingdom of Castile, with the help of the Royal Council. The Spaniards were gradually moving away from their recently acquired national consciousness to assume a more international character, as events dictated. In all of Spain, the talk was of the wars against the infidel, the pope's alliances, the maneuvers of the kings of England and France, the German questions: in short, all the known world had become the private concern of every Spaniard. Little wonder that in such an atmosphere those returning from the Indies should find themselves pandering to the national pride with their tales of wondrous achievement, and they had the gold to prove it; gold to procure those expensive luxuries and indulge those refined tastes that the Europeanized Court of Charles the Fifth had introduced into the once frugal surroundings of the Spanish Court of the Catholic kings.

The arrival in Seville of Hernando de Soto and his friends was an occasion for great festivities in all classes of society. Everyone talked of the great deeds of the famous captain and of his enormous riches, which he took good care to husband, though not to hide. He started, rather ostentatiously, by setting up house in great style in Seville, acquiring a splendid and costly wardrobe and visiting the town notables with an impressive retinue.

On the day he landed, he wrote from Seville to Doña Isabel, Pedrarias's widow, who spent part of the year in Madrid, in the house of her brother-in-law, Count de Puñonrostro. He included in his letter expressions of affectionate regard for her daughter Isabel and asked to be allowed to visit her, making it plain that he fully intended to bring to fruition the great dream of his life that had taken shape in Darién.

Doña Isabel de Bobadilla still held a high position in the empress's entourage. Her noble and graceful daughter Isabel was at her side, still dreaming of her captain, waiting for him through the long and tedious conversations she had with the ladies of the Court, or during the sewing or painting exercises with which she tried to occupy her mind. When Hernando received the pleasant and encouraging reply that he expected, he started to make preparations to journey to Madrid.

Count de Puñonrostro, Don Juan Arias Dávila, was Pedrarias's younger brother and he had gained fame in the king's service by putting down a Commoners' Rebellion. His drawing room, austere and sought after by the most distinguished people of his epoch, was open to the chosen few, among the superficially elegant of the day. Noble courtiers and a few intellectuals attended his receptions. It was a time when people still talked of *La Celestina*, the start of the picaresque style of writing, the first stirrings of Erasmian thought. The imperial aura was present everywhere, with the victory over Barbarossa's pirates, Spain's expansion throughout Europe, its growing prestige in European matters and its competition with France and England; all this was the subject of extravagant debate in the drawing rooms of Spain. Most of all, the fabulous conquests in America had caught the popular fancy, especially the feats of Cortés, Pizarro, Magellan and many others, among whom de Soto stood out as the hero of the day. People crowded into the streets and public squares just to see him go by: tall, strong and smiling, he cut a dashing figure with his hand resting on the pommel of his sword and a heavy gold chain draped over his doublet. Spain was proud of him, while a thousand rumors, grown out of all proportion, told of his fabulous riches brought back from the Indies.

In that late afternoon, in October 1535, a carriage was entering the Plaza del Cordón, in Madrid. It drew up at the door of the town house of Count de Puñonrostro. A footman stood at the door; apparently the visitor had been expected. De Soto's assistant and secretary, Rodrigo Rangel, stepped down to open the carriage door.[6]

Hernando appeared, commendably elegant in his sober finery. He motioned to Rangel to wait for him with the carriage, then followed the footman up the paved driveway that led between flowered borders to the mansion. As he climbed the splendid stairway, he must have felt his heart pounding faster. He had probably thought of this moment a thousand times, yet he was just as flustered as if he had never expected it. Another footman awaited de Soto at the top of the flight of stairs. Bowing deeply, the footman led him to the main drawing room. Moorish suits of armor lined the corridors and the walls of the huge drawing room were hung with the portraits of the distinguished ancestors of the Arias family. The door was flung open and Count de Puñonrostro strode in, followed by Doña Isabel.

After such a long absence, there were many items of news to be exchanged. Hernando had grown into a mature man. Doña Isabel de Bobadilla, the daughter of the countess de Moya, had kept her proud and noble bearing. Her silver hair added luster to her impressive appearance: and she truly looked the great lady of the Imperial Court that she was. Neither did she hide her pleasure at seeing de Soto again.[7]

The handsome knight, hero of many exploits had often been the subject of conversation and his return must have caused a stir in the household. Yet etiquette prevented Isabel from being on hand to greet him. Hernando learned that Isabel's brothers and sisters were well: Arias Gonzalo held office as the high constable of León. Two sisters were in convents, Beatriz and Catalina. Elvira lived in Segovia with relatives.

When Isabel finally appeared, Hernando stood up, making an effort to remain calm. Moving toward him from the end of the room was the woman of his dreams, Isabel, the most constant object of his thoughts, approaching with extraordinary grace and noble bearing. This was the sight that haunted his memory, the meeting he longed for all through his active life, as a humble gentleman dreaming of the day he could claim her with the confidence of a conqueror. Isabel was dressed severely in black, which enhanced her graceful silhouette. She was almost thirty years old. She was also proud and found it impossible to show her feelings.[8]

The exchange between Isabel and Hernando was courtly, yet charged with emotion, while de Soto answered all kinds of questions concerning the Indies and the remote places that had kept him away from Spain for so long. Fifteen years had elapsed since their last meeting and time was needed to renew the ties that had been formed long ago. Isabel was afraid of the future, of the other interests, dreams and quests that filled Hernando's life, and she needed time to come to know him again.

Nevertheless, de Soto's happiness was plain for all to see, but the etiquette of the day demanded that he take his leave immediately: after all, this was the first visit.

When he left, his lips touched the hand of Isabel, who withdrew it, but not before gently tightening her fingers on his hand.[9] The count invited Hernando to dine the following week.

Inside the carriage, Hernando gave vent to his great joy, confiding in his friend Rangel,[10] on his way back to the elegant inn where they were staying. The following day, he sent presents that were truly princely. For Isabel, there was a beautiful Inca collar made of gold, with ornaments in the shape of small seashells; for her mother, a pair of delicate pearl pendants from Panama; and for the count, a magnificent emerald that came from the Inca's ransom.

During the dinner, he spoke with Doña Isabel, who gave her consent in principle to making arrangements for the wedding as soon as possible. The count thanked him for the emerald and told him that he was just as much impressed by the great services de Soto had rendered the Crown as by the gem, and that he felt confident of being able to obtain for him the Order of Santiago.

De Soto was aware of the old count's motives: in order to be admitted to the Order of Santiago, Spain's highest ranking order, a most thorough investigation of de Soto's antecedents was necessary. The proud count no doubt wanted to delve into Hernando's family history before the provincial, albeit famous, captain was admitted to his ancient and mighty family. It amused de Soto to think of the surprise that lay in store for the count, since Hernando's family, judged "by the standards and customs of

Spain," as to its titles of nobility, had "neither strain of converted infidel, nor villain," which gave it an edge even over the count's family that numbered among its ancestors, as was well known, a certain Diego Arias, a convert and former itinerant merchant from the province of León who finally settled in Segovia.[11]

Now that there was a promise of marriage, he lived through several weeks of happiness, staying close to Isabel and visiting her daily. The captain undertook a journey to Extremadura to visit his family. His father had died several years earlier, but his mother was still alive and delighted in being able to enjoy the company of her son for a few days. He had beforehand laden her with gifts, with his usual generosity. He visited his relatives in Badajoz and Barcarrota. Jerez had changed, now calling itself a city, confirmed by a charter granted by the emperor.

To attend to his affairs and also to enjoy the company of his friends while the wedding preparations went forward, Hernando returned to Seville where his elegant house was nearly completely fitted out; he wished to see to the final details himself; he expected to live there after his wedding. He spent time with his friends Nuño de Tovar, Luis Moscoso de Alvarado, Juan Rodríguez Lobillo, Juan de Añasco and his equerry and secretary, Rodrigo Rangel. They were the young "Indians," who would stride into the taverns and order wine all round, thus getting an immediate audience, ready to listen to their tales of adventure. But they were not empty-headed and childish braggarts. They were quick-witted and fearsome swordsmen who were respected and admired. Free-spending and generous, they gave out gold by the fistful, looking down upon the other knights who were also pillars of the empire, recently back from the wars in Africa or Europe. They were the Imperial Knights of the Indian Kingdoms, huge and mysterious, distant lands.

Hernando went along with his select group of friends on several occasions, but never tarnished his name in quarrels or scandals. He would rather spend his time visiting the noteworthy citizens in town, who flooded him with invitations, or put the finishing touches to his house. In the context of the social conventions of his time, he considered his marriage as a conquest too: the modest provincial nobility of Jerez joining the noble houses of Bobadilla and Arias, and he wanted his house to be worthy of the woman of his dreams.

Hernando often saw Isabel during her stays in Madrid. He visited her at her house in Seville and frequented the social circles in both towns. By her side, or away from her, he never missed sending her tokens of his love. Doña Isabel decided to spend the winter of 1536 in Valladolid, where Charles I held court. All preparations had finally been made and a date was set for the wedding in November. Hernando left Seville with a splendid retinue bound for Valladolid. He wanted all his friends and relatives to share with him this happy moment. The marriage contract was signed in Valladolid, on the fourteenth of November; the contract specified that "there had been an agreement and contract of union by marriage, as witnessed by those present, between Doña Isabel de Bobadilla, and yourself, Captain Hernando de Soto, present in this Court." She gave him as a dowry the herd of cattle and the round mansion of Panama, as Pedrarias had wanted and stipulated in his will; this came to seven thousand ducats. De Soto in turn undertook to give her six thousand ducats.

The whole Court attended the lavish ceremonies. The ladies were extremely eager to see the famous captain who had seen Atahualpa's apartment full of gold and had shared in the spoils; the valiant conquistador who had won so many battles and of whom it was said that he was the second-best lance to have gone to America. His fame as a conversationalist had also spread abroad.

Those were days of intense happiness. Life would, no doubt, have other paths for him to follow in the future, but for the time being, the attainment of this goal meant complete fulfillment.

The emperor himself had shown interest in meeting the young captain. Doña Isabel made arrangements for the interview, which Hernando attended dressed in resplendent raiment, accompanied by his wife and his mother-in-law. Charles the Fifth was at the peak of his power when he summoned de Soto. In April of that year, he had addressed the pope and the cardinals in Rome, and, in an attempt to avoid bloodshed and war, he had made a gesture, worthy of the knights of the day, by publicly challenging Francis the First of France to a single combat, staking Burgundy against Milan on the outcome of the contest. The challenge had not been accepted and the Frenchman had continued to prepare for war. Charles the Fifth attacked through Provence, and his other imperial forces marched in from the Low Countries, from Narbonne and across Champagne, while Doria's fleet threatened the coastline. No major victory had been gained, however, and Charles the Fifth had returned to Spain in low spirits. He needed to see imperial knights bearing good tidings. Since there were no favors to be asked at this meeting, the interview with Hernando went off without haggling, in the most cordial atmosphere. The emperor asked for firsthand news of the Indies. The most powerful man on earth greeted the captain with his well-known simplicity, and questioned him at length about Panama, Nicaragua, Peru and—this seemed to worry him—about the Pizarros' power and their rivalry with Almagro. He talked with feeling of Atahualpa and showed displeasure of his treatment praising de Soto's position which had been to bring the Inca to Spain. Finally the emperor told him that although he had already rendered great services to his country, he would nevertheless have to continue to work for Spain. The emperor's skill as a practiced negotiator showed when, at the mention of the gold of Peru, he immediately asked de Soto for an advance in specie against certain taxes and revenues expected from silks in Granada and de Soto promptly agreed, saying that he considered himself greatly honored by the request.[12]

A little later, the newlyweds visited Segovia and other towns before finally settling in Seville. Segovia must have been a revelation to de Soto.[13] He marveled at the extraordinary aqueduct, at the grandeur and harmony of its Roman proportions, comparable in a way with the timeless Indian fortresses of stone, fitted together without mortar, which he had discovered in Peru. The huge alcazar, which seemed to rise from the rocks and reach to the sky, also greatly impressed him; it was from here that Isabel the Catholic had set off to be crowned queen of Castile. Next to the alcazar and other Gothic monuments, de Soto admired the tall Moorish tower of the Arias Dávila family, with its crenellated battlements and lookout towers conjuring up visions of the quests of the knights of old. Hernando, with his romantic temperament, must have felt that his adventurous spirit and love of action drew him close to this chivalrous past. They also visited the convent of San Antonio el Real, with its beautiful fifteenth-century Stations of the Cross, and saw Catalina, Isabel's sister, who had been a nun there for some years past and who greeted them with great affection.

Seville welcomed them with open arms. Isabel liked the elegant mansion very much and she immediately set about organizing it and improving it, with the help of the ladies who attended her. But more than anything else, more than any material comfort, more than the social honors and attention, more than the beauty of the country and the surroundings, one thing gave the most happiness:[14] the satisfaction of her great love, the romance that entered her life with the man she had waited for all these long years. It was as though Oriana and The Youth from the Sea had linked their destinies forever. As though Amadís had conquered the kingdom of her heart.

THE NEW TEMPTATION

XVI

Let your spirit rest, your ardor abate;
leave the glory of battle and the luster
of honors to those who are beginning to
climb the high wheel of fickle fortune
and be content with what you have achieved
so far . . . and you, Amadís of Gaul who,
from the day when King Perion, your father,
made you a knight, at the request of your
damsel Oriana, you have bested many knights
and giants strong and brave, at great risk
to your own self . . . from now on, rest your
straining limbs . . . start life anew, being
more attentive to governance than to contest.

Amadís of Gaul,
bk. IV

The gentleman of Seville seemed to lead a serene and harmonious life, entirely given up to the enjoyment of happiness at the side of his loved one. How different this was from the adventurous life he had led for twenty-two years, constantly struggling against the unknown, in a welter of events, where only presence of mind and perseverance could bring success. Now all this had changed and his obligations had taken a social or domestic turn. An unending succession of Arias and Bobadilla relatives came to visit them in Seville. Radiant with happiness, Isabel liked to show off her hero to her relatives and friends. In her blind devotion to the man of her dreams, she was forever singing his praises and addressing him with terms of endearment, caressing him all the while, to such an extent that, to his rough campaigner's taste, it all seemed quite overwhelming.[1] Countless times, he was required to recount his tales of the Indies, especially those of Peru and the Inca, that his visitors invariably wanted to hear. Playing down his own role, Hernando would sketch out a few episodes with quick, well-turned sentences, and would in every way comply with Isabel's wishes, with tolerance and understanding.

In Seville's social circles, the couple's charm had earned them a place of favor: they were always the most popular couple at the tournaments, the jousts, at the cathedral's solemn services which they frequently attended, as well as in the mall of the Corral de los Naranjos, or at the play, watching, on moonlit evenings, the new *pasos* of Lope de Rueda, then staged by a troupe of itinerant players. Hernando also frequented the Casa de Contratación, Seville's Board of Trade of the Indies, where his opinions were respectfully sought. He was usually greeted at the door with a series of bows by the guards who would usher him in deferentially; he would then move on, to be greeted with more bows by an army of postulants who crowded the halls, stairs and passageways, hoping for enrollment in some Indian enterprise, or negotiating deals, requesting charters, settling accounts, checking references or else reporting at the end of their missions. The referees and officials of the Casa de Contratación de las Indias, famous all over Spain, valued de Soto's counsel, not only because he was an independent party, but because his experience in matters concerning the New World had made him an acknowledged authority on such questions. Friar García de Loaysa, the archbishop of Seville, was president of the council and was at that time assuming responsibility for matters usually handled by members of the King's Council. The officials of the Casa de Contratación would, for instance, have to deal with cases such as the crimes committed on the outward or homeward voyages to and from the Indies and, as they would themselves aver, they would invoke the old laws of Alfonso the Wise, which stipulated that "no son of a good family could be detained or imprisoned for debt." In the course of these meetings, de Soto would gather detailed information about the latest happenings in the regions he knew so well. He thus learned of the progress of Almagro's expedition to the land of Chile, of Manco Capac's rebellion, of the siege of Cuzco, of the massacre of the Spaniards on his plantation, and of Hernando Pizarro's battles to conquer and subdue the Indians, with the help of his old partner, Hernán Ponce de León. War was different now, for the new Inca, whom Hernando had helped place on the throne, could no longer be defeated quite so easily with superior weapons; the reverse was the case. The Inca now went to war mounted on a horse that was caparisoned from head to tail, and he frequently routed the Spaniards. Juan Pizarro had lost his life in one such encounter.

Not a day went by without de Soto being appraised of some new matter concerning the Indies by his friends, particularly Moscoso, Tovar and Rangel, who were reaching the end of the treasures they had brought from Peru and made no secret of their longing for new ventures. They kept praising de Soto's great qualities and talked of his success, in the hope of inducing him to dwell on thoughts of new conquests. Naturally, Moscoso and Tovar realized that these were not matters to be broached in Hernando's house, and they therefore waited to discuss them with him in the Casa de Contratación, or in such places where gentlemen congregated, in the malls and hostelries they frequented, for instance. They knew that the subject would not be to Isabel's liking and they tried to keep it to themselves.

As for Isabel, she was completely under the spell of his deep black eyes.[2] She saw in him the courteous knight, ever ready to entertain her with his amazing tales, or most amusing anecdotes; most of all, she realized he was utterly devoted to her. He would listen with great interest to her stories about her entourage, the latest Court rumor, the winsome pranks of nine-year-old Prince Felipe, the latest changes she made in the running of the house, and the way she dealt with the daily domestic problems. He was always ready to set off on visits to his mother-in-law, or Isabel's sisters. And yet, her feminine intuition must have told her that all was not well behind the outwardly serene appearance of her captain. She would sometimes observe him from afar, strolling along the mansion's terrace, seemingly lost in thought, or staring in the distance, as though straining his sight and imagination to make the leap across the vast expanse of the ocean and rejoin his comrades-in-arms in the lands of America. Such was indeed the name people were beginning to apply to the New World, even though the appellation was open to controversy. Certain German cartographers, enthusing over Amerigo Vespucci's accounts, had published a number of his reports, with map illustrations of the land, and they added the following comment: "There seems to be no reason why we should not call the region America, that is to say, the land of Amerigo." The Strasbourg Account, which was reprinted in 1522, also mentioned America, which reminded de Soto of his friendship with Giovanni Vespucci, who had already given up his cartographer's post in Seville and moved to Florence.

During his many talks with Isabel, Hernando must have found his mind straying once more. As a man of action he could not hide the fact that his thoughts dwelt on adventures past and new challenges. He felt the need to draw Isabel into his world[3] and talked of showing her the many things she never saw in Darién. Trying to allay her fears of setting off on new adventures, he would say that by now almost everything had been explored, all kingdoms conquered and subdued by Hernán Cortés and Pizarro. The immense region of Florida remained to be explored, but so little was known about it that no concrete plans could be formulated by anyone in this regard.

Yet those were the very things that frightened Isabel, and, though she did her best to hide her anguish at the sight of those dark clouds on the horizon of her happiness, she nevertheless discussed the matter with her mother, her sister the nun and her uncle the count. They all agreed that whatever de Soto decided, Isabel should support him. And, as a last resort, if he decided to undertake an expedition for the glory of King and Country, she should accompany him. Such was the exacting duty of a daughter of Pedrarias.[4]

Matters soon came to a head with the arrival in Seville
of a famous explorer of the Indies, well known for his
accomplishments and his exploits. His name was Álvar
Núñez Cabeza de Vaca. Tall, spare and sunburned, he
told awesome tales of astounding deeds, of courage in
inhospitable lands, of aggressive warriors and daring explorers. Out of a force of six hundred men who had sailed,
ten years earlier, bound for Florida, only four had come
back. He described rich lands where gold had been found,
but where most of all new kingdoms were to be established. He soon came to frequent Hernando's house and,
despite Isabel's undisguised aversion for him, spent long
hours there, seated at a table, amply supplied with generous wines, with Hernando and his friends Moscoso,
Tovar and Rangel plying him with questions and asking
him to recount over and over again the tale of his adventures and misfortunes in the country north of Cortés's
lands, that huge, unknown expanse known as Florida,
which reached from Labrador to the Gulf of Mexico and
covered all the northern part of America.
    The fact was that, despite numerous expeditions, each
more daring than the next, Florida was still unexplored.
Three main attempts had been made, all of which had
met but scant success: by Ponce de León, by Lucas Vázquez de Ayllón and by Pánfilo de Narváez, the latter with
the ill-starred participation of Cabeza de Vaca.
    Juan Ponce de León had been a page of King Ferdi-
nand and was already a grown man when he sailed with
Ovando to the Indies. He had created the colony of Puerto
Rico, under the authority of Admiral Diego Colón, and
had gone on in search of the island that was said to hold
the Fountain of Eternal Youth. He landed at Bimini and,
on Easter Sunday, the day called Pascua Florida, in the
year 1512, he struck the land that was to bear that name.
He returned to Spain and obtained from King Fernando
the title of adelantado of Bimini and governor of Florida.
When, after a hazardous crossing, he disembarked in 1513,

he was driven back by hostile Indians who killed most of his men. Undismayed, he returned to Spain and mounted another expedition. In 1521, he landed in Florida, near what is now Charlotte Harbor, at the head of 250 men and fifty horses. Once again, an army of intrepid warriors, the Calusa Indians, opposed his landing so vigorously that the invaders were decimated and the aging conquistador was seriously wounded by a poisoned arrow; he was then carried to Cuba among only seven survivors and there he died.[5]

Lucas Vázquez de Ayllón, a judge and justice of the Court of Appeals of Santo Domingo, had, with six other rich men of the island, decided to charter two ships and set up an expedition to explore Florida. He had come across a few good-natured Indians with whom he had been able to trade a little merchandise and, realizing how trusting the Indians were, he subsequently contrived to seize them while they were on board his ship and carried them off as slaves. One boat foundered on the way to Santo Domingo; the other gained small profit from its load of slaves, for they all "fell into a state of listnessness, bred of their disgust at having been deceived under the pretence of friendship, and they starved themselves to death."[6] Back in Spain, Vázquez de Ayllón nevertheless asked to be allowed to conquer and govern the province of Florida. Having chartered a fleet of three ships, he landed in Florida in 1524, where he was met by a native tribe which greeted him in a friendly manner; after two or three days of festivities, however, the Indians made a surprise attack on the band of Spaniards and killed nearly all of them. Vázquez de Ayllón barely managed to escape with four or five companions, acknowledging that the Indians were only paying him back for "what he had done to them on his earlier trip."[7]

Pánfilo de Narváez left Spain in 1527 with five ships and six hundred men, to explore the vast region surrounding the Río de las Palmas in the Gulf of Mexico, going up into Florida. He had with him Cabeza de Vaca as his treasurer and high constable, at the head of a magnificent expedition. Narváez had previously been the captain general of the force that Diego Velázquez, the governor of Cuba, had sent to conquer Mexico. Some years before this, he had tangled with Vázquez de Ayllón, and he had also lost all his men and his fleet of eighteen ships to Cortés who had cleverly wrested them from him at Cempoala. He lost an eye in the brief encounter.

During the Florida expedition, ignoring Cabeza de Vaca's warnings, Narváez led his troops away from the ships on an ill-fated trip along the coast, where he lost all six hundred men and the hundred horses. On one island, the Spaniards suffered such dire privations that they resorted to cannibalism among themselves. In Narváez's expedition, only four survived, including Cabeza de Vaca, who wandered for nearly nine years through the inhospitable regions, and was captured and held prisoner by the Sioux Indians. They did not kill him, because he showed some skill at healing the sick. He managed to escape eventually, and fled to Mexico, then to Spain.

Such was the tragic picture that Florida offered: it was an extensive land, heavily populated by Indians that were different from those of Mexico or Peru. It was rich agricultural land, for the most part unknown, since none of the expeditions so far had been successful. In the whole of the sixteenth century, the area then known as Florida was never properly defined; rather, it was said that "no one knows where it ends, nor whether it borders on seas or other lands."[8] All that was known was that, to the west, it led to the land of the Seven Cities of Cibola (now northern New Mexico). It was realized that what had until recently been thought to have been an island, was, in fact, a peninsula, a part of Florida that lay very close to Cuba and was mostly surrounded by coral reefs; that it had many lagoons around which grew mangrove trees; that its flora and fauna were of a special kind, strange to

Spanish eyes. De Soto was swayed by Cabeza de Vaca's description of this land and must have already heard within himself the call of new conquests.[9] That others should have failed mattered little; on the contrary, it left the field open for anyone to try his luck. And this time, he could be the leader of the expedition, the absolute master, not the second-in-command serving the fame and wealth of others, as he had in the past.

De Soto consulted his friends Tovar, Moscoso and Rangel to get their opinion on the character of this strange captain and the veracity of his accounts, as well as the possibilities of his wanting to set up his own undertaking. He decided to meet Cabeza de Vaca and suggest a joint expedition to Florida.

Cabeza de Vaca replied evasively and showed no enthusiasm for such an association. He protested his own weariness and the difficulties of the undertaking, saying that he first had to see the king and make his report before even considering further projects.[10]

Hernando thought the matter over and a few days later decided to embark on an expedition to Florida, whatever the difficulties. He talked the matter over with Isabel, who acceded to his wishes and assured him of her support. They both decided to travel to Madrid to speak to Isabel's uncle, the count, before petitioning the king.[11]

The preparations for the journey were soon completed. Two days later, they left Seville. Before their departure, Hernando had taken the time to acquaint Bishop García de Loaysa with his plans. The prelate had given his full approval and promised his support when de Soto made his official request.

Count de Puñonrostro was vain and domineering. He repeatedly stressed his own part in obtaining for de Soto the Order of Santiago, which now made him proud of his relationship with the famous captain. He was most enthusiastic about the new undertaking. He immediately advised de Soto of the things that would have to be done in order to enlist the interest, not only of the king, but also of the highest gentlemen at Court, so that they would wish to join. He already took it for granted that it would be the most brilliant expedition ever to sail from Spain.

Doña Isabel alone remained silent. She understood her daughter's anguish. She knew how many years Isabel had waited for these few months of happiness that she now enjoyed. And she knew from her own experience how a woman can suffer, waiting for the man she loves, through the uncertain times of such campaigns. Seeing Hernando and Isabel so determined, however, no doubt prompted her to conceal her misgivings.[12]

The count now urged de Soto to ask not only for the title of governor and captain general of Florida, but also that of marquess, as Pizarro had done before; Pizarro, the man from Trujillo, of very humble condition, now Marquess de los Atavillos. De Soto was of the opinion that the governorship of Cuba, which was at the time as good as vacant, would be of much greater benefit, since Cuba would be called upon to support the Florida expedition and holding the governorship would be the best way of protecting the operation from the rear. The count fully agreed and promised his support.[13]

Hernando argued with his friends[14] that King Charles would probably welcome the fact that the veteran of Peru should take an interest in Florida and there was no need for Doña Isabel's recommendation, but by mobilizing the Pedrarias household he was giving the undertaking an air of family support. He knew that this would make things more acceptable to Isabel. He wanted her to share in the initiative from the very beginning. Indeed, his happiness depended on hers.[15]

THE GREAT FLEET

XVII

And wishing to embark on worthy enterprises and follow his noble aspirations, he asked the King to be allowed to conquer and pacify Florida; the King readily granted him his wish, with all the conditions he set, for he was a Man of experience and good presence, with the right build, age and strength to bear the strains of War.[1]

Antonio de Herrera

The king was enthusiastic about entrusting the governorship and undertaking of Florida to de Soto.[2] Recently there had been no one to come forward and face such a difficult venture and, if anyone in Spain was qualified to bring such an under-taking to a successful conclusion, de Soto was the man. The king, de Soto's age, was plainly attracted to this merry, personable citizen of Jerez,[3] whom everyone liked and spoke of with enthusiasm. He instructed the Casa de Contratación to give him all possible help and also hinted to the high dignitaries of the Court that they should take part in the venture.

News of Hernando de Soto's plans spread all over Spain. The famous conqueror of Peru was undertaking a second conquest. Rumor had it that he would find greater empires than those of the Aztecs and the Incas, and de Soto's name seemed to be a guarantee of success, because of his knowledge of the Indies, his proven valor and also because he was expected to invest in the enterprise the hundred thousand ducats he was known to have brought from the New World. This started a rush at all levels of society to join the enterprise with money and personal services. Illustrious names, young soldiers just back from the European wars against France or the Moors, workers and tradesmen, clerics and adventurers, all wanted to go and used whatever influence they could to meet de Soto, or his close friends, or hand him letters of introduction from people in high places. To reach their goal, they did not hesitate to sell or mortgage their arable land, their houses, jewels or businesses; all this to join in the mad whirl of adventure with a blind appetite for heroic deeds, for the unknown, for the difficult tasks, not unlike the gambler's lust for wagering, and certainly in keeping with the truly Spanish spirit of the times.

Charles the Fifth had granted Hernando de Soto the title of adelantado, with that of marquess of the land that he would eventually conquer in Florida. There he would hold a stretch of land thirty leagues long by fifteen leagues wide, in his own name, wherever he chose to stake it. He was also made governor and captain general of Florida—a country that was little known in those days—"and its annexes on the Mainland"; it was supposed to extend from the island, or peninsula of what is now Florida, up to the remote regions of the northern seas. Finally, he was also made governor of Cuba, or Fernandina Island, so that the rich isle could give him the necessary support for his undertaking in Florida.

This was, for Hernando, a great accumulation of honors and titles, greater than had been given to any conquistador of the Indies. With respect to Fernandina Island, he was taking over from Admiral Luis Colón, who had made Gonzalo de Guzmán his lieutenant in the governorship of the island, the highest authority in the land for the colonists. He had been given access to the nobility by his knighthood in the Order of Santiago, and now he also carried the title of marquess.

From the time de Soto decided to sail for Florida, Isabel must have tried to be closer to him, despite the many obligations of the undertaking he had to comply with. It was as if she wanted to enjoy every possible minute with her adored captain, whom everyone now addressed as "The Most Magnificent Lord Governor."

In the letters patent granted in Valladolid on April 20, 1537, the emperor's pleasure was that de Soto should start the conquest within one year, with at least five hundred men, fully armed, with the horses and supplies that may be necessary. He was to take victuals sufficient for eighteen months from Cuba to Florida. In fact, as was the custom of the day, the king required all costs of the expedition to be borne by de Soto himself. As to what might be gained from the conquest, the king was most generous: he authorized de Soto to draw fifteen hundred ducats per year, plus five hundred ducats more as a contribution toward expenses, or as a grant. He also added to the other titles he gave him that of high constable, which carried the wardenship of three fortresses, with a revenue of a hundred thousand maravedis per year for each fortress.

The king made a special recommendation, stipulating that de Soto should not take with him a lawyer of any kind, or a solicitor or barrister, since he knew the trouble and strife they stirred up; he also requested that de Soto not forget the now classical Requerimiento, to be read several times to the Indians before undertaking any violent action, the reading to be done through interpreters, since the Indians must be treated as "free persons" who must be helped to forsake "the heinous sin and perversion of eating human flesh."[4]

A little later, on May 4, came the appointment as captain general and adelantado of Florida, "entitling him to all the honors, graces, mercies, franchises, liberties, excises, precedence, prerogatives, immunities and others such, due to his rank."[5] The *gobernación* and *capitanía general* of Florida was not subordinated to any *audiencia*; by law, de Soto reported directly to the Royal Council of the Indies, in Madrid.

Hernando de Soto gathered his closest friends to organize the enterprise with the dispatch and practical qualities that he usually displayed. Nuño de Tovar and Luis de Moscoso would be the key men of his expedition. With them, he set to work in his house in Seville to make ready the required fleet; this meant finding the right ships, buying them, equipping them and arming them. He also had to make a careful selection of men, bearing in mind that it would be a difficult venture, as he well knew. Yet they all reveled in the fact that no one had tackled such a daring adventure and that men of real worth would be needed to prevail where so many others had failed.

Every detail needed consideration. This was not to be an expedition like that of 1514, where Pedrarias had drafted quarrelsome captains and unctuous courtiers, who were more trouble than they were worth. Now, de Soto needed strong men to explore the country and, if need be, fight, but he also needed workers to settle the land. Furthermore, times had changed: no longer were plunder and the slave trade allowed. The law had evolved in the Indies, mainly under the influence of such preachers as the indefatigable Las Casas; de Soto would therefore have to follow and enforce the new laws. In 1531, Empress Isabel of Portugal[6] had signed a long list of instructions favoring the American settlers. They provided for free passages for workers who brought their wives and children; the state further undertook to support them during the first year of their stay in the Indies and to exempt them from all taxes for a period of twenty years. These measures were the result of a new way of looking at things: rulers no longer thought of conquering new kingdoms easily and at the point of a sword, but rather they preferred exploring the vast expanse of unknown territories, hoping to extend the empire by bringing new peoples into the already universal Spanish community.

Progress had gradually been made in the choice of ships and by now a fleet of five vessels had been fitted out: one galleon, two caravels and two brigantines. Luis Moscoso was responsible for procuring the endless variety of stores, tools, seeds, arms, ammunition, livestock, medical supplies, religious items and the many other sundry requirements of a fleet. Nuño Tovar was given the task of interviewing the volunteers, collecting their contributions in cash, acquainting them with their jobs and assigning them rank and duties in the expeditionary force. It was an overwhelming responsibility, since it soon appeared that the minimum requirement of five hundred men would be greatly exceeded. This made for an ever more stringent selection, where young men were given preference over the others. Hernando took care, of course, to choose people who would be loyal to him and for that reason he invited a number of kinsmen to join him. From Extremadura, his relatives belonging to the gentry and the clergy came to enroll under the banners of the lucky citizen of Jerez, whose reputation now filled the whole district with pride. For instance, he welcomed Don Carlos Enríquez, who had married a niece of the adelantado and governor, Doña Isabel de Soto; a nephew, Captain Diego de Soto; a cousin, Friar Luis de Soto, from Barcarrota; his cousins on his mother's side, the brothers Arias Tinoco; as well as Alonso Romo and Diego Tinoco, from Badajoz.

It looked as though the expedition was going to be a thousand men strong, with the following chain of command:

Hernando de Soto, adelantado, governor and captain general both of Florida and of Cuba; Nuño Tovar, lieutenant general; Luis Moscoso y Alvarado, camp marshal; Baltasar de Gallegos, first magistrate; Alonso Martín, first pilot; Juan de Añasco, comptroller; Luis Hernández de Biedma, agent; Diego del Corral, treasurer; Juan Gaitán, treasurer; Pedro de Villegas, inspector; Diego de Arias Tinoco, chief ensign of the army; Francisco Osorio, alderman; García Osorio, alderman; Andrés de Vasconcelos, captain; Diego García, captain; Arias Tinoco, captain;

Alonso Romo de Cardeñosa, captain; Pedro Calderón, captain; Rodrigo Rangel, secretary to the adelantado; Alonso de Ayala, majordomo of the adelantado. To discharge the important religious duties of the mission there were a number of ecclesiastics.[7]

To meet the rising costs of the expedition, the adelantado most willingly invested all his fortune. He had a note covering the loan he made to the emperor, and a draft for three hundred thousand maravedis against the annual revenues from the silks of Granada. De Soto negotiated this draft with the town merchants, together with other bills, to raise more ready cash, although he prized the draft as a token of a service the emperor had requested of him. Doña Isabel also offered to sell her jewels, but de Soto courteously declined, pointing out that he now had enough with his own contributions and that of the captains who were paying for their own passage, to meet the costs of the expedition.

De Soto was full of attention for the men of the splendid expedition. The year 1537 was already advanced, when de Soto decided to "parade" his army through Seville. It was by now a large and impressive formation of young and resolute soldiers, determined to overcome any trouble or danger, impelled by their thirst for fame and riches and living under the spell of the magic name of de Soto, whose presence was in itself a guarantee of success. De Soto was most generous in the matter of helping his men with their expenses and he often would supply them with double rations; others, however, would see to their own requirements. Garcilaso[8] was to say later: "The general's munificence was such and so great was his pleasure at having such noble and valiant people with him, that he held of small account the expenses he incurred to gratify his desire to bestow gifts." For the moment, de Soto had so much money that he did not spare expenses, though he insisted on quality and fitness in what was bought.

Five ships had grown to ten ships, which were full of victuals and equipment at the start of 1538. The appointments of dignitaries and military personnel had been completed. Each man knew what was expected of him. The holds contained iron, mattocks, spades, hoes, rope, shovels, bars, axes, saws, hammers, pincers, pots and frying pans. There were supplies of harquebuses, falconets, powder kegs, swords, lances, paper, seeds and medical supplies. There were a great number of horses, swine and various domestic animals, in pairs, aboard the vessels, together with barrels of wine, oil, vinegar, fruit, sails, anchors and boxes of glass beads to trade with the native populations.

The *San Cristóbal* of 800 tons was the flagship on which the adelantado would sail. The other large vessel, the *Magdalena,* would be under the command of the lieutenant general, Nuño Tovar; on the *Concepción,* of 500 tons, sailed the camp marshal, Luis Moscoso y Alvarado; the galleon *Buena Fortuna,* also of 500 tons, carried Andrés de Vasconcelos and his jaunty Portuguese friends; the *San Juan* was entrusted to Captain Diego García; the *Santa Bárbara,* to Captain Arias Tinoco; a caravel, under the command of Captain Pedro Caldo, carried the Genoese Cristóbal Espíndola, Cabeza de Vaca's relative, who was in charge of the sixty halberdiers of the adelantado's personal guard; the *San Antón,* a smaller ship, was under the command of Alonso Romo de Cardeñosa, the adelantado's relative, and also carried the ensign general, Diego Arias Tinoco. Two smaller brigantines also acted as escorts. Not counting the sailors and cabin boys, the expedition was 950 men strong.

As the sailing date was drawing close, the governor received instructions that he would also have charge of another fleet, that of New Spain, made up of twenty ships sailing for Mexico, that were to escort de Soto to Cuba, then leave him to sail on to Veracruz. At that time, the Granada citizen Gonzalo de Salazar would take command of the fleet; he had been one of the conquistadores of Mexico. Salazar came to pay his respects to de Soto, with great demonstrations of consideration and deference.

Finally the moment came to embark. A most solemn Sailors' Mass had been celebrated on land, in the Andalusian style, before a statue of the Virgin of Barrameda, and the general confession of the members of the expedition had been heard by the monks of the Order of Saint Jerome of Sanlúcar. The expedition bound for Florida embarked that morning of April 1538, to the sound of trumpets and salvos of artillery, marching under the royal standards that finally were carried on board the flagship. The Casa de Contratación officials and the councillors of the Indies went aboard to wish the governor goodbye in the name of the king. The adelantado was dressed in his most impressive finery. He walked up the gangplank with great dignity, in company with his wife, admirable as always and looking most beautiful in a lavish dress of scarlet brocade, with white satin sleeves. The last well-wisher to leave the ship was Count de Puñonrostro, who had been good enough to come down to Seville to bid his niece and his favorite kinsman good-bye. Sad and lonely, Doña Isabel remained in Madrid; she had sent her blessing to her daughter and her incorrigible explorer and adventurer, always seeking new horizons and difficult assignments. At the last moment a sad piece of news reached Hernando, which must have taxed his usual self-control, in order to avoid interfering with the progress of the enterprise. He learned that his mother had died in the distant town of Jerez.

On April 6, 1538, they slowly made their way toward the bar of Sanlúcar. The thirty ships of the most powerful and impressive fleet ever to sail for the Indies made a beautiful sight. The members of the expedition must have felt a pang of regret and sadness, watching the Spanish mainland recede as the expanse of water stretched around them. The horizon held the mystery of their future. With stout hearts, they were sailing toward the unknown, knowing full well what they were about, from the captains to the youngest cabin boy, yet filled with that truly admirable spirit of the knights-errant of those days.

The most daring of all, the most tenacious and the most inspired, the adelantado and captain general, was watching from the bridge of his flagship the Giralda Tower of Seville disappear in the distance, while the luminous mass of water grew ever more imposing around him, ready to bear him once again to the New World, seemingly the final objective of his destiny. Holding his hand, silently shedding the tears she could no longer contain, stood Isabel. They were like Amadís, who had forsworn the quiet life, and Oriana, who accompanied him on the adventure.

FERNANDINA ISLAND

XVIII

*On reaching Juana, I followed the coast
westward and found the island to be of
such size that I thought it to be the
mainland of the Province of Cathay . . .
its sea coast has many havens that are
without comparison with any other that
I know in Christian lands and large
rivers too, good and wide, that are
marvels to behold . . . and there are
large fields, and honey, and many birds
of various kinds, and a great diversity
of fruit.*[1]

Christopher Columbus

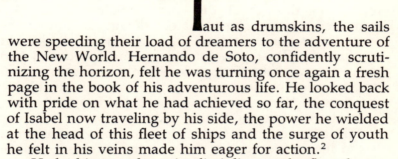

aut as drumskins, the sails
were speeding their load of dreamers to the adventure of
the New World. Hernando de Soto, confidently scruti-
nizing the horizon, felt he was turning once again a fresh
page in the book of his adventurous life. He looked back
with pride on what he had achieved so far, the conquest
of Isabel now traveling by his side, the power he wielded
at the head of this fleet of ships and the surge of youth
he felt in his veins made him eager for action.[2]

He had imposed a strict discipline on the fleet, knowing that the slightest letup would lead to discontent.
Moreover, he wished to make useful soldiers of the motley
band of men he had gathered from so many different
origins. Like all other expeditions to the Indies, his contingent was an amorphous mass of inexperienced people.
On the first day out, at nightfall, he summoned one of
his trusted soldiers, Gonzalo Silvestre: "Give the sentries
their instructions for the night watches. Let the chief artificer have all the guns manned, ready to fire without
warning on any suspicious looking vessel that may appear
before the flagship. We cannot afford to take any risks if
we run across privateers."[3]

The rules were that no ship was to pass the flagship
of the governor and at night each captain was to make
his position known by megaphone. It so happened, how-

ever, that about midnight the main ship of the Mexican fleet, with Agent Gonzalo de Salazar aboard, either trying to show the speed he could muster, or making it clear that his, too, was a flagship, sailed ahead of the *San Cristóbal*. Gonzalo Silvestre, who was on watch at the time, did not recognize it and gave the chief artificer the order to fire; he could not imagine any vessel of the governor's fleet committing such a breach of discipline which, as everyone knew, was punishable by death under normal sea practice. It was therefore assumed that an enemy ship had been sighted, and it was duly fired upon. The first round tore through all the sails of the unknown ship, from stem to stern, immediately slowing it down. The second round brought down part of the upper works, but by then the flagship was making good speed and had greatly reduced the distance between the vessels, so that voices could now be heard crying for mercy, identifying the crew as fellow travelers and compatriots and calling upon heaven to come to their aid.

The commotion woke de Soto who, going out on deck, found his men grappling with another problem, that of avoiding a collision with the disabled ship that would damage both vessels. He quickly ordered his soldiers to use their lances to ward off the accident. Several hundred pikes were broken in the attempt, but the measure was effective: the two ships merely grazed each other, though their rigging became hopelessly entangled, much to the governor's annoyance. He had his men use sharp spars to cut through the snarled lines and the sails that were thus caught up; this made it possible for the *San Cristóbal* to free itself from the other ship, which by now was recognized as the Salazar vessel. De Soto threatened to have Salazar beheaded at dawn.

The bystanders shuddered with horror on hearing this threat. Of those who knew only the kind and gracious side of the adelantado's nature, few could have imagined him capable of anything so drastic. The news spread quickly through the disabled ship and Salazar himself begged to see the governor to explain what had happened.[4] At his captains' insistence, de Soto agreed to hear the agent out. Salazar arrived in a small boat and, climbing on deck, threw himself at the adelantado's feet, making great protestations of submission and respect, explaining that it had all happened while he was sleeping and that it was a pilot's mistake, with no disrespect intended for the governor's authority.

De Soto treated Salazar harshly, declaring that negligence and inattention were as inexcusable as insubordination and disrespect, since the lives of thousands of men and the good name of the Crown were at stake. Yielding, however, to his officers' entreaties and to Isabel's tears and expression of horror, Hernando agreed to accept the agent's explanations and his act of submission.[5]

The episode firmly established de Soto's authority in the eyes of all members of the expedition, while at the same time showing the soldiers the firmness and magnanimity of their commanding officer. The winds were fair and the crossing went well. They soon reached the Canaries, where all Spanish fleets usually repaired for supplies, before setting off on the long leg of the Atlantic crossing. It was Easter Sunday, the 21st of April, the day of la Pascua Florida, when they reached the island of Gomera, some fifteen miles off Tenerife. As soon as the port was sighted, preparations were made for going ashore: this landing had been arranged beforehand, de Soto having been specially invited by the count and governor of Gomera, a relative of Isabel's. The count, a colorful bon vivant, dressed in white, was at the quayside to meet them; he had prepared to greet them with great pomp and a profusion of festivities, as was proper at Easter time.

The generous count spared no effort to make them welcome, and he had organized a lavish parade for the fleet of his illustrious kin. Beautiful local girls danced the traditional island dances for the men of the expeditionary force, evoking the strange, mysterious lore of the sunken continent; the dances alternated with popular songs called *folías*, to the gifted accompaniment of Gomera guitar players.

Isabel, whom everyone was already calling "Marquesa," or "Madam Governor," met one of the count's many offspring, a beautiful seventeen-year-old daughter, Leonor de Bobadilla, and she took a great liking to her. After consulting Hernando, Isabel formally asked leave of the girl's father to take Leonor with her as her lady-in-waiting, to help manage the group of ladies and servants of her company. Isabel was sure that at the appropriate time she would find Leonor a husband of a suitably high station in the new lands they were about to explore. The count raised several objections about parting with his favorite daughter, but he soon yielded before Isabel's insistence and that of the adelantado himself, who as good as promised to adopt her as his own daughter, and before Leonor's own enthusiasm; thus he finally consented to let her go with his relatives.

Supplies of fresh water, firewood and victuals, especially meat, had now been stowed on board, the boats had been checked, the livestock they carried were rested and well fed. Governor de Soto had completed his mandatory inspection and the fleet was ready to weigh anchor. It set sail for Cuba on April 24, heading southwest for the long crossing, riding the Canaries' current that was to carry them across the Sea of Columbus, the Northern Sea, as the Atlantic was known then.

No significant untoward event marred the remainder of the voyage, which took the rest of the month of April and lasted well into the month of May. For those newly out of Spain who were crossing the Atlantic for the first time, everything seemed captivatingly new.[6] The water's phosphorescence, the gradually changing skies, the nights under the stars, the strange fish and the eternal mystery of the sea were all subjects of conversation that helped while away the long hours of sailing and fed everyone's dreams about what was in store in the new lands of America. They soon entered the much talked about Sargasso Sea, which had won the admiration and raised the hopes of the crews of Columbus's caravels; the great concentrations of algae, with their yellowish or greenish hues, gave the impression of being floating meadows, as once in a while a lobster or other creature was seen moving over the drifting masses.

At the end of May, the first pilot informed de Soto that they should be two days' sailing off the island of Cuba, or Fernandina Island, and that, if he so decided, he could now authorize the Mexican fleet to break formation and sail off alone to New Spain. De Soto did so, glad to be rid of the unreliable agent Gonzalo de Salazar, who, in turn, was longing to assume authority over his own ships.

The outline of the coast of Hispaniola soon came into view. They had given a wide berth to the island of Tortuga, which was already becoming known as a pirates' and smugglers' lair, and they reached the coast of Cuba. The governor gave orders to follow the shore and to disembark at Santiago. The ships were approaching the port when there occurred an incident that could have had serious consequences. The flagship was sailing in, at the head of the line of ships, when a man was seen riding a horse along the beach and shouting at the top of his voice:

"Veer to port, to port!"[7]

The pilots were surprised at such strange instructions; they knew the coast was fraught with the dangers of rocks and shallows. The *San Cristóbal* nevertheless started to heave to, with the other ships following suit. By then, a sizable crowd had gathered on the beach, watching the fleet with great curiosity, when the same rider suddenly began to shout new instructions, together with some of the watchers on the beach: "To starboard! To starboard! Beware of the reefs!"[8]

The pilots quickly tried to come about; this made more sense to them. It was more in keeping with what they knew of the coast and with the indications on their maps. This was an easier maneuver for the other ships than for the *San Cristóbal,* which was already close inshore; it was unable to avoid striking a reef with a jar that caused a general commotion, especially among those unaccustomed to the working of a ship. Everyone thought the hull was sprung and a scramble started to lower the boats for the women, while others worked the pumps to save the ship from sinking. The crew were shouting in alarm. The women wanted to jump into the water. The friars intoned their orisons. More than one frenzied male tried to gain admittance to the boats, to be on the first trip ashore with the women. Friar Hernando de Mesa, a Dominican, even lost his balance while climbing aboard and fell into the sea, before being rescued by the sailors.

Hernando maintained his usual calm composure throughout the ordeal and personally went below to see how effective the pumps were. There he found out that the bilge they were drawing was nothing but the wine and vinegar that had run out of the broken jars at the time of the impact. He was told that the ship was otherwise sound and undamaged, so that he was able to restore calm and order the disembarkation to proceed normally.

De Soto's first act on stepping ashore was to find out the reason for such dangerous directions to his ships. With great demonstrations of repentance, the rider and the bystanders confessed that they had formed this unfortunate plan to sink the ships in self-defense, as they thought they were about to withstand another pirates' raid. Hardly ten days had gone by since the town had witnessed a battle between a Spanish merchantman and a French privateer. Both ships had fought within sight of the population, observing the rules of the day which resembled those of cavalry encounters: at the end of the first day's battle, when night fell, the two captains ceased fire and exchanged greetings and presents of food and drink. At daybreak, they resumed battle; at nightfall came the exchange of courtesies once more, and so it went, until on the fourth day the Frenchman broke off and vanished.

The governor reprimanded—not without a chuckle[9] over the novel stratagem—those who, with the best of intentions, tried to run his ship aground. He then proceeded to instruct all persons aboard the fleet to come ashore and make for Santiago, some seven miles inland.

The population did its best to welcome the new governor. The town council came to pay homage to Hernando and his wife. Within a matter of hours, all two hundred houses in Santiago were decked with garlands of flowers and rich bunting, the wealthier citizens trying to make amends by presenting the governor with a magnificently harnessed horse, and the marquesa with an equally well-equipped mule.

Hernando had at last reached his own island. He was the supreme authority on the Isla Fernandina, the former Isla Juana, the pearl of the Indies which Admiral Columbus had declared to be the kingdom of Cathay. It was the first jewel of the Crown to leave the colonial administration of Hispaniola, to come directly under the authority of the king; it was the first kingdom that Hernando lay at the feet of Isabel, calling her publicly "Madam Governor." With typical industry and initiative, he immediately decided to put his troops through a course of training and discipline, while preparing for the expedition to Florida.

One of his first concerns after establishing his headquarters in Santiago was to form a body of cavalry, with the two hundred horses he had brought with him from Spain to which he would add whatever could be found on the island. He soon had four hundred men on horseback undergoing strict training. To stimulate interest in the riding exercises, he organized all kinds of events, horse shows, jousts and races, to keep his men alert and the population in good spirits.

He also took care to send one of his captains, Mateo Aceituno, to the port of Havana, at the other end of the island, with instructions to start the work of rebuilding the town in the wake of the great destruction he had just learned of, and that were due to the incursions of the French privateers. Aceituno was a countryman of his, from Jerez, and familiar with construction work. De Soto's instructions were to rebuild the houses and also to start work on a fortress, to be known as Castillo de la Fuerza, to protect the port of Havana, for which the governor offered to send a few pieces of ordnance.

De Soto began a tireless round of visits to the villages of the island, ascertaining the state of the colony, taking an interest in farming and appointing his own lieutenants to run the peaceful and industrious administration he wished to maintain.

About that time he was visited by Don Vasco Porcallo de Figueroa, the richest man in the district, who lived in Trinidad township. He was a member of the illustrious Feria family, a veteran of the Italian and Indian wars and a plantation owner and businessman of considerable standing on the island who enjoyed wide esteem and respect. Porcallo de Figueroa behaved with natural candor and gaiety when he met de Soto, expressing his surprise and his joy, as one would upon meeting a friend. The two men struck up a mutual friendship, though Porcallo was already past fifty years of age. He was duly impressed by the sight of so many admirable, fine-looking captains in the governor's splendid expeditionary force; he was won over by the knights' contests and competitions, the martial fanfares and the pageantry, so that he was moved to ask to be allowed to join the expedition, offering to bring a number of men, arms and horses equal to that of whoever had contributed most in Spain.

"I should be very pleased to be able to count on your sword and your prestigious support," the governor told him appreciatively, "and I assure you, you shall be given the high rank your merit deserves. "Your knowledge of the land and its people will be invaluable to us."[10]

Porcallo's contingent comprised thirty-six horses for his personal use and that of his guard, and fifty more for the other soldiers of the expedition, together with a following of servants, equerries and soldiers, of Spanish, Indian, black and mestizo blood, all of whom were loyal to him and had stayed by his side throughout his adventures and labors. Porcallo had been the candidate proposed by Governor Velázquez to replace Hernán Cortés during the conquest of Mexico, when the latter decided to give fate a nudge and launch into a wild adventure against the orders of his friend the governor.

Meanwhile de Soto's old friend and kinsman, Lieutenant General Nuño de Tovar, was displaying his fine qualities as a horseman, a consummate dancer and a ladies' man at all the festive events of Santiago de Cuba. His finery, his richly wrought arms, his gift for the well-turned phrase made him a great success everywhere: in the drawing rooms, at the hunt and at all social functions. His eminent position and his relationship with the governor, as well as his rank, made him a desirable escort for the beautiful Leonor de Bobadilla, who seemed to be happy at his side, dazzled at being able to enjoy the favor of her distinguished relatives and of the fashionable courtiers, and at attending the long succession of festivities that seemed to be the main daily occupation of the expedition.

The governor's wife soon noticed that Nuño de Tovar's assiduity at Leonor's side exceeded the bounds of mere courtesy. She tried to investigate and discovered that in a few weeks, matters had gone very far indeed. She decided that Hernando had to be told. The credulous Leonor had trusted Tovar and his promises and now they were both striving to hide the true nature of their relationship. Hernando was greatly disappointed on learning of the breach of trust by his relative and his friend of so many years; he immediately sent for Tovar. He ordered Tovar to marry Leonor the next day and dismissed him as lieutenant general of the expedition.

De Soto felt a real sense of loss. After giving such a high position to his friend, his comrade-in-arms, his confidant in the expedition, he was now conscious of the emptiness Tovar's departure left in his heart.[11] He felt the void all the more keenly since he was himself a true and loyal friend, given to cherishing lasting associations. By breaking his trust, Tovar had added an injury to the pain of losing a genuine friend.

One can easily imagine the difficulties posed by the sentimental aspect of the question. The two men were veterans of the wars of Peru and they were related to each other. De Soto owed Tovar favors, even his life. Moreover Tovar had expressed a strong wish to remain with the expedition, as a private soldier. De Soto nevertheless stood by his decision to dismiss Tovar and he appointed Vasco Porcallo de Figueroa to replace him, assigning Tovar to the Cuban garrison. It is interesting, however, to note that he mentioned Tovar in the will he made before leaving for Florida.

De Soto next wrote to the governor, Count de Gomera, telling him of Leonor de Bobadilla's marriage. He then attended to the preparations for the departure for Havana. He sent his wife, the other women, the ecclesiastics and part of the infantry with the fleet, under the command of his relative, Don Carlos Enríquez. He chose a first group of fifty horsemen to go with him by land and reconnoiter his island, and decided to leave at the end of August. As for the remainder of the cavalry, numbering approximately three hundred horses, they were to leave in successive groups of fifty, with appropriate supplies of

food and fodder, to make for various posts he would designate on his exploratory vanguard journey.

For most of the Spaniards, this first overland ride in tropical territory was a fascinating experience, leading from one surprise to another. The huge Fernandina Island, which for so long had been thought to be a continent and, of course, a part of Asia, had been fully explored since 1508 by order of Ovando;[12] Diego Velázquez had pacified it as early as 1511, and glorious expeditions, such as that of Hernán Cortés, had used it as a point of departure. The Spaniards thought of it as being 875 miles long from Point Maisi, opposite Hispaniola (now Haiti at that point), to Cape San Antonio at the western end, facing Yucatán. Its narrowest part they guessed was 150 to 175 miles wide. The overland journey from Santiago to Havana, a distance exceeding 800 kilometers, they covered in several days' exploratory trek, stopping at little villages or hamlets and plantations previously settled by Spaniards. All the while, Porcallo de Figueroa's help proved extremely useful and his natural charm and powers of persuasion served to lead many of the people they met to join the expedition, which they felt was bound to be a success.

The land was mostly flat and the journey proceeded without much trouble. The Spaniards were able to admire the exuberant tropical thickets, the graceful palm groves and the shady pine copses; they marveled at the abundance of native fruit, such as the pineapples, the papayas, the guavas, the fruit of the cocoa tree, the peanuts, the wild grapes, as well as the numerous varieties of trees, edible roots or tubers, such as the cassava, that the Indians used to make bread, the Indian corn or maize and the plantain bananas that were already spreading across the island. There were pleasant streams, where the water was clear and the fish plentiful. In a word, here was a green paradise, where beauty and fertility and abundance were everywhere to be seen: a privileged island indeed. They also knew that copper and gold were now being mined, and the district of Santiago was famous for its plentiful cattle.

The Spaniards stopped at the village of Bayamo, 80 miles from Santiago, close to a river which they found to be wider than the Guadiana River of Spain. They were surprised to find it harbored the enormous, quasi-mythological iguanas, which they took to be lizards or "a kind of four-legged snake,"[13] but they did not demur at eating the flesh, despite the fear these apocalyptic monsters inspired. From Bayamo, they traveled 160 miles farther on, to Puerto de Príncipe, whence the governor went by sea to visit one of Vasco de Porcallo's properties. News reached him there of his wife and of the fleet led by Carlos Enríquez. De Soto must have learned with some anxiety that they had had to skirt a heavy storm which must have carried them far out to sea, but that they were probably coming into sight of Havana by now. He therefore decided to proceed by sea to join his wife and instructed the various cavalry detachments to continue their overland ride through Sancti Spíritus, Trinidad and the other inland villages.

The beautiful Bay of Havana lay calm and sparkling in the sun when Hernando de Soto arrived. His wife, all members of the government and the entire population came down to give him a splendid reception, despite the scars left by the recent incursion of the French pirates. The town founded by Diego Velázquez in 1515 on the feast day of Saint Christopher, was then known as San Cristóbal de la Habana and had approximately five hundred inhabitants. Once the customary courtesies were over, Hernando smothered Isabel with affectionate kisses. She looked magnificent in a black velvet dress, with a crimson bodice, the sleeves and front made of satin. She had been longing for him to arrive and had found their separation hard to bear. The governor displayed his usual activity: he first inspected the rising rectangular fortress which, thanks to Master Aceituno, was already taking shape, with bastions and ramparts ready to withstand eventual assaults. He also made arrangements for the churches to be repaired, but since the district was poor, he provided for all this out of his privy purse, in addition to the contributions of the richest settlers, like Porcallo, so that the work could proceed at a fast pace.

He now set his mind to the exploration of Florida, first sending a reconnaissance party in two brigantines under the leadership of the purser of the royal estates, Juan de Añasco, who was also a cartographer and an excellent seaman. He gave de Añasco instructions to survey the land, havens and bays and try to secure the services of a few Indians who would serve as interpreters. The cautious de Soto would not commit himself to making a general crossing without first collecting all the necessary information and making some kind of contact with the local population.

Two months later, Juan de Añasco returned with a lengthy report on the coast of Florida. He brought with him two Indians to whom he was beginning to teach Spanish. The governor felt he needed to know more about the land. Añasco was to return for further explorations, especially to find a suitable bay where the whole expedition might go directly, without time-wasting probes along the coast. Añasco spent three months on his new assignment, during which time he ran into a great deal of trouble, having to struggle against strong winds and currents. A storm once drove him to an inhospitable island where he and his men were obliged to live off periwinkles and sea gulls, with all the attendant difficulties one can imagine upon catching the birds and clubbing them to death. They were finally able to repair their ships and set sail once more on calm seas, to explore the eastern and western coasts of Florida. This time the information they collected was more detailed and more extensive and they were able to bring back two more Indians. Their return to Havana created a stir, since their prolonged absence had bred the belief that they had run into trouble. Upon coming ashore, all crew members knelt on the ground and wended their way on their knees up to the church to hear Mass: such was the vow they had made in their time of trial. Only after Mass did Añasco go to pay his respects to the governor and give him the full report he expected.

Havana was a mandatory port of call for all vessels sailing to or from Mexico: thus de Soto learned that the viceroy of New Spain, Don Antonio de Mendoza, was considering sending an expedition to Florida. De Soto, who knew from experience what strife could come from such questions of bailiwick in the matter of explorations, as had been the case with Pedrarias, Pizarro and Alvarado in Peru and Central America, promptly sent a trusted messenger, the Galician San Jorge, to speak to the viceroy and acquaint him with his own commission and plans. The reply he received a short while later was worthy of the chivalrous viceroy and it fully satisfied de Soto. Mendoza said that his plans were quite different from Hernando's and concerned regions totally removed from those de Soto intended to explore. He wished de Soto every success and offered to give whatever help he could in support of the great undertaking.[14]

By now, all the cavalry detachments had reached Havana, the ships had been checked over and the supplies were practically up to capacity. The expedition, in whose interests Porcallo had been most active, was nearly ready to leave for Florida. The governor now bought one more ship, the *Santa Ana* that plied the Mexico route and held eighty horses. This he added to the already powerful fleet.

Hernando then started to make arrangements for the administration of Cuba in his absence. Isabel knew that she would have to stay behind. She was to remain in

Havana, as governor, with the support of Don Juan de Rojas, a most capable man, who would be her lieutenant; Don Francisco de Guzmán was appointed lieutenant in the town of Santiago. Both men were distinguished members of the local gentry, who had previously held those positions and continued to enjoy the respect of everyone. Isabel was grieving at the prospect of the coming separation, but she was ready for it and she looked upon it as her duty to make every sacrifice, barring none, to help her husband in every possible way.

Another incident occurred at about that time, in which Hernando could clearly discern the hand of fate. One day when the sea was rough, a ship came into port that had obviously been trying to avoid putting into Havana harbor, but had been obliged to do so in the face of strong winds and heavy seas. When the ship moored, news of its arrival quickly spread through the town and soon reached the governor's ears: it carried a high dignitary on board who apparently had not wished to call in at Havana. It was Hernán Ponce de León, de Soto's partner and friend, the companion of his early campaigns in Nicaragua, Panama and Peru. He was on his way back to Spain, with great riches and a store of gold. He must have preferred not to come near his old partner, to avoid giving de Soto an account of the vast interests entrusted to his care when Hernando left Peru, as confirmed by a rider to the old contract executed in Panama. For de Soto, the only thing that mattered was the return of his old friend. He immediately sent greetings and gave assurances that he would not use his authority, but rather would give him whatever he had. Such was indeed the selfless and generous nature of the man, that he would always set friendship and understanding above all else.[15]

Ponce de León made a few excuses, alleging fatigue after the voyage among other reasons for putting off a visit to de Soto immediately, as he had been asked to.

Hernando was greatly pained at such behavior; surprised though he was, he resigned himself to waiting for his friend's visit the next day. With characteristic shrewdness, however, he posted guards along the coast, lest the ship should attempt to slip its moorings under cover of darkness. As it happened, a group of Ponce's men stealthily left the ship at midnight and made for the shore in a small boat, taking with them a large bundle and two chests, which they evidently intended to bury. They were in fact carrying the treasure that Ponce de León wished to stow safely before entering into negotiations with de Soto. Hernando's men promptly surrounded the boat's crew once they had pulled the chests ashore and started to dig a hole near the first line of trees. After a brief scuffle, the sailors were put to flight and the chests were taken to the governor. The incident upset de Soto, as it clearly showed the deceit of his comrade for whom he still had a great deal of affection. Hiding his feelings, he waited to see what the next day would bring.

Hernán Ponce was very much put out by the loss of his fortune, which in gold, pearls and gems amounted to some forty thousand pesos of gold. He nevertheless paid his respects to the governor, with whom he talked for several hours.

Two soldiers entered the hall bearing the two chests. They raised the lids to allow the embarrassed Ponce to check their contents. Ponce apologized profusely and was all the more filled with confusion when de Soto assured him that he considered the partnership still in force. Ponce immediately proffered ten thousand pesos to be remitted immediately to Doña Isabel as his contribution to the expedition, with a promise of further contributions, when available, later on.[16]

Hernando affectionately embraced his fickle friend. The next day, they signed the contract extending the old brotherhood and all the while the two friends reminisced about their absent friend, the deceased third member of the enterprise of dreams of Panama, the good Campañón.

The 13th of May 1539 was the date on which they signed their agreement, whereby Hernando once again renewed his friendship with Ponce. His friend had otherwise always been a man of happy disposition, a great conversationalist and quick-tempered fellow, although his covetousness had become more pronounced with the passing years. Under the stipulations in the contract, and in view of the fact that Ponce was returning to Spain, Hernando gave Ponce power of attorney to redeem and collect the revenues on the securities worth three hundred thousand maravedis per annum, from the silks in Granada, that Charles the Fifth had given him in exchange for his gold loan.

That same day, Hernando made his will as he was about to leave. The document is as revealing as it is moving, springing from the thoroughly good and honorable nature of the Jerez man, yet proof of his clear mind. In it, he requests that he should be buried in his beloved Jerez de los Caballeros and that his tomb be covered with a black pall adorned with the red cross of the Order of Santiago and four shields bearing his arms. He names as his heirs his relatives, friends and servants, remembering among them his daughter in Nicaragua as well as another offspring. Strangely enough, he does not mention—perhaps he was unaware of her existence—young Leonor de Soto, the daughter of the princess of Cuzco, who was to honor his name and remember him all her life.

On the eve of the day of departure, the governor and adelantado handed over full powers to his beloved wife Isabel and tried to dispel the fears that assailed her. Don Carlos de Gallegos would be at her side and so would the wife of Don Baltasar de Gallegos, while Don Juan de Rojas would, as she knew, be her lieutenant in the administration of the island, just as he had been before her arrival. A stern Isabel soon had to exercise those powers when Ponce, in a legalistic move characteristic of the man, requested her through an attorney to "state once and for all if she agreed to comply with the contract entered into with my lord . . ." and he proceeded to ask for the return of the ten thousand pesos he had handed to her in Hernando's presence. Isabel was a true daughter of Pedrarias, besides being de Soto's wife, and she was certainly not about to allow herself to be used. She firmly instructed that Ponce should be informed that there would be no such restitution and that if he did not wish to end up in jail, he had better fulfill his obligations with all due diligence. Ponce promptly took the measure of the woman he was dealing with and undertook to make good the contract, renewing it with even more documents and promises.

It was Sunday, the 18th of May, when the fleet weighed anchor and sailed out of Havana harbor. The governor had climbed aboard his flagship, while Isabel waved her kerchief from the shore and gave free rein to her sorrow. By her side stood her relative Leonor de Bobadilla, also in tears. Her husband, Nuño de Tovar, had finally obtained permission from the governor to sail with the expedition as a private soldier. De Soto sternly gave the order to cast away and sailed toward the land of his destiny. The mighty fleet comprised nine ships, five square-riggers, two caravels and two brigantines. The ships carried among them 350 horses: eighty were on the *Santa Ana*, seventy on the *San Cristóbal*, forty on the *Concepción* and lesser amounts on the other ships, like the *San Juan*, the *Santa Bárbara* and the *San Antonio*. Thanks to fair winds and a calm sea, they caught sight of Florida within seven days, at the point selected by Juan de Añasco. It was Whit Sunday, May 25, the day of Pentecost, la Pascua del Espíritu Santo. Because of the sand banks, they sailed farther on and landed on Friday the 30th a few leagues away from the village of an Indian chief named Uscita.[17] The governor gave the order to disembark and himself went ashore with great pomp and ceremony, to take possession of his land.

This was the start of his great adventure. For the first time, Hernando de Soto had set foot in North America.

NORTH AMERICA

XIX

Of all the enterprises undertaken by this spirit of daring adventure, none has surpassed, for hardihood and variety of incident, that of the renowned Hernando de Soto and his band of cavaliers. It was poetry put in action. It was the knight-errantry of the old world carried into the depths of the American wilderness.[1]

Theodore Irving, 1835

Tierra Florida, Land of Flowers, it carries its name very well! Look at those flowers, as well as the fact that it was named after Easter Sunday, la Pascua Florida, but all the same, all this stillness makes me uneasy, friend Perico," Juan García Pechudo said to his fellow-sentry Perico de Badajoz, the best guitar player of the expedition.

It was three o'clock in the morning and the soldiers were lying on the beach, sleeping off the strain and excitement of this first day of disembarkation. It had been a day of ceremonies, a day when the first explorations had taken place and now they were all trying to restore their strength after living for so long in cramped quarters aboard ship. They were in the Bay of Espíritu Santo, near Tampa.[2]

"Pechudo, my friend, it makes me uneasy too," replied Perico. "We have had so many reports of the fearful cruelty of the Indians of these lands, from the accounts of Cabeza de Vaca and Vázquez de Ayllón. You may be sure that they have been watching our every move from their hiding places all around us, just waiting for their chance."

"I trust our General de Soto and, what is more, we have our ships over there within sight. Should anything happen, we would receive reinforcements immediately.

All we need do, is keep a watchful eye. But wait! Something is moving between the shrubs. I could have sworn that that bush, between the flower patches, was not there a moment ago! Better go and have a look; but keep your harquebus ready. . . ."

The gigantic Juan García Pechudo, whom they had nicknamed "La Pechuda," as his mother had been known, did not have time to approach the bush in question. It just rose out of the ground and turned into a red-skinned Indian who fell upon them, uttering war whoops that were soon echoed by hundreds of warriors springing from the darkness with fantastic leaps, brandishing their flint hatchets decorated with plumes, or drawing their bows. These were tall, strong Indians, with shaved skulls, leaving only a tuft of hair on top of the head, where they wore eagle feathers as a decoration. A rain of arrows soon pelted the Spaniards; they in turn sounded the alarm on their trumpets, not so much to arouse the three hundred soldiers, who were already up and armed, as to give notice to those on board the ships that reinforcements might be needed.[3]

Among those left on board, the first to react was the lieutenant general, Porcallo de Figueroa who in no time came fully armed and with his horse in the first boatload of soldiers he ordered ashore. Men and horses jumped into the water and waded into the fray, eager for action. Those already on land had formed a square and did their best to fend off the Indian attack, while edging toward the landing spot. Several Spaniards had already been wounded by arrows. But the harquebus shots were effective. Porcallo de Figueroa led the column of reinforcements with great courage and amid cries of encouragement managed to put the Indians to flight. He pursued them until they disappeared in the thickets. He then gave the order to return to camp, but noticed that his horse was bleeding and was having trouble moving forward. The brave mount faltered and fell dying shortly afterward, mortally wounded by an arrow that pierced the padding and the leather flaps of the saddle and penetrated the animal's flank.

"This sorrel has served me well," said Porcallo, "but I take comfort in the fact that mine was the first horse to fall and the first lance to stave off the Indians."[4]

Thereupon the governor came ashore and gave orders to attend to the wounded. He congratulated Porcallo, doubled the sentries and calmly instructed all those left on board to proceed with the general disembarkation, more in fact to restore the forces of the stumbling horses, weakened by the long sea crossing, than anything else. These were the three hundred fifty animals that were to become the source from which would spring the noble equine population of North America.

Meantime, Vasco was sent to explore the recesses of Tampa Bay with his brigantines, sailing in the direction of old Tampa. There, several detachments, under the command of captains Añasco, Osorio and Lobillo, made a few incursions into the territory and found the land to be difficult, consisting of thorny brushland or more frequently of treacherous swamps.

On Sunday, the first day of June, the Feast of the Holy Trinity, the army by now fully rested, marched past its general in a splendid parade before undertaking its march to the north. The intention was to go overland to meet the detachments that Porcallo had set ashore and reconnoiter the country on the way. The adelantado's aim was always to explore, to keep exploring, wherever they went. He had enough gold and he was already covered with honors; now, he wanted to present his king with the most extensive tract of land in the New World, to reveal to Imperial Spain and the rest of Europe it represented, the mysteries of a region which had proved so hostile to the Spaniards who had tried to venture there. He wanted to open up as much as possible of what was already being referred to as North America.

On their way north, the expedition came across an agglomeration called Ocita, the main center of the tribe headed by Chief Hirrihigua, who had fled to the high ground. The Indian guides whom Añasco had brought back from his initial explorations explained to the governor[5] that Hirrihigua was a brave and cruel man, who loathed the Spaniards ever since a captain visited them some time ago, with troops, arms and horrific animals, just like his. They were referring to Pánfilo de Narváez, who had committed all kinds of outrages, going so far as to cut off the chief's nose, after killing and cutting off the hands of several of his men. De Soto nevertheless wished to repair the damage and improve relations with the chief. He therefore sent him one of the prisoners with a friendly message and bearing several gifts, to invite Hirrihigua to show himself as the great leader he was and come to talk of peace. In the message de Soto acknowledged[6] that there were good Spaniards and bad Spaniards, just as there were good and bad people everywhere and that de Soto wished to dispel with proof of his friendship the impression left by others, whose misdeeds he wanted to remedy. The chief spurned de Soto's offer.

The adelantado understood that he had to be doubly cautious; he could see that the Indian chief was laying waste the land around him. De Soto therefore had the agglomeration of Ocita reinforced and cleared the bush around the village to ensure that they would not be taken by surprise and to leave sufficient room for the cavalry to maneuver freely. One of the guides informed the adelantado of a rumor that there was a white man living with another tribe that was related to Hirrihigua's; he was a survivor of Narváez's expedition and was living under the protection of Chief Mococo, a man well known for his kindness. De Soto immediately wished to rescue his compatriot, if he were still alive, and to this end, dispatched the brave captain Baltasar Gallegos at the head of a troop of forty horses, to seek out the Christian and make friendly overtures to Mococo.

After various incidents, and trying to make sure that the guides did not waylay them, Gallegos and his men finally came within sight of a group of some thirty warriors in red paint, with their skulls all shaved but for the tuft at the top of the head where they wore the traditional feathers. Gallegos sent his men galloping toward the group of Indians who seemed to be waiting with supreme indifference. Alvaro Nieto, the brave Spaniard who led the charge, drew level with one of the Indians who carried bow and arrow and wore a loincloth like the others, but who startled everyone by shouting:

"Seville! Seville! In the name of God and the Blessed Virgin do not kill me, I am a Christian!" Whereupon he knelt on the gound and made the sign of the cross.[7]

The Spaniards drew rein and surrounded the strange warrior who spoke Spanish. They had found the compatriot they were looking for. The thirty Indians meantime withdrew to a safe distance without drawing their weapons.

"My name is Juan Ortiz," exclaimed the jubilant Spaniard, finding it somewhat difficult to remember the words, "and I shall thank heaven for this day, all the rest of my life. It has been many years since I have spoken Spanish, but I shall soon get back into the habit with you, noble gentlemen."[8]

He then explained that his master, Chief Mococo, had learned from his scouts about the arrival of the Spaniards and had sent the foremost warriors of the tribe to assure the general of their friendship and to deliver Ortiz, whom he was freeing, into their hands. Gallegos sent friendly messages to Mococo in return and invited him in the name of the governor to visit them at the camp, adding that he would there receive tokens of their gratitude for having freed a Christian. The inscrutable Indians made slight bows and returned to their village, while Gallegos and his men returned to camp, with Ortiz riding behind one of the horsemen. They arrived at nightfall.

The appearance of Ortiz, with his preposterous war paint, his bow and arrow, his tattoos, his dyed skin, his quaint Spanish, was a subject of considerable mirth and rejoicing among the members of the expedition. Ortiz was much courted by his compatriots, who learned that he was the scion of a noble Seville family and that he had spent twelve years with the Indians. What is more, he would be a tremendous asset to the expedition as an additional interpreter who knew all the idioms of the region. These dialects were of the Timuquan family, not unlike the Arawak dialects spoken by the Cuban Indians.

Ortiz could hardly contain his joy. The governor greeted him affectionately, as a father would a lost son, giving due credit to Gallegos for finding him. He gave Ortiz a suit of clothes made of velvet, a breastplate, helmet, arms and a splendid horse. Then he ordered that he be brought the best food possible, pork and Spanish wines. Ortiz had washed off the war paint in the river and had put on the clothes he had just been given, but they only served to make him look very awkward, since he obviously was ill at ease in European dress. He was quite overwhelmed and burst into tears when Perico the guitar player and his merry cronies regaled him with Andalusian folk songs and brought him up to date with the gossip and the anecdotes that the local wits of Seville had produced since his departure.

At the governor's bidding, Ortiz gave a firsthand account of his extraordinary life and adventures. He had been one of the young soldiers serving under Narváez, who not only had mutilated Hirrihigua, but had also killed his mother before her son's very eyes. While Hirrihigua watched, she had been tied to a post and torn apart by the dogs. Ortiz had arrived by boat to rescue Narváez, ignorant of the fact that Narváez had already left.

The chief, bent on revenge, had sent reassuring messages to the occupants of the boat from his position on the beach, to the effect that he had been instructed by Narváez to wait for them. He would send four worthy warriors to them as hostages, while the soldiers in the boat disembarked and enjoyed his hospitality. The Spaniards were suspicious of so much courtesy and sent only four soldiers ashore, among whom was Ortiz. They were taken prisoner as soon as they set foot on land. The four Indian hostages had surreptitiously jumped off the boat into the sea and had quickly reached the coast. Ortiz explained that these Indians belonged to the Calusa tribes that peopled practically the entire Florida peninsula. They were fearless warriors, skilled bowmen and excellent fishermen. In war, they would swiftly remove with their flint knives the scalps of their fallen enemies, dead or alive, and carried these terrible trophies in their belts as a mark of valor that commanded the respect of the other members of the tribe. They were a stern and hard people who trained their boys in the arts of war and left the women to work in the fields and attend to the heaviest tasks.

During the celebrations that took place immediately after the boat's departure—there being no way to rescue the four soldiers—the chief had ordered the young warriors to line the length of the main street of the village. Then the four soldiers were made to run, one by one, from one end of the street to the other, so the warriors could shoot their arrows at them, taking good care not to inflict mortal wounds, so that the torture could last longer. Ortiz's three companions had perished in the attempt, unable to survive the hail of arrows. When his turn came, the chief's wife and daughters took pity on him and asked for his life to be spared, so that they might keep him as a slave. Grudgingly, Hirrihigua yielded, fully intending to make life intolerable for the hated Spaniard. As was to be expected, whenever celebrations took place thereafter, Ortiz was made to run daily through the village, while being kept jumping to avoid the arrows shot at his feet. This would continue till he fell from exhaustion and was carried away to have his countless wounds dressed by the women who protected him. One day, however, it seemed that Hirrihigua had made up his mind to do away with Ortiz, and at the height of the day's festivities, he had Ortiz slowly roasted over a fire that had been lit in the middle of the marketplace, to the great enjoyment of all the warriors. Luckily, the women once again interceded in his favor, voicing such loud protestations that they managed to turn the chief from his original intention and induce him to stop the torture. Ortiz was so badly burned along one side that he would always carry the huge scars of the ordeal on his legs and hips. Thanks to the care and medication of the Indian women, he was at last able to recover his health and his strength. His destinies now took a different turn: he was charged with the supervision of the tombs of the village. The villagers used to place their dead in various kinds of wooden huts built of planks, that were far from proof against the incursions of the pumas that roamed the neighborhood. It appeared that the wild beasts frequently made off with the dead under cover of darkness. Ortiz knew that his life depended on his putting an end to these occurrences. Yet one night, unable to keep from falling asleep, he let a puma slip into one of the shacks and purloin the body of a child that had been laid there only two days earlier. Ortiz woke up to the full horror of the possible consequences of his neglect of duty. He therefore set off in search of the puma and, finding its tracks, followed the beast to a place where it was starting to feed on its prey. Commending his soul to all the saints, he drew his bow; by good fortune, the arrow struck home, though he had to wait until dawn to find the carcass, shot through the heart. Gathering the remnants of the boy's body, he took it back to its resting place, then carried the puma back to the village, with the arrow still in its heart.

This earned him the high honors that the Apalache Indians render their valiant warriors.

Hirrihigua still could not forget the injury he had suffered, nor the outrage done to his mother and, consumed by a burning desire for revenge, he decided to have done with Ortiz once and for all, in the course of a ceremony to be held in the village. He informed his wife and daughters of his decision. They realized that their protégé could not be spared this time, unless he escaped, and they urged him to do so, and to seek refuge with a distant relative and friend of theirs, Chief Mococo. They helped him get away, and when he reached Mococo, he won compassion with his account of the countless tortures. Furthermore, Hirrihigua's daughter's pleas in his favor carried great weight, since Mococo was engaged to be married to her. Ortiz received the chief's assurance that he no longer had anything to fear, because he would henceforth live under Mococo's protection, a promise that would be kept faithfully. He became the chief's personal servant and accompanied him on all his expeditions. Ortiz had thus lived some two years with Hirrihigua and about ten years with Mococo. Mococo told Ortiz, before he left to look for the governor, that the time had come to seek de Soto's protection for Mococo, in return for the protection Mococo had afforded Ortiz.

Three days later, Mococo arrived in solemn procession with the notables of his tribe. He was handsome and lean, about thirty years of age. He moved with grace and, bowing before the governor with great majesty, he kissed de Soto's hand. Then, asking Ortiz to tell him the rank of each of the Spaniards present, he greeted each one in turn, saying he had come to assure them of his allegiance to the king of Spain in the person of the governor and to request protection and help in the name of his people. He in turn offered de Soto the modest fruits of his land. Both the adelantado and Lieutenant General Porcallo gave the chief repeated assurances of friendship and heaped gifts upon the chief and his retinue.

It was not long before Mococo's mother descended upon the camp to protest her son's detainment. She thought he was being held under duress and she would offer herself as a victim in his place, should they intend to behave as Pánfilo de Narváez had done. De Soto told the old woman with a great deal of patience and affection that he had no intention of doing anyone any harm and he courteously gave her presents. The woman stayed three days but never relented in her mistrust.[9] Mococo remained a week before returning to his village, having offered his white friends food and aid. He later returned on several occasions to see de Soto and converse with him about Spain, a subject that seemed to interest him very much.

The great topic of amusement just about that time was the discovery of a woman in the camp, the only one among a thousand soldiers; she was Francisca Hinestrosa, who had arranged with her husband to travel in disguise. She was living in dread of the adelantado's wrath, since he had given strict orders that no women were to accompany the expedition. However, the clerics, the high ranking captains and a few relatives interceded with the adelantado and obtained Hinestrosa's pardon: she was assigned to cookhouse duties and infirmary work.

Before proceeding with the exploration of the interior of the country, the adelantado ordered seven of the eleven ships back to Havana. He then sent the *San Antonio*, a caravel and two brigantines, under the orders of Captain Pedro Calderón, to follow the coast round the Bay of Espíritu Santo. Pedro Calderón was a veteran of the Italian wars, where he served under the orders of the Great Captain.[10] The governor had written a long letter to the king on the 9th of June and he now sent it off, in care of the ships returning to Havana. He also sent special messages and presents for Doña Isabel, the lady governor of the island.

He now attempted to secure the friendship of the arrogant Hirrihigua and sent him new messages of peace, but to no avail. He did however receive a reply that spoke well for the Indian chief's good judgment. His message was that the injuries received at the hands of other Spaniards prevented him from sending a favorable reply, yet the governor's courtesy prevented him from sending an unfavorable reply, so that, on balance, he was making no reply at all. Nevertheless, incidents that occurred when soldiers strayed from the main body of troops and temporarily fell into the hands of Hirrihigua's men, without having to rue the fact, led one to believe that relations were improving. De Soto was a realist; despite the decisions of the Council of the Indies, he had refrained from imposing the useless formality of the reading of the Requerimiento, and he had given the appropriate orders to his men to abstain from doing so for the whole of the expedition. Rather, he lost no opportunity of sending messages of friendship, attempting to give the Indians a better impression of the white man.

Whenever an Indian was taken prisoner, de Soto invariably sent him back a free man, laden with presents. One incident caused a great deal of merriment and gave rise to many jokes when a soldier named Grajales, a manly and jolly trooper, fell into the hands of a group of Indian women. They fussed over him and fed him, but insisted on dressing him in a loincloth, which he wore when he was rescued by his friends. Acting under the governor's orders, the Spanish soldiers let the Indian women go, but from that day on, they referred to him only as "our Indian Grajales"[11] throughout the expeditionary force and never lost a chance to warn him not to stray from the camp, lest he should lose his pants!

Once the ships had left for Havana, the governor was

ready to undertake the exploration of the whole of the territory, starting in a northerly direction. He therefore ordered Captain Baltasar de Gallegos to lead seventy horses and seventy foot soldiers into the northern districts, which were known to be ruled by Chief Urribarracuxi. Juan Ortiz was to go with them. At the same time, he ordered Lieutenant General Porcallo de Figueroa[12] to take a detachment of one hundred men and try to make contact with the elusive Hirrihigua and bring him to the camp, if possible of his own accord, otherwise forcibly. The good Porcallo undertook his mission with great enthusiasm, ignoring the numerous messages that Hirrihigua sent him in an attempt to dissuade him and the numerous warnings following the messages. Closing in one day on what he thought to be the Indian chief's hideout, the energetic Porcallo felt his horse losing its footing and sinking into a marsh; it fell over in such an unfortunate position that one of Porcallo's legs was caught under his mount and he could neither swim, nor struggle free, nor get help from his men. It was only with a tremendous amount of effort that he was able to work himself out of his predicament and pull himself from the foul-smelling stagnant water, covered with mud from head to toe. So great was the lieutenant general's fear of appearing ridiculous before his men that he gave forth with lusty curses, wondering why he had ever thought of joining the group, how he had been led to put himself in such a position, when at his age he had rich plantations, friends and a pleasant life waiting for him in Havana.

"That is where I should be, enjoying my wealth in the few years I have left," he was shouting, "rather than chase after these savages with their eccentric names Hirri, Hurra, Erre, Burra, Coxi and other such foolishness."[13]

He ordered the detachment back to the camp, where he reported to de Soto what had happened, and also told him of his determination to leave the expedition and return to Cuba. Hernando, showing his affection for his loyal, generous and courageous friend, did everything to help him obtain what he wanted and placed the *San Antonio* at his disposal. Before leaving, Porcallo divided up his arms, horses and trappings among his friends and left two horses, arms and servants to a son of his, born of a Cuban Indian. Hernando gave him letters he had written to his beloved wife, asking him to deliver them when he reached Havana. De Soto then divided the functions of Porcallo between Luis Moscoso, camp marshal, and Captain Baltasar de Gallegos, who was later to succeed him.

Gallegos had meantime made contact with Chief Urribarracuxi, who was more powerful than the chiefs they had dealt with so far. He made peace proposals to Urribarracuxi and invited him to visit the captain and governor. The chief offered tokens of friendship, but never kept his promise to visit de Soto.

The governor gave the order to move out and on June 15 they left Ocita, the town and port of Espíritu Santo, where they left Pedro Calderón with the two brigantines and forty mounted lancers, with eighty foot soldiers, partly drawn from the infantry, partly from the ships' crews. De Soto had organized his column for the vast project of exploring North America: in addition to Luis de Moscoso serving as camp marshal, the three cavalry troops would be under the command of Captains Vasconcelos of Portugal, Arias Tinoco and Alonso Romo, his kinsmen; the infantry units were to be placed under the orders of Captains Francisco Maldonado and Juan Rodríguez Lobillo. The vanguard would be made up of a detachment of scouts, which de Soto hoped would make contact with Gallegos's advance party. De Soto would himself be in the center surrounded by his guard of halberdiers and closing the rear would come the artillery and the supply services, with the enormous train of swine that kept multiplying, to serve as a food reserve whenever local supplies should fail.

The first march led them to Chief Mococo, of whom

they took their leave in his own village. The generous Indian, who had already learned of the expedition, came out to meet them with his most eminent warriors and offered them his hospitality. De Soto however declined, for the large body of men he led would involve his friend Mococo in too much expense.

"Your leaving us is very sad, commensurate only with the joy your presence here has given us," the Indian said, rather poetically. "May the sun go with the pale faces on their journey and may their undertaking be crowned with success."[14]

Gallegos was waiting for de Soto in the village of Urribarracuxi, but the shy chief did not appear. He was hiding in the hills and sent his warriors to observe the movements of the intruders. The governor did not wish to waste any more time and pushed on toward the north. He soon came upon the first obstacle to be crossed, in the form of a marshy lagoon that extended in the neighborhood of the village. The Indian guides did their best to waylay them and on several occasions, it was necessary to resort to the dogs, well versed in attacking the Indians, to frighten them into showing them the right path. After spending several days looking for a suitable passage, de Soto himself found a way.

The whole expedition finally came together in the province of Acuera, where they found the crops to be plentiful and the region likely to provide sufficient supplies. It was impossible, however, to secure the chieftain's friendship, since there, as elsewhere, the chief had fled and kept harassing the expedition from the woodlands. To the many gifts and peace offerings de Soto sent, the chief replied that his experience of white men's earlier expeditions had been unfortunate and that he would wage war on them unless they moved on without delay.[15] The governor imposed the strictest discipline on his marching column, since any straggler soon fell a victim to the arrows or sudden onsets of the small roving bands of Indians.

Unavoidably, some Spaniards did stray or fall back, soon to be killed and have their mounts stolen. Fourteen men were lost in this way.

The march continued until they reached the village of Ocala where the ground was slightly less marshy and difficult. The landscape was fascinating, groves of strangely beautiful semitropical trees grew along water inlets where the admiring Spaniards glimpsed flamingos and herons and many other birds that inhabited this paradise land. Huge oak trees, draped in moss, stretched out their ghostlike arms, while the palm trees brought to the very edge of the water the endless fencing of their leaves. There were palm trees of all sizes growing around the swamps that were also hemmed in with mangroves and bushes. Farther on, pine groves shot their trunks into the sky in strict alignment and cypresses kept watch over their cool shadows. Everywhere there was water to be found: on the surface, in lakes, rivers and marshes, swamps, or underground streams, or medicinal springs. De Soto remembered that Ponce de León had talked of the island of Bimini and of the "island" of Florida, where there were fountains that restored men's youth. Yet, the paradise was harsh and hostile. The village of Ocala turned out to be a real town of six hundred houses, but they were all empty, since the chief, his warriors and their families had taken refuge in the hills. De Soto pitched camp to enable his column to rest and recover its strength, taking advantage of the stores of food he found there, mostly maize, plums, pumpkins and various fruit. After a few days of forays and counterforays by scouting parties on both sides, the chief of Ocala himself came to the camp. De Soto greeted him with his usual civility. He was an Indian of enormous size and amazing strength. All de Soto wanted of him was the loan of a few men to help build a bridge that would enable them to cross the wide river that ran near the town. The chief agreed to go with de Soto to inspect the site, but when they arrived, some two hundred

Indians sprang from the thickets and amid great noise and confusion shot a volley of arrows in the direction of the governor who fortunately wore his armor and helmet. The chief tried to excuse their behavior by saying that since he had befriended the foreigners, his warriors would no longer obey him. Brutus, the dog de Soto had brought with him, had charged the bowmen, but was struck by nearly forty arrows before he could manage to drag himself back to die at the feet of the governor and of his master, the general's young page, Carlos Enríquez.

Under the direction of the Genoese, Master Francisco, the bridge was soon completed and the expeditionary force was able to leave Ocala and the territory of the Timuquan Indians, who lived there. They were tall, athletic people, who went about clad in nothing but a loincloth; they adorned themselves with complicated tattoos and were extremely skillful with bow and arrow. Their villages were laid out in a circular pattern and were closed in with stockades; in the center was usually a covered enclosure that served as an assembly hall for the population. They lived under stern military rule, made human sacrifices and were in the habit of scalping their victims.

A new province now lay before the Spaniards, the present Alachua County, surrounding Gainesville. It was ruled by Vitacucho, a man of warlike disposition who was addicted to magic practices. With the help of his medicine men, he tried to cast all kinds of evil spells on the unwanted intruders. On several occasions, he had sent his horn blowers to take up positions around the Spaniards, in the hope, no doubt, of calling down the wrath of heaven upon them. Gallegos retaliated with a raid on one of their villages where he took seventeen prisoners, among whom was one of Vitacucho's daughters. She sent messages back to her father, in which she told him that she was being well treated and that all her captors wanted was sufficient food to enable them to cross his land on their way north.

Vitacucho finally agreed to meet de Soto. The following day, he made a solemn appearance at the head of two hundred of his best men; like his captains, he wore a most elaborate feather headdress. In answer to de Soto's friendly overtures, the chief finally agreed to escort the Spaniards across his land. Thus the two men traveled side by side the rest of the way.

On one occasion, however, Ortiz, who understood the tribal dialect, overheard something that indicated that treachery was afoot. Vitacucho was preparing to kill the Spaniards in a sudden swoop by his warriors. Ortiz got word of this to de Soto, who warned his captains to be doubly vigilant, both during the marches and in camp.

"White Chief," Vitacucho said to him one day, "if you are not afraid to accept my invitation, come and watch a parade of my ten thousand warriors in a plain nearby."

"My men are afraid of nothing," de Soto answered calmly. "Not only would we enjoy watching your army, but my men will march side by side with your men. Thus our soldiers will have an opportunity of fraternizing."[16]

De Soto and Vitacucho were walking together when they suddenly came upon a plain that opened up before them: there, ten thousand Indian warriors were already lined up in battle formation, wearing war paint and brandishing their weapons. The Spaniards entered the valley cautiously, the mounted lancers formed in troops, the infantry ready for battle. A dozen guards escorted the white chief and the Indian leader, and while each pretended not to notice anything, each watched his rival with the utmost attention.

Vitacucho then raised his hatchet and a great war cry rose from the ranks of his men. De Soto lifted his hand for the prearranged signal: a harquebus shot rang out and the trumpets sounded the attack. At the same time, an equerry brought the governor his horse Aceituno. De Soto was soon mounted, and armed with his famous lance, he charged the center of the formation of the warriors, leading his own men, while his escort fought Vitacucho's guard, finally capturing the chief.

The battle spread far afield, with great losses for the Spaniards, while their own systematic cavalry charges and the crossbow and harquebus fire wrought havoc in their opponents' ranks. De Soto showed his mettle as an accomplished lancer and opened great swaths in the enemy lines. He then felt his faithful mount stagger beneath him, struck by eight arrows. Struggling under the weight of his armor, he managed to free himself from the horse, just as a rousing cry of victory rose from the ranks of the Indians, who thought that the White Chief had been defeated. However a man called Biota, a native of Zamora, gave his horse to de Soto, who promptly climbed back into the saddle to lead another charge that routed Vitacucho's men, leaving hundreds of casualties on the field. Some escaped to the hills, others, still shooting their arrows, took refuge in a nearby lagoon. De Soto surrounded these men and shouted to them that he would spare their lives if they surrendered. Standing waist deep in the water, with the white men lining the banks, the besieged men had to lift one another to be able to shoot their arrows. They kept up the fight for fourteen hours and won the Spaniards' admiration. A group of exhausted men, hardly able to stand, finally gave themselves up at dawn. This only left a dozen or so determined men, who though they barely had strength enough to stand, found enough courage to brandish their hatchets and threaten the Spaniards who were trying to surround them. The whole morning went by in this manner until, at about three o'clock in the afternoon, they appeared to be unable to stand any longer and seemed ready to drown rather than surrender. De Soto then ordered a dozen Spanish swimmers into the waters of the lagoon to save the brave and determined warriors, who were thus brought to the safety of the bank against their will, in a state of complete exhaustion. The governor ordered that they be given food and shelter and be allowed to regain sufficient strength, so that he could later question them. He particularly wanted to know why they had fought with such determination and with such senseless heroism. The oldest warrior gravely replied:

"Timuquan warriors know how to show their chiefs that they can be trusted. They must give their sons the good example, ready for the time when the youngsters will themselves have to fight. Now please arrange for our execution, for we cannot live under the shame of defeat."[17]

De Soto ordered that the Indians be untied and invited them to sit at his own table. He also sent for Vitacucho, who made many protestations of loyalty, assuring him that the battle had been a misunderstanding. De Soto then gave the order to move on, taking all the prisoners with him as hostages while they crossed the province. Yet Vitacucho kept plotting the destruction of the hated white men. On the day after the departure, he surreptitiously gave all the prisoners to understand by signs and gestures that they were to try and attack the Spaniards by surprise, kill them and escape. One of the heroic warriors who had defended the lagoon was one day seated, facing de Soto, as they enjoyed a meal together. The Indian suddenly jumped up and fell upon de Soto, punching him in the face with tremendous force. Vitacucho who was present, also tried to escape, while the other prisoners spread great confusion throughout the camp. A few seconds later, the governor's captains rallied and cornered Vitacucho who fought bravely before finally falling under the blows of the Spaniards, as did the Indian brave who had struck the governor in the mouth. Many were wounded in the fray and four Spaniards lost their lives.

De Soto ordered the column to hurry northward, to leave this region where they had been given such a poor reception and which left them with such unpleasant memories. They reached the Suwannee River, where they had once again to build a bridge under the supervision of

Master Francisco, in order to get across. On the other bank, they camped in the village of Uzachile (Suwannee Old Town) and later in the village of Aucilla, which was also deserted, since the chiefs would rather flee than have anything to do with the white man. For all that, the chiefs did not neglect harassing the Spaniards from the cover of nearby woods, especially when they were busy fording rivers or lagoons.

The Spaniards were now entering the region of the fearsome Apalachee warriors, who had annihilated Narváez's expedition. The Apalachees were treated with the utmost respect by their neighbors of other tribes, who held them to be the most intrepid of all Indian braves. Despite the many obstacles in their way, the column finally reached the village of Ambaica Apalachee (Tallahassee) toward the end of October. It was the capital of the province and its chief, the famous Copafi, had also fled the village of approximately 250 lodgings, with a central covered longhouse, a strong stockade wall and conical roofed huts. The Indians of the village belonged to the Muskhogee nation; the name, in the Choctaw language, means "the people from the other bank." They drew on a great abundance of oysters and shrimp and they lit their houses with resin from the ground, the first petroleum product the Spaniards had come across.

After organizing the camp to let the wounded recover and everyone rest, de Soto ordered Captain Añasco with forty horsemen and fifty foot soldiers, to reconnoiter the country, with a view to finding out how far the coast was, since several Indians had mentioned the sea, as though it were close by. Other scouting parties went north and brought back encouraging information about the quality and fertility of the land. Añasco had to contend with the duplicity of his guides, but made progress all the same, relying on his instinct as an explorer and a sailor. He soon reached the sea at the spacious Apalachicola Bay, where he found remains of the forges and crosses left by the

Narváez expedition. This was the site that Cabeza de Vaca had called the "Bay of Horses": still there, sprawled in the sun after twelve years of bleaching, were the bones of the horses Narváez's men had eaten while they were building their five boats on which they hoped to leave this inhospitable land. Añasco left numerous marks on trees and stones, so that if need be the men in the expedition who had remained on board the ships could find their way.

De Soto thought that since the month of November was well advanced it would be preferable to spend the winter in the village and plan a systematic exploration of the country. With the information that Añasco brought back, he decided to bring the ships that were in Tampa up to Apalachicola Bay, and therefore he instructed Añasco once more to choose twenty-nine men and make contact with Calderón. Then Añasco was to sail the ships and Calderón was to proceed by land, led by one of the men of the expedition acting as a guide. In this manner, all would be familiar with the country and more information would be gathered. Moreover, the trusty Gómez Arias was to sail for Havana with one of the caravels, to give letters and gifts to the governor's wife and deliver slaves from the heads of the expedition.

The adelantado's orders were carried out, through a succession of exploits made necessary as much by the harshness of the winter as by the hostility of the villagers scattered along the path of de Soto's army. Toward the end of December, Añasco finally reached Apalachicola Bay with the two brigantines and personally reported to de Soto. A little later the brave Calderón arrived by land and gave an account of his experiences to his chief. De Soto himself managed to carry out an expedition aimed at capturing Chief Copafi, who turned out to be a man of such monstrous proportions, and so obese, that he had to move about on all fours; yet he was not entirely devoid of a certain agility and skill. Although he kissed the general's hand, as a sign of obeisance, he plotted against him on several occasions, and one day managed to escape.

De Soto continued to gather information about the country, the object of his undertaking being exploration before attempting to settle the land. He was by now convinced that there were no vast empires nor great hoards of gold in these territories, and the Indians who lived there, he knew, were stronger and more warlike than those he had found in the Inca empire, or even in Panama and Central America. On the other hand, the land seemed to be fertile and likely to attract settlers and become great governorships. Apart from the various inland parties he sent out on scouting duties, he also dispatched a group under Maldonado's command to reconnoiter the coast.[18] Maldonado returned a few weeks later and reported that he had found a wide haven called Achusi, 210 miles from Aute, in Apalachicola country. Armed with such information, de Soto decided to send Maldonado back to Havana with the two brigantines, with new information for the authorities and passionate letters for his beloved wife Isabel. He then instructed Maldonado to return to Achusi Bay in October the following year, or thereabouts, bringing the two barks and the caravel he had earlier sent off with Gómez Arias, so that he could make use of their support for the forthcoming explorations.

About that time, two young Indians arrived at the camp, who, in answer to the soldiers' questioning, declared that there was gold aplenty in the province that lay to the north, called Cofitachequi. De Soto, who had always intended to resume the march to the north, lost no time in so doing as soon as the winter was over. He left Ambaica Apalachee on March 3, 1540, moving in a northeasterly direction into what is now the state of Georgia.

At the province of Atapaha, they were given a warm welcome. This, coupled with the fact that the land was in itself most attractive and offered beautiful sights to

behold, made the country appear as one of the most agree-
able lands peopled by most hospitable tribes. They crossed
the Ocmulgee River in the neighborhood of what is now
Hawkinsville, as they were crossing Georgia diagonally
in a northeasterly direction. They went through Cofa territory, where the local chief also greeted them in a friendly
manner, providing food, shelter and the run of his hunting grounds, which were particularly well stocked with
deer. He even lent them arrows. De Soto gave a few
demonstrations of the cannons he had brought with him,
filling the Indians with alarm and consternation in the
process, though they were careful not to show it. In fact
they kept their composure and stoically maintained an
imperturbable appearance, as befitted worthy braves. De
Soto had a purpose in displaying his might: he wanted
the power of the white man's "medicine" to be conveyed
far and wide. Then he made a great show of assuring the
chief of the Cofa Indians of his affection and trust and
presented him with the cannon in the course of an impressive ceremony where he made him the trusted keeper
of the "Channel of Thunder."[19] De Soto had, in any case,
reached the conclusion that the cannon was of little use
to him during the march, while it took many men to
transport it. The chief gave de Soto facilities for settling
in his region, to which de Soto replied that he first wanted
to explore the land before returning to organize the territory. The chief then gave him seven hundred men to
carry the expedition's supplies, under the command of a
herculean leader named Patofa, who was instructed to
lead the Spaniards to the kingdom of Cofitachequi, renowned for its size and its wealth. The expedition moved
northward once again. The Pizarros and Almagros had
pushed the frontier southward; de Soto wanted to spread
the European ideals to the north and bring back knowledge of those regions.

They crossed many rivers along the way, such as the
Oconee, where they made bridges for the enormous ex-

pedition. They underwent great hardships crossing an inhospitable desert, where Patofa himself confessed he was lost. Thanks to several scouting parties, they finally found their way out and de Soto sent the Indians home, resolving to lead his army on his own to the land of Cofitachequi. They came across a very large river, the Savannah, which they crossed on May 1, 1540, for the first time in the neighborhood of the present Augusta, Georgia. There they were met by a group of Indians. Six warriors, splendidly dressed in deerskins, guarded a beautiful girl who seemed to be their chief. They showed no emotion and certainly no fear before the white men's powerful expedition. Speaking through Ortiz the interpreter, the young girl asked if they were coming in war or in peace. Upon being assured of de Soto's friendship and peaceful intentions, the young girl answered that she would inform their queen and would decide whether to accede to de Soto's request for help. She then retired with her guards as majestically as she had come, to the bark canoes that took them to the other side of the river.[20]

A few hours later, the sentries informed de Soto that a group of Indians was approaching. Many canoes were crossing the Savannah River, and the occupants quickly formed a group on the riverbank before approaching the Spanish camp. Herculean warriors carried a beautiful Indian girl on a litter. She was dressed in transparent white cotton and wore a headdress of eagle feathers. Eight girls, almost as beautifully dressed as their queen, surrounded her. Near the camp, the beautiful woman set foot on the ground. A young girl followed her, carrying a small carved wooden seat which she set down for her sovereign to use. Their faces betrayed no emotion. The warriors looked like granite statues; guards and young girl attendants took their places around her in prearranged order.

"My kingdom has known some very difficult times," said the young woman. "This year's maize crop has been small and there have been epidemics; nevertheless we can

accept the Palefaces' friendship and will give them lodgings in our village. They will share our food and my own
house shall be at their disposal."[21]

"Not only do I thank you from the bottom of my heart,
beautiful lady," the general replied, "but my king, who
will be told of this, will also be grateful to you and will
reward you."

The beautiful Cofita won the admiration of all the
members of the expedition. She had an imposing profile,
with a high-bridged nose. Her jet-black eyes held a joyful
expression, but could at times harden into a stern glare.
Her blue-black hair made a fascinating contrast with the
pure white of her dress. Her fine hands, her delicate
ankles, her graceful gestures all betokened her self-as-
surance, her breeding and her experience of power. She
told de Soto that she had come to the throne only a short
time ago and that she wanted to govern in peace; that
she had heard rumors about the white men's expeditions,
but that they had never before reached her lands. De Soto
in turn gave her an idea of what Spain was like, what
kingdoms he had seen and the aims of his expedition.
Cofita then rose and slowly took off a very long pearl
necklace that was wound several times round her neck.
She slipped it over de Soto's head. He received it, helmet
in hand, bowing courteously. The governor in turn took
off a large ruby ring he was wearing and gave it to Cofita.
Upon taking her departure, she offered to send canoes
the following day so that the whole expedition could cross
over to the village.

The days the expedition spent in Cofita's village were
days of peace in a near paradise. The Indians belonged
to the powerful Creek tribe and spoke the Muskhogean
language. The women were of medium height, fine boned
and shapely, the men extraordinarily tall. The tribe was
proud and frugal and taught the Spaniards the games
they played with a ball, showed their hunting skills, their
dances and their music. They were the most splendidly

dressed Indians the expedition had yet met. The chiefs wore bright copper diadems ornamented with plumes and they tied their deerskin tunics around the waist with beautiful, brightly colored cloth sashes, interwoven with animal and plant designs. The women wore white cotton tunics and a great variety of pearl headdresses. All wore embroidered moccasins and carried a pouch around their neck which contained the "medicines" prescribed by their sorcerers. The greatest feast of the year was the beginning of the solar cycle, when they took "the new fire," a ceremony they explained to their astonished guests, namely the offering of fire for the coming year made by a local priest to all families, to be kept in each hearth.

Cofita noticed the expeditionaries' interest in gold, but she explained that there was none to be found in her land. When she noticed, however, how covetously they admired the pearls, she smiled deprecatingly, saying that they did not attach much importance to such things.[22] She told de Soto that he could have as many as he wanted and indicated two houses that the governor went to see with his captains. He found that it was the resting place of the dead notables of the tribe. The corpses lay in carved wood and, next to them, in large willow baskets, were enormous quantities of pearls, together with marten pelts. De Soto stopped Rangel from carrying everything away.

Cofita was impressed with the delight de Soto showed at her gift, as much as she was by his not taking everything. She then told him that pearls were easy to come by in her land, and that he should visit a burial place close by, where he could take as many pearls as he wished and that if he needed more, he could simply ask her men for them.

When, one league away, they reached the village of Talomeco which she had mentioned, they found an enormous funeral shrine where the mummified bodies of the former rulers of the land were kept, together with great quantities of arms, shields, totem symbols and work utensils. Baskets filled with a huge quantity of pearls, graded according to size, were everywhere to be seen, intermingled with bundles of fine pelts. De Soto nevertheless refused to take any, since it would have been necessary to use all the horses to carry them. In any case, he thought it best to keep the goodwill of the population, in anticipation of his plans to settle the land in the future.

His good judgment was having an effect on young Cofita, who was obviously very much taken with the white chief, whose bearing, majesty and natural kindness impressed all who approached him. Whenever she spoke to de Soto, she could not help betraying her feelings and she was forever showering him with gifts and thoughtful attentions.

Hernando was very much impressed by the beautiful and powerful princess. He fancied at times that his adventure could have a different ending.[23] He could remain here, settle the land and organize a Spanish province, give up the violent life of conquest and struggle against the unknown. But he knew that this was impossible. To remain would have meant to submit to Cofita's manifest intentions, return her affections as she deserved and devote himself to sharing her kingdom with her. This could not be; his loyalty, his rank, his obligations to his king and his lady, his very nature, all conspired to impose upon him the role of an Amadís, unable to take a different course of action. He therefore decided to leave as soon as possible.

When he told Cofita of his plans that same evening, the Indian girl composed herself, as her elders had taught her to do, but her gaze hardened and she gave her captains orders to get an escort ready, food, guides and supplies for the expedition. She also sent messengers to the various villages of her dominions to request them to render assistance to her friends. Then, without taking her leave, she left the room.

The following day, the army assembled, ready for

departure. De Soto inquired where he could find Cofita to take his leave. Her aides told him that she had left to visit other villages. He regretted having curbed his own feelings toward her, yet he knew that he had done his duty to himself and to his beloved and faithful Isabel.[24]

The path of the expedition now lay through what are now the states of South and North Carolina. They later penetrated Tennessee, where they crossed the river bearing that name, on May 26, 1540, at the present site of Franklin, North Carolina, after negotiating the inhospitable Blue Ridge Mountains. De Soto still enjoyed the effects of Cofita's protection, since the Indians everywhere came out to welcome him with presents and food and offers of shelter. The expedition finally reached Cherokee territory and the village of Guajule, where the chief also came out to welcome them. The Cherokees were highly civilized compared with the other tribes of the region. They had originally lived in caves, a fact to which they owed their nation's name. However, they now tilled the red soil of the region, built walled cities of wood, were highly organized and made pottery of intricate designs. Cofita's messages had been effective and de Soto's troops were so well treated that they henceforth called their luckiest throw at dice "a house in Guajule." From there, they went to Ichiaha, at the confluence of the Tennessee and the Little Tennessee rivers, in the present state of Tennessee, where a chief of another branch of the Cherokees also greeted them with great kindness. Although he was not one of Cofita's subjects, he must have heard of the welcome given the white men in other regions and he probably had not wished to seem less hospitable than the others. Moreover, no other white man had yet reached these parts, and no earlier precedent existed that could have caused resentment. De Soto had, of course, driven far deeper inland than any previous Spanish explorer. Neither Ponce de León's short incursion in search of the Fountain of Youth, nor that of Narváez himself, which had lasted all of six months, could compare with his own adventure which, over a period of more than a year, had taken him in a wide semicircle through vast unknown regions of North America.

The Indians offered the Spaniards the succulent fish from their river, where they abounded. The Spaniards also learned to appreciate turtle fillet and the sweet meat of the iguana, and of the delicious wild turkey, an animal they found disconcerting by its large size. They learned to eat amaranth seasoned with salt and dwarf palms served up as salad. Maize had already been adopted by the Europeans, who could not get wheat. Some of the Spanish dandies, who were either inept or reluctant to resort to manual labor, would content themselves with roasting the dry kernels in earthenware pots and eating them without further ado. The more enterprising would follow Indian custom and grind the grain in wooden mortars, with the help of makeshift pestles, and sift the flour through their coats of mail, which they found to be ideal for the purpose; they then made the typical Indian flapjack, or tortilla, which gained acceptance everywhere and became a part of the troops' regular rations.

A group of scouts sent north by de Soto in search of minerals and, it was hoped, gold, returned with reports of a range of steep mountains, the Lookouts, which were a part of the Appalachian chain. However to the veterans of the Peruvian campaign, there was no comparison possible between the gentle mountain slopes of these lands and the massive bulk of the Andes, through which they had wended their way up to Cuzco. Another strange fact they related was seeing a large unusual cow with very big hooves and a humped back, the first time Europeans met the great American bison.

De Soto thought he would now turn south in a wide curve, for it was time to join his ships in the gulf and get news of Cuba. The Cherokees lent him five hundred men to serve as carriers and he set off, exploring large stretches of Alabama, along the banks of the great river Coosa. The land here was governed by Chief Cosa, who ruled over the districts of Talladega, Coosa and Tallapoosa, where orders had been given to treat the explorers well. On July 16, they reached the main town, Talladega, where they spent a pleasant two weeks. Cosa, however, refused to lend them Indian carriers. On the other hand, he invited de Soto to remain to settle a colony and organize a province. De Soto, who had carefully studied the land during his journey, first wanted to complete his tour before deciding where to establish a settlement. He also wanted to secure his lines of communication with the sea and his ships. He therefore told Cosa that he would rather come back later and, before leaving, gave him a few pairs of animals: horses, hogs and poultry.[25] He then moved on to Talise, the last Cherokee village, now called Tallassee, on the Tallapoosa River. There he rested, to gather more information and prepare for the resumption of the march south, through different country, that of the harsh Chief Tuscaloosa of the renowned Alibamus tribe.

De Soto spent the last night before his departure in quiet, solitary meditation, reviewing his achievements and thinking about what lay ahead.[26] His men were sleeping peacefully around him, fully relying on him, while he fully trusted his lucky star. Above him, the tops of the pine trees etched their silhouette against the sky, where they traced a delicate lacework of moonlight.

The peaceful phase of the exploration was drawing to a close. Even if a new warring phase were to lay ahead, he would at least have done what he had set out to do: open up as much as possible of the mysterious lands of North America.

THE FATHER OF THE WATERS

XX

It is by far the most important stream on the globe, and would seem to have been marked out by design, slow-floating from north to south, through a dozen climates, all fitted for man's healthy occupancy, its outlet unfrozen all the year, and its line forming a safe, cheap continental avenue for commerce and passage from the north temperate to the torrid zone. Not even the mighty Amazon (though larger in volume), not the Nile in Africa nor the Danube in Europe, nor the three great rivers of China, compare with it. Only the Mediterranean sea has played some such part in history, and all through the past, as the Mississippi is destined to play in the future.[1]

Walt Whitman

September 1540 found the column advancing along the site of Montgomery, Alabama, and continued by the banks of the Alabama River, in search of the land of the dread Chief Tuscaloosa, whose name in Choctaw language means "Black Warrior," a name the river of that region now bears. A thousand stories were told of the legendary chief of the Alibamus, a group of the Muskhogean Indians, of the Creek Confederacy. De Soto recommended that special precautions be taken and he decided to lead his column, accompanied by his trumpeters and by Ortiz, the interpreter.

A scout reported a group of Indians on the road ahead. De Soto decided to press on, and soon sighted a cluster of armed men gathered on a hill, seemingly waiting for them. De Soto calmly marched on and, as he approached, gradually discerned that they were Indian braves, standing motionless, pretending not to see the Spaniards, their gaze fixed on the horizon, as though they were made of stone. They were tall people, but two veritable giants stood out among them; one could have been six feet six inches tall, and judging by his insignia of rank, he seemed to be the supreme chief. The other giant was a younger man who resembled the chief and must have been his son.

The Indians all appeared to be chiefs, or distinguished warriors; they wore bright headdresses of eagle feathers and deerskin clothing with richly embroidered white moccasins. On their shoulders, some wore cloaks of vivid colors, embellished with complicated designs. Behind the main chiefs stood an Indian with a staff from which hung a kind of deerskin pennant, also colored with the tribal devices on black and white quarters. Tuscaloosa stood out unmistakably from the group of chiefs; he was in the center, seated on a wooden throne carved from a tree trunk. He wore a kind of red turban and from his shoulders hung a bright mantle of feathers reaching to the ground.

Recalling his first interview with Atahualpa, de Soto ordered the cavalry to move forward in a display of horsemanship and, riding up to the group of Indians, to form a circle around them. Tuscaloosa and his men remained motionless, as though they saw nothing, and they would no doubt have remained so for a long time had not de Soto himself moved in close to the group. When he was twenty paces away, Tuscaloosa rose; de Soto then dismounted and Tuscaloosa started down the hill to meet the white chief, ceremoniously lending himself to the embrace the latter gave him as a token of his friendly intentions. De Soto was one of the tallest among the Spaniards, yet Tuscaloosa towered a whole head above him. Apart from being well proportioned, he had fine, virile features; so did his son.

He waved de Soto to a seat next to him and, speaking with great majesty, said:

"Mighty lord, I greet you as a brother. Of this, I will not speak much, since it is not fitting for brave warriors to waste words on what can be said briefly. I am ready to help you. In the next village, which is not our main town, lodgings have been prepared for you and your men."[2]

"Great Chief," de Soto answered, "in all the villages

I have visited upon my king's instructions, I have heard of your exploits and of your hospitality. I did not want to leave these lands without meeting you and offering you our alliance. I should be happy if we could become friends and I invite you to ride with me to the next village, on one of our horses."

Tuscaloosa nodded in assent, though he had never seen a horse before, let alone ridden one. But the real problem was finding a sufficiently strong horse to carry the giant. Finally, one of de Soto's finest and largest horses was brought around and Tuscaloosa mounted it without the slightest difficulty. He was so tall that his feet hung loose and nearly reached the ground.

It was not long before they came to the village and Tuscaloosa pointed out one of the houses that de Soto could use and he himself retired to his own house. Both were within the stockade. Before resuming their march, the soldiers rested for two days at the Indian chief's invitation, and under his direction they reached the main town of Tuscaloosa, from which he took his name. The journey had lasted three days. The town was built on a spur, around which flowed a river, so that they entered the town after crossing on rafts, a difficult and tedious maneuver.

Two Spaniards, one of whom was Juan de Villalobos, disappeared during the march, giving de Soto cause to worry. Villalobos was indeed one of those unruly, independent men who would rather set off on scouting parties of his own; he was always straying from the main body of troops on such sallies. Nothing more was heard from them and when de Soto indirectly asked Tuscaloosa about their whereabouts, he received the testy reply that the Indians were not the white men's keepers. De Soto inferred that they had been killed in some remote place and he consequently gave orders to take greater precautions and to watch the Indians' movements.

The governor crossed swords with Tuscaloosa on another occasion, when he sent Moscoso to ask for help in carrying the supplies. The giant answered tersely that his men had never served anyone but himself. De Soto then spoke to the chief, asking him to accompany him south on the expedition, down to the town of which he had spoken as being the largest of his tribe. As de Soto conveyed this invitation, he was ominously surrounded by his captains in full armor, a clear indication to Tuscaloosa that he could consider himself the Spanish chief's prisoner whereupon the Indian wisely changed his attitude. He assigned four hundred men to carry the supplies and said he would send messengers to the big town in the south he called Mauvila, or Mobile, where he would take them, marching at the white chief's side.

De Soto then gave the giant a cloak of red velvet, which he donned immediately with great pride, though without a single word of thanks to the governor who also gave him a pair of enormous boots that no one in the expedition could possibly wear, but which were a good fit for Tuscaloosa's wide feet. On the way, the governor explained to Tuscaloosa that the name of Mobile stirred memories for him,[3] since the book of Amadís's adventures told of a royal princess called Mabilia, who was the niece of a king and a brave and beautiful girl; it was from her hands that the hero of the novel received his knighthood. Tuscaloosa listened silently to de Soto's words translated through the interpreter, about the grandeur of Spain, and his own good intentions in the matter of colonizing the country and becoming his friend. The port of Mobile was not far from the sea and the Tombigbee River, but farther up the Alabama River than it is today, near Choctaw Bluffs. Canny as always, de Soto dispatched two men to Mobile; his equerry, Diego Velázquez, and Gonzalo Cuadrado Jaramillo were sent to find out if it were true that many people were assembling in the town; the adelantado suspected this might be the work of Tuscaloosa's emissaries.

Leaving the main body of troops under the command of Moscoso, de Soto took a hundred infantrymen and a hundred horsemen and accompanied Tuscaloosa, or rather stayed very close to him, feigning perfect concord and amity. The day before his arrival, the governor's messengers returned and reported that they had indeed seen great activity, heavy concentrations of people, stockpiling of arms and supplies. The Indians had hidden in the largest houses of the town and had even been drilled recently, to ensure that all the tribes assembled in the district were accustomed to each other's fighting methods.

On the morning of October 18, the Feast of Saint Lucas, de Soto came within sight of Mobile in Alabama. The town was surrounded by a high stockade, to protect the many log houses within, some of which were single-family dwellings, others huge assembly halls, built to house hundreds of people. De Soto decided that when his army arrived, it would bivouac in the plain next to the town. He then marched into the city at the head of his two hundred men, and with a small guard, took up residence in the place Tuscaloosa had reserved for them. He cautioned his captains, warning them not to lay down their arms and, if possible, not to break formation when they bivouacked. Meanwhile, he showed his appreciation at the dances and singing that the inhabitants prepared for him and he greatly commended the townswomen for their beauty.

The Indians seemed to be waiting for the right moment to spring a violent attack on the newcomers. When de Soto sent Juan Ortiz to invite Tuscaloosa to lunch with him, the giant happened to be holding a war council with his lieutenants in preparation for the attack. One of the Indians then burst out of the house and started to berate Ortiz and all white people, predicting that not one would be left alive before long. Baltasar de Gallegos, who was standing close by, drew his sword and the Indian shot an arrow, whereupon several Indians rushed from the nearby houses and a general scramble ensued. The Spaniards then sounded the alarm, and, as they were already on the alert, it was not long before the cavalry formed in battle order. Nevertheless some cavalrymen were unable to harness their mounts in time and had to cut them loose and send them galloping across the plain outside the stockade, to avoid being struck by the Indians' arrows. For the time being, only a small part of the column and all the supplies had reached the town, the supply carriers having had previous instructions from Tuscaloosa. Several hundred Indians seized the supplies and, amid great cries of triumph, stowed them in the houses of the town.

De Soto had only one third of his troops with him, since Moscoso had not yet arrived. He nevertheless marshaled his forces around him in the plain and launched a traditional charge against the Indians who, driven by their eagerness to fight, had by now left the enclosure of the stockade. Their bravery was most impressive. Without the slightest trace of fear, they stood their ground, while the cavalry charged them at full gallop, lances at the ready. They would then grasp the lances in midair and endeavor to drag the riders off their mounts, not without some measure of success. The Spaniards, however, who were better armed and who were mounted, forced the Indians to retreat behind their stockade, leaving many dead behind. From their refuge behind the wooden stakes, they shot their arrows amid cries of defiance, brandishing the bleeding scalps they had culled from their Paleface victims, as well as the articles of clothing and other equipment they had filched from the bundles of supplies.

De Soto decided to make Tuscaloosa pay for his duplicity. He was determined to take the town of Mobile and to recover his supplies with all his men's belongings as well as Cofita's gift of two hundred pounds of pearls. He therefore mounted a full-scale attack, with the infantry in open formation, the cavalry spearheading the onslaught and himself, as usual, leading his men, sure of his skill in the saddle and with the lance. Many Spaniards fell; some died and a great number were wounded, but in the first hour of the battle, they killed several hundred Indians. Yet neither side would yield an inch.

Don Carlos Enríquez, the native of Jerez de Badajoz, married to one of de Soto's nieces, distinguished himself in the field and fought with his customary courage. He tirelessly drove one attack after another against the huge, ten-thousand-strong Indian host. As he came up to the stockade during one of the assaults, an arrow penetrated his horse's breastplate. To save his mount, he transferred his lance to his left hand and, bending over, tried to pull the arrow from the wound without leaving the saddle. While he was thus engaged, he bared his neck, leaving it unprotected by either shield or armor. This was the chance an Alibamus bowman seized upon. He brought down Don Carlos bleeding profusely. Captain Enríquez's fall caused great consternation among the Spaniards, who held him in high esteem. He was taken to the rear, where his condition grew steadily worse, until all hope of saving him had to be abandoned. He died the following day.

De Soto, enraged, launched one final charge which dislodged the last Indians from the plain and sent them scurrying behind the stockade. Then de Soto drew up another plan of attack. He ordered his cavalry, his best men, to dismount, and, armed with sword and round shields, to advance with the support of the infantry. The infantry carried axes to cut down the wooden stakes of the stockade, after severing the ties that kept the logs together. They moved forward, protected by their roundels from the hail of arrows, while formations of harquebusiers and crossbowmen kept the Indians out of sight behind the parapets.

De Soto was concerned about the fate of the group of Spaniards who remained in the town, some of whom were his own bodyguard. They had barricaded themselves in the house they had been assigned to. The group consisted of eight soldiers, two clerics, two black servants and one Indian from another region. The soldiers were armed with three crossbows and five halberds and the Indians with bow and arrows. The Indians paid little attention to them while the battle raged in the open field, but when the gates and the stockade gave way, they sent a detachment to liquidate the white men in the central house. Sensing the danger his trusted men now faced, de Soto fought with renewed vigor to free them.

The men in the house managed to achieve the impossible and kept the Indians at bay, even when the Indians climbed on the roof to drop through the holes they made. Spanish crossbows and Indian arrows made short work of dispatching any intruder. The siege had already lasted for about half an hour when de Soto and his men arrived on the scene, after fighting foot by foot through the town. They surrounded the house and soon freed it without losing a single man.

The battle had to be carried into every street and every house. The Indians neither fled nor gave themselves up; rather, they shouted their war cries of encouragement at each other, fighting the Spaniards with hatchets and arrows, or simply leaping from the rooftops to crush their opponents to the ground. De Soto ordered a troop to return to the rear and remount, while he personally took the lead with Nuño Tovar, and cleared the streets of the remaining pockets of resistance. Some Indians, realizing that the eight-hour-long battle was apparently close to ending in the Palefaces' favor, chose to be killed, or perish at their own hands by setting fire to their houses. The straw roofs quickly fed the flames and spread sparks and smoke through the whole town. De Soto's trumpeters kept sounding the alarm, hoping to reach the ears of the last detachment of the column, for, although another third of the expedition had by now joined the battle, there were about two hundred men still expected. Toward four o'clock in the afternoon, after seven hours of uninterrupted fighting, the awaited detachment appeared and made a most welcome reinforcement for the final assault. With them came the governor's nephew, Diego de Soto, Carlos Enríquez' brother-in-law, who, upon learning the fate of his kinsman, charged into the middle of the town square that was defended by hundreds of resisting braves, aided by swarms of armed women. No sooner had Diego entered the fray than he was shot through the eye. He spent the night in agony and died the next morning, next to his brother-in-law. The sun was setting and the battle nearly over when the soldiers realized that de Soto himself was wounded in the thigh. De Soto nevertheless managed to stay in the saddle and fight on relentlessly for two more hours, despite the loss of blood and the pain caused by the wound. The last of the Indians now occupied one street, their comrades having apparently fled. No trace could be found of Tuscaloosa. One man de Soto recognized as one of the giant's lieutenants hanged himself from the top of the stockade, a supreme example of the courage that inspired the Alibamus warriors.

De Soto considered this to have been the greatest battle he ever fought against the Indians, in all his adventurous life in the Americas. Neither in Peru, Panama, nor Nicaragua could any veteran recall anything to compare with the fearful battle of Mobile. More than twenty-five hundred Indians had been killed. The number of wounded the Indian survivors must have carried off with them could not be known. The town had been destroyed. The Spaniards' supplies had been burned, together with the precious load of pearls. There were approximately thirty Spaniards dead, over 250 casualties in serious condition and nearly everyone had been wounded with varying degrees of severity. They had, moreover, lost forty-five horses. Night was already upon them when de Soto gave orders to pitch camp on the battlefield. Arrangements were made to attend to the wounded under the supervision of a single surgeon and the care of the clerics.

It was a dreadful night of suffering, distress, pain, prayer and agony.

The governor now faced other problems. With military thoroughness, he re-formed his troops, posted sentries and forward lookouts, and gave instructions that the men should take turns resting, lest Tuscaloosa renew hostilities. He also needed time to recover his strength. He had lost more than a hundred men since landing in Florida. He therefore decided to let the wounded recover in Mobile, where he rebuilt the stockade and repaired the largest houses to be used for quartering his troops. Upon questioning the Indian prisoners, he learned that Tuscaloosa had fought untiringly and withdrawn after being sadly afflicted by the death of his son who fell under a Spanish lance. From that day forward, he would be a legendary figure among the Indian people of the district. According to the information de Soto had been able to gather, practically all the chieftains of the region had lost their lives, in what historians believe to have been the greatest battle the North American Indians of those days had ever fought.[4]

De Soto's men spent the following days burying the dead, attending to the wounded, helping each other and guarding the camp with all due military vigilance. Several of the more severe casualties died, mainly because nearly all had been wounded in the head, eyes or mouth. The Indians had in fact discovered that these were the most telling targets for their arrows, rather than the armor or coats of mail. As food supplies were short, the Spaniards dried the flesh of the dead horses and in this way managed to keep themselves fed. All the wheat and wine had been lost, together with the sacramental vestments and plate, so that the ecclesiastics had to celebrate Mass without the essential requirements of the rite. Chasubles had to be improvised out of deerskins, and the Mass, reduced of necessity to a commentary on the Gospels, was called the "Dry Mass."

They found food in the neighborhood and discovered Indians who had fought in the battle recovering from their wounds in the surrounding villages.

De Soto then learned that they were five days' march away from the sea, where their ships waited for them under the command of Captains Gómez Arias and Diego Maldonado, who in turn were looking for him to make contact and deliver supplies, in the coastal province of Achusi. De Soto, who had made plans for founding a colony in this country, with a base near the sea and another settlement some seventy miles inland, ordered the Indian who had brought the news and Ortiz the interpreter to keep the information strictly to themselves. At the same time, he freed one of the prisoners, the son of one of the chieftains of the region of Achusi, telling him that he would come to visit his village a little later to talk about founding a town and inaugurating an age of industry and friendship that would bind their two nations together.

De Soto changed his plans when, on one of the quiet night strolls he usually took around the camp to measure the morale of his troops, he discovered that desertion plans were being hatched by a number of men under the leadership of Treasurer Juan Gaitán, Cardinal de Loyola's nephew; apparently he and other officers were bent on leaving de Soto and making for Mexico or Cuba as soon as they reached the boats. They argued that there was neither gold to be had, nor kingdoms to be founded, and it was time to forget this senseless adventure which had brought nothing but hardship, hunger and danger to all through these many long months.

De Soto realized that if he continued to draw near the coast, his army would disband, and he would perhaps remain alone, or with just a handful of loyal men. With his usual resolve and despite the deprivations his decision would entail, he feigned to know nothing of what was afoot and gave the order to leave Mobile on November 18, 1540, heading once more in a northerly direction, away from the sea, much to the despair of the conspirators. His action was in a way reminiscent of Hernán Cortés's daring decision to burn his ships, thus eliminating any chance of return. They were about to penetrate the northwestern part of Alabama. They left Tuscaloosa's territory after three days' march and entered the province the Indians called Chicaza, which was also the name of one of their chiefs. They reached a village called Cabusto, in what is now Greene County, on the mighty Black Warrior River. Despite opposition from the Indians on the other bank, de Soto had a few boats built to start crossing to the other side. The first boat, under the command of the valiant Diego García, reached the other side without meeting any armed opposition and the whole column gradually moved across, then continued through deserted regions until they came to another river, the Tombigbee, which they also crossed. On December 14, 1540, they passed the sites of Columbus and Aberdeen, Mississippi. Later they reached the village of Chicaza, built by the Chickasaw Indians at the fork of two rivers that ran down from the Lowery region, the Yazoo and the Tallahatchie. The village, some two hundred houses strong, was well provided with food, but had been abandoned by its inhabitants. De Soto decided to spend the winter there and gave orders accordingly.[5]

At first, the Chicaza chieftain ignored the governor's repeated messages of friendship, but eventually consented to pay him a visit in the village. He was a corpulent Chickasaw Indian. He made de Soto a present of several hundred rabbits and many pelts and cloaks, that the Spaniards were glad to put to good use, since many of them had lost all their clothing in the battle of Mobile.

When March came, and the cold weather was over, the governor asked Chicaza for two hundred men to help carry the supplies.[6] This visibly displeased the Indian, who anyway seemed to have other plans in mind for the

Spaniards. Sensing what might happen, de Soto ordered his troops to sleep under arms. Events proved him right. During the small hours of the following morning, the Chickasaw Indians launched a surprise mass attack on the village, amid a great confusion of war cries, beating of drums and sounding of horns and bells, and they shot flaming arrows at the huts.

De Soto immediately armed himself and, mounting his horse, led a dozen cavalrymen to stem the attack. Some Spaniards fled in confusion, but the brave Nuño de Tovar checked them with his derisive shouts.

The whinnying of the horses and the squealing of the hogs mingled with the cries of the wounded and added to the confusion. However de Soto soon had his troops drawn up in formation in the field next to the village, where the Indians were concentrated, and was able to launch a full-scale charge, which by now his men had been trained to carry out. Tovar and Vasconcelos were the heroes of the battle. De Soto fought bravely, but, through an aide's negligence, suffered a fall from his horse whose cinch had been improperly tightened. He recovered himself, somewhat bruised, but was otherwise unharmed. By the time dawn broke two hours later, the assailants had been routed. The soldiers started to gather the wounded and put out the fires the Indians started. Among the dead were twelve soldiers and the brave Francisca Hinestrosa, the only woman in the column, who had rendered such valuable services taking care of the sick and distributing the food. Fifty horses had been lost, many frightened away by the confusion, never to be recovered: they went to swell the fund of such animals de Soto contributed to the country all along his trek.

De Soto relieved his friend Moscoso of his responsibilities as camp marshal,[7] that is, his second-in-command, as a disciplinary measure. He had given him instructions as to the precautions that were to be taken and that would have avoided such great losses in lives, or at least reduced the casualties. In Moscoso's place, he appointed the brave Baltasar Gallegos. Once more he ordered the march to proceed and left this ill-fated place. They bivouacked at a neighboring village, called Chicacilla, where the wounded were able to rest and regain their strength. A forge was also improvised there, with a bearskin for bellows, and the men set to repairing their arms, horseshoes, saddles and other pieces of equipment. On April 26, 1541, the column moved forward again, through a country of plains and small villages.

On the strength of a scout's reports, de Soto went north to reconnoiter a strange structure, the fort of Alibamo. Tall wooden stakes marked out an area of approximately three hundred feet square. There seemed to be successive barriers inside the outer wall and a stream ran before the entrances of the strange structure. De Soto decided to capture the fort, and with two-thirds of his column, he formed three troops to attack the three main entrances to the stockade. It was not long before Indian warriors appeared on the top of the trunks that formed the walled defenses. They looked different from the other Indians encountered by the troops. They wore feather headdresses, but they also wore horns as well as feathers. Some wore red or black paint on their faces. These were the valorous Muskhogee braves. They started to shoot arrows at the three columns that were under the command of lancers Guzmán, Cardeñosa and Silvestre. A group of Indians sallied forth to join battle in the vicinity of the fort and there soon was a general melee. De Soto, with Añasco and Vasconcelos charged to support one of the columns, promptly put the Indian formation to flight and managed to slip into the fort with his men as they retreated to the safety of the stockade. Soon the battle was raging inside the fort, too, but the Indians began to escape toward the river which they crossed over a fragile bridge. De Soto remained in possession of the fort and he ordered all his men inside the perimeter.

The Indians wre regrouping, uttering their defiant war whoops from the other side of the river, which was the Tallahatchie, near New Albany. De Soto decided to disperse them and launched an attack. He had no trouble taking the bridge and attacked the Indian ranks with the cavalry; the Indians disbanded after a brief resistance. Nevertheless eight Spaniards lost their lives in the skirmish and twenty-five were wounded. They stayed four days to recuperate at the fort.

The main problem they had to contend with was lack of food. Some men were suffering from outright starvation, others showed signs of salt deficiency. The army marched the first days of May through rough country. They came to a village called Quizquiz, whose name reminded de Soto of one of the Inca's generals. The Indians now spoke different tongues that Ortiz had difficulty in deciphering, even with the help of several interpreters. Soon de Soto managed to make friends with the chieftain and obtained the food he needed. The old chieftain, ailing and withered, spoke slowly to de Soto of his country and of his dominions, where no foreigner had yet set foot and he urged de Soto to continue on his way, mentioning a mighty river to the north.

De Soto must have felt a strong emotion, as though he were on the eve of a great discovery. He was in a land where no Spaniard had ever been before, a country of mystery. The chieftain had told of the existence nearby of a great river of colossal proportions. He therefore decided to gather a plentiful supply of food and to move forward. He had stayed six days in Quizquiz to restore his strength and he now headed north to find the great river.

On the fourth day's march, on May 8, 1541, from a height now called Sunflower Landing, de Soto, who was marching at the head of his army, raised his hand to give the signal to stop. He had just seen in the distance the enormous, majestic outline of the huge river. Plainly the actual sight was even more marvelous than he had been led to expect. So this was the Río Grande, the Father of the Waters, the "Mississippi" as the Indians called it in their singing language, reminiscent of a birdsong! Its slow waters, the color of gold, ran with incomparable majesty between steep banks, overgrown with luxuriant vegetation. De Soto fell to his knees and thanked heaven for allowing him to make such a find. This discovery brought back memories of the old friend whom he admired so much, Vasco Núñez de Balboa, whose eyes had also rested on another of the world's secrets, that of the Southern Sea, under whose spell he had fallen for all time. The clerics addressed their prayers to heaven, echoed in turn by the assembled troops.

De Soto immediately felt an irresistible impulse to cross to the other side, so that his expedition might be the first to navigate these waters and to give European eyes a chance to look upon it as the Indians had done for centuries. To this end, he decided to make the necessary preparations in a suitable place, which he immediately set out to find, pushing through thick clumps of yellow pines. The river must have held all the expeditionaries under its spell. They had never imagined anything of such grandeur. It was nearly two miles wide, and from one bank, it was hard to distinguish a man on the other side. The Indians had also told them that the river held an infinite variety of fishes.

When they found a suitable site, the governor gave orders to bivouac, install a forge and on May 21 start building the rafts to cross the Mighty River. The work gave the men of the expedition renewed courage,[8] and optimism soon returned, especially with the help of the jokes and good humor of the Andalusians.

A delegation of Indians came to greet de Soto in the name of the local chieftain and offered to bring food, but they never said anything definite about a visit from the chieftain himself. It was only later, when de Soto had already built four large rafts fitted with sails and oars, that two hundred Indians appeared in solemn procession, packed in enormous canoes, dressed in feather head-dresses and painted with ocher and black, all of them displaying the dignified bearing of veteran warriors. The chieftain arrived in a larger canoe, richly decorated and decked with an awning. He said his name was Aquixo and he presented de Soto with a large quantity of fish and cakes of prune paste that had a very pleasant taste. The governor thanked those present and asked the chieftain to disembark, so that they could get acquainted, but Aquixo did not respond and retired.[9]

De Soto spent twenty days building his rafts and with great trepidation he prepared to cross the Mississippi. On June 18, 1541, the expedition actually made the crossing of the Mighty River on rafts constructed with their own hands.

The first thing that de Soto did once the crossing was completed was to order all rafts carefully dismantled and all nails and other hardware preserved for future use. Following a path that ran parallel to the river, he led the expedition in a northerly direction until, five days later, they arrived within sight of a large village in the province of Casqui that was inhabited by the Kaskaskis Indians whose chief sent a deputation on a friendly mission. De Soto took the opportunity to rest for six days in the village, enjoying the attentions of the Indians who not only provided food and shelter in the form of hutches built especially for them out of branches, but also entertained them with the music and dancing of their attractive women. The Indian chief, addressing de Soto with the strict economy of words that marked practically all Indian speech, said:

"We know that you are the Children of the Sun: your weapons are more powerful than ours, and so must your religion be. Our recently sown fields are in need of water: ask your God for rain and we will worship Him."[10]

"Our God can give you rain, He is all-powerful," answered de Soto. "We shall build His symbol on that hill, facing the Mighty River."

He immediately set Master Francisco the Genoese to build a tall pinewood cross on the hill, where it could be seen from the surrounding countryside.

Three days later, the cross was blessed with great solemnity. The ecclesiastics with their chanting and ceremony excited the admiration of the ten to fifteen thousand Indians congregated there for the occasion. The moving tones of the Te Deum rang out for the first time over the land and river of the Mississippi, and the Indians, visibly impressed, imitated all the Spaniards' gestures during the ceremony, kneeling and rising as they did, and doing their best to make the sign of the cross. When the Spaniards returned to camp, they were well satisfied with the outward sign of their Faith they had just given.

There was a truly astonishing sequel to this ceremony when, the following day, the sky clouded and an abundant rain drenched the fields.

The white men's God had performed the requested miracle. But the river gods were also to demand their tribute of sacrifice.

THE SPELL
OF THE RIVER

XXI

*I call out to you, whom I so earnestly
strain to reach, fleeing from the sea and
Poseidon's spite. Even the immortal gods
should show some mercy to a poor wandering
wretch who comes, as I do, worn by so many
trials, to bathe in your stream and clasp
your knees. . . .'' Then the hero's limbs and
sturdy arms gave way, for he was exhausted
by the struggle.*[1]

Homer
Odyssey, V

H ernando de Soto had crossed what is now the state of Mississippi and was then in Arkansas. A few Indian prisoners—traders from distant provinces—had told him of the mountains in the northeast, where there were minerals and salt to be found. The governor sent two soldiers, Hernando de Silvera and Pedro Moreno, to explore the coveted land where they might even find precious metals. He then followed the right bank of the Mighty River, entering the Great Plains, where he found few settlements, but came across great herds of bison, which aroused the Spaniards' curiosity and provided them with succulent food for a long time. He realized that the springs of the Mighty River lay much farther north and that it was definitely not a canal joining the two seas, as some were led to believe.

De Soto returned to the Capaha camp and found that the two soldiers he had sent to the mountains were already back with several loads of crystallized rock salt and copper ore, but they found no trace of gold.

De Soto gave orders to head west. He still had lingering hopes of finding in that direction the Seven Cities of Cibola mentioned by Cabeza de Vaca. Thus he followed the banks of the broad Arkansas River for several days, until he reached the area where Little Rock stands today. The local chieftain gave him a friendly welcome and presented him with maize. From there, the army first marched south, then veered to the west. Along the way, they came across saline ground and spent many hours washing the salt out of the sands and distilling the water in order to collect the crystals of the precious commodity. Some devoured the salt by the fistful, to the point of illness, after being starved of it for so long. Moving on, they came to the province of Tula, the richest of the region.

The Tulas were Indians of the Caddoan family. They tilled the land, were hunters and skilled at making pottery. In their world of magic, they adored the forces of nature, the Mighty River and the stars. When they saw the Spanish column marching into their village, with their shining armor and their horses, an animal they had never seen, instead of showing fear, they assembled, men and women, took up arms and lunged into battle. The fight continued until dark, at which time de Soto chose to fall back and rest his troops, ready for a new assault in the morning. Retreating into the hamlet, they found the place deserted and took up quarters in the houses so that everyone might rest and attend to the wounded. Among the wounded was the valiant Hernandarias de Saavedra, the marshal of Seville's grandson, who died a few days later.

The Indians returned after three days, under cover of darkness, and the battle that took place in the night was indeed an eerie episode. The Spaniards fought with great courage and in the end the combination of valor and superior weapons gave them the upper hand. The Indians were quite exhausted and had to retreat at daybreak, dragging many wounded with them.

The next day, the Tulas sent a deputation with presents of pelts from their chief who expressed his regrets at having met the foreigners with violence. He now offered hospitality and assistance for the future. As a token of sincerity, he sent a quantity of food, especially sundried meat, or pemmican, which the men of the expedition found delicious and which sustained them for twenty days. But above all, de Soto was grateful for the services of an interpreter, whom he had asked the chieftain to provide, to converse through the resourceful Ortiz.

They now had to find a suitable place to spend the winter. Inquiries so far indicated that the Autianque country, which lay to the southwest and which was said to hold a great quantity of maize, would be an appropriate choice. De Soto called a council of his captains and decided to travel there, all the more since the country was said to lie close to a great expanse of water, rivers perhaps, or even the sea. At the end of the winter, de Soto said, they would build boats to send to Cuba for reinforcements, drawn either from the island itself, or from New Spain, and then, newly armed and with fresh supplies, they would continue to explore the West. For there lay new, fertile lands, spread over vast plains, where many Indian nations maintained themselves with hunting and fishing. There at last would it be possible to found cities and establish a governorship.

De Soto keenly felt the joys of discovery. Thinking of posterity, he would link his own name to such famous explorers as Columbus, Vespucci, Pinzón, Magellan and Balboa.

After eleven days' march, probing along the way, they reached Autianque which, though deserted, justified their expectations and had sufficient houses to accommodate them, besides having good stores of food. It was November 21, 1541. Designating a section of the settlement as his troops' winter quarters, de Soto had it fenced in for greater security, starting the fence at a nearby river that circled the village.

A chieftain of the district, a crafty man, who walked with a limp, came to visit the governor and brought him presents of bison hides and food, mostly maize, beans, nuts, plums and rabbits. But there was no sign of his superior, the great chief of Autianque, who kept sending scouts to watch the white men's movements, in expectation of their departure.

De Soto had his men settle in, expecting three months of winter. To keep them active, he ordered a general refurbishing of all arms, which gave a great deal of work to the armorers and associated tradesmen throughout the column. He charged others with learning to hunt rabbits and expected them to provide the main cookhouse with a set quantity of game every day. He finally staged mock attacks at odd times, such as midnight or the small hours before dawn, to test his men's discipline and speed at falling in at their appointed places, fully armed and mounted, ready for any emergency. Others were given the task of gathering firewood, an absolute necessity during the cold weather. They had already put up with snow for more than a month and were suffering a great deal from the cold. At the same time and with true Spanish gusto, they organized parties, where entertainment was provided by those who played the guitar, and those who made and sold beautifully decorated playing cards for the benefit of the many cardplayers.

As the end of the winter approached, de Soto set off, in spite of the freezing winds that still blew, to scout the province of Naguatex, with fifty horsemen and sixty infantrymen. They reached a village and stopped there, though it was uninhabited. They were soon met by deputations from the chief of the village, bringing food and hides for clothing. Later, there came a group of important-looking Indians, with more than five hundred servants to carry the Spaniards' supplies, all of whom de Soto received with gratitude, insisting however on meeting the chief personally, to conclude their pact of friendship. He never appeared. De Soto then decided to return to Autianque to prepare to return to the Mighty River and there carry out his plan of fitting up boats and trying to make contact with the Spanish colonies in Cuba before founding cities. Shortly after their departure, they came to Hot Springs, and thereby became the first Europeans to set eyes on the thermal springs.

They had been on the move for some time when they noticed that one of their companions was missing: the distinguished Sevillian, Don Diego de Guzmán, one of the most handsome and elegant squires in the expedition; he was also an excellent soldier, a good conversationalist, a redoubtable wine drinker and a born gambler. De Soto halted the detachment and organized a search. They wasted several days before finally learning from the Indians that Guzmán was alive, in the hands of the chieftain of Naguatex, who had given Guzmán his very beautiful daughter in marriage. In reply to a letter from a friend and countryman, Baltasar de Gallegos, Guzmán sent a message on deerskin vellum to say that no one should worry about him and that he wished to be left alone, since, having found a beautiful woman, being protected by the chief of a tribe and having plenty of food, rest and riches, he felt he had fulfilled his destiny. He had no wish to continue with the exhausting expedition. De Soto abided by the letter, especially since the huge gambling debts Guzmán had run up all over camp may have influenced his decision. De Soto felt that there was no point in trying to rescue someone against his will, especially when the Indians were to be expected to defend him. He therefore ordered the detachment to move back to base, leaving behind the first settler, a prisoner caught in the snares of Indian love.

On reaching Autianque to raise camp, he was greeted by the sad news of the death of Juan Ortiz, the faithful, ever-obliging interpreter of a hundred tongues, who had perished of starvation. Everyone grieved at the burial, for Ortiz was well liked. They continued with the help of an Indian interpreter who had joined them in the province of Cofitachequi. The return to the Mighty River, whose discovery de Soto must have remembered as the climax of his life's work, took them along a different route, through new country. Hernando had crossed what is today Arkansas and was now keeping a southerly course, as much to reach the sea as to see new territory. He was about to enter the vast expanses of present-day Louisiana, following the Ouachita River downstream. They found the terrain difficult to negotiate; they first came to a large lagoon, possibly Catahoula Lake and crossed it on rafts they built on the banks. They then landed in the vast province of Anilco. De Soto tried to make contact with the chief of the Indians of the district, but he was told that the chief was absent. On the other hand, bands of warlike Indians set about the Spaniards whenever a group separated from the main body of troops. The valiant Nuño de Tovar was sent with a platoon of lancers to get rid of the snipers, which he did. They then entered the village of Anilco, where they settled comfortably in the four hundred houses they found there. Counting the six hundred Indian servants that had joined them from various districts, the expedition now had thirteen hundred men. To all cordial messages from de Soto, Chief Anilco replied with haughty defiance that de Soto would do better to move on and leave his people in peace.

When the men were rested, de Soto gave the order to set off once more. He wanted to reach the Mighty River as soon as possible, to carry out his project. They first had to cross another broad stream, which once again required the construction of rafts. The river marked the limits of the vast and rich province of Guachoya, which they now entered.

For four days they trudged through tropical forests and swamps, infested with alligators and insects—malaria country at its worst. Finally working their way through Guachoya country, they reached the vicinity of the Mississippi. Hernando de Soto had the comforting feeling[2] of coming back to a known region that seemed as familiar to him as an old friend.

The largest Guachoya village numbered some three hundred houses and stood on the right bank of the Mississippi, perched on a knoll and guarded by two hillocks, one on either side. From its main square, the view carried over the mighty, immensely wide river. High above the waters probably hovered the great bald eagles,[3] winging their slow, precise circles, watching the fish hawks. The area is the site of Ferriday, in the state of Louisiana. As soon as the white men made their unexpected appearance, the villagers rushed to take up arms and defend themselves. But assessing the Spaniards' strength, their arms and equipment, they promptly left the village, leaping into their graceful canoes, and drifted downstream in the direction of the opposite bank of the Mighty River. This suited de Soto's plans admirably well, for it enabled him to bivouac in the village and set about thinking of a way to build the two boats to carry out his project of contacting Cuba and settling the interior. He bivouacked on Sunday, April 17, 1542.

Three days later came a deputation from the Indian chieftain Guachoya who, having heard of the punishment meted out to his traditional enemies, the Anilcos, found it highly advisable to make friends with the white chief and offer him hospitality, help and supplies. Through their interpreters, the Indians solemnly told de Soto that they craved his forgiveness for not visiting him earlier, and they promised all sorts of facilities and assistance in his work. They gave proof of their good faith by bringing enough fruit and fish to feed the whole army.

They were Quapaw Indians who were related to those of the Capaha district, through whose country de Soto had traveled on his way to discover the Mississippi. They enjoyed an advanced culture. Their village was walled in by a stockade. Their houses were raised on small mounds of earth, and this feature took on a particular charm in

the midst of their luxuriant surroundings, which they thus
embellished in their own way. They sowed fields around
the village and were keen fishermen. When Chief Guachoya himself arrived the following day in his great ceremonial canoe, surrounded by his lieutenants, the spectacle was impressive.[4] Several of his men had their bodies
painted in various colors and they wore tufts of feathers
and bobcat furs, with the tails hanging down their backs,
while more furs circled their ankles. They carried bells
made of gourds, or wore seashells on various parts of
their bodies, and also brought their calumets to smoke a
ceremonious pipe of peace with the white chiefs. The
proud Guachoya wore a deerskin mantle decorated with
bird and animal designs. When de Soto had placidly drawn
four puffs of smoke from the pipe and blown smoke to
the four cardinal points, as he had already done on several
similar occasions, Guachoya gave a theatrical sneeze and
spoke with great solemnity:

"White Chief, may the Sun shine upon you and defend you. Your magic powers are well known to us and
we seek your friendship. At first, we committed the error
of thinking of resisting you, but only foolish men persist
in their errors. Wise and rational men know when to
change their mind. We are here to wish the Palefaces a
happy stay and help them, whatever they may need."[5]

De Soto answered the Indian with his usual courtesy
and kindness. He thanked him for his offer of friendship
and gave him the little he had to give. He then asked
which way the sea lay and what news there was of the
neighboring districts. The Indian replied that he did not
know about the sea, but that several leagues farther down,
on the other bank of the Mississippi, was a powerful
kingdom ruled over by Chieftain Quigualtam. His people
were at war with the Anilcos who had given the Spaniards
such a bad reception, and Guachoya was ready to supply
as many warriors as de Soto needed, if he would send a
detachment to crush the hated tribe. De Soto replied that

for the time being he wished to get on with building his boats.

Then de Soto told Guachoya of the reason for his journey. He explained the interest of the king of Spain and then summarized the main tenets of the Catholic Faith. The Indian listened attentively. He in turn explained to de Soto the beliefs held by his tribe about the influence of the forces of nature, to which magical powers were attributed. In everything dwelt a superior force, called "Manitú," whose greatest manifestations were Thunder and the Mighty River. Everything fell under its sway, its dominion: nothing could escape it. Anyone who had seen the River, or lived by it, or owed his livelihood to it, already belonged to it and it was useless trying to go against its will.

De Soto was much impressed and he pondered Guachoya's words. He must have felt the full weight of his responsibilities at having brought his men here, having violated the secret of the river in the name of the Europeans. He felt a vague sort of relationship, a mutual belonging, a close kinship with the river that had offered itself to him. In a way, he identified his life with its stream. The Mississippi, the Father of the Waters, was his and he in turn belonged to the river; their relationship was binding.

For Guachoya, however, matters were much simpler. In his magical world of animated and visible powers, the white chief, with his beard and shining armor, dispensing thunder and death, was the font of special powers that commanded respect. As the few tribesmen knew who were privy to the secrets of their traditions, there obviously had to be a connection between the powers of the white chief and those of the River gods and the Sun. The white chief must surely be immortal, or at least his spirit was destined to roam forever over the wide prairies and the imposing river, to guide other men.

Bowing deeply, the chieftain took his leave of de Soto

and offered to send supplies every day, not forgetting to repeat his offer of men on a punitive expedition against the Anilcos.

De Soto decided to send scouts downstream to the other side of the water. Eight men left under the command of the brave Añasco and returned a week later, not very much the wiser for their pains, since the marshes and swamps, the cane fields and dense forests, had hampered any thorough exploration. They had not come across any villages, nor found any sign of the sea or anything that might have justified further investigation by the main body of troops.

De Soto then sent an Indian emissary to greet Chieftain Quigualtam, telling him who they were and inviting him to visit them. The haughty chief sent back a very curt reply: he would only believe in the white man's magical powers if he were capable of drying up the Mighty River. Moreover, he was not in the habit of going to visit others, but rather others came to see him and brought tribute. If de Soto so wished, he could visit and the Indian would know how to receive him, whether he came in peace or in war, but in no case would he make a move to meet the Paleface.

The Indian's cutting reply stung de Soto, and in other circumstances he would have launched an expedition to punish such insolence, but he had been feeling the first symptoms of an illness that left him tired and depressed. He sometimes had feverish spells, and at other times, felt dreadfully cold, which led him to overdress and perspire. He felt exhausted. He had caught an illness from the unhealthy miasma of the country, malaria, the swamp sickness, and though he tried to conceal it from his men, hoping to throw off the symptoms by sheer force of will-power, he was unable to do so and had to take to his bed.

Meanwhile, Guachoya's messengers called every day, laden with the promised supplies. Despite his illness, de

Soto maintained the strictest discipline in the camp. While men were sent to gather wood and twine to build the boats, the watches were scrupulously kept, horse patrols regularly carried out day and night, and the stockade gates, as well as the rafts on the river, were guarded by detachments of crossbowmen, who continuously took turns at keeping watch. All these measures, carefully noted by the Indians, may have contributed to the fact that the Spaniards were not attacked by their newfound friends.

In the face of Anilco's recurring depredations, and yielding to the insistent solicitations of Guachoya, whose friendship would, after all, be needed, de Soto decided to send a troop accompanied by some Indians to make a brief raid on one of Anilco's villages. He told Nuño de Tovar to take fifteen horsemen overland and Juan de Guzmán to accompany Guachoya's rafts and men. He directed them to act with restraint and to be satisfied with a brief display of Spanish might that would be remembered with profit. Both groups, later joined by several hundred friendly warriors, moved forward under cover of darkness. The besieged braves were not given a chance to muster in time to fight back and their undoing was complete. Amid loud war cries, Guachoya's men plundered the houses and made off with a large booty, in utter disregard of Tovar's admonitions. Tovar and Guzmán limited themselves to a few prisoners and some clothing they badly needed. When they returned to report to the governor, they found that he had already heard from Guachoya himself how bravely the Palefaces fought and how much their arms had been admired, whereupon the Indians renewed their assurances of peace and promises of help. De Soto, however, who had intended only to make a token show of strength, was appalled at the cruelties and outrages of Guachoya's men, who, as it was later learned, even violated the Anilco graves, scattering the remains of the ancient tribal chiefs.

All the while, the work of preparing materials to build

the boats was progressing apace. Three years had passed since his departure and it would soon be a year since he had discovered the Mississippi. An infinite lassitude, commensurate with the incredibly long path he had trodden, was now beginning to sap his strength and weaken his iron constitution.

He had discovered huge territories that spread over close to eight degrees of latitude north and south, and some twelve degrees of longitude, the whole journey amounting to 2175 miles approximately. He now had a general idea of the country where he would settle his governorship and had found it to be good, arable land. Settlers were needed urgently, people who knew the work and were used to it, not young adventurers, eager only for easy gains. There were many in his army who were ready to settle down as farmers and till the land as they would never have had a chance to in their home countries.

The tribes of the prosperous Natchez territory, on the other side of the river, were the subjects of the haughty Quigualtam. They held sway over more than eight towns close to the Mississippi. They adored the Sun, and the chief's authority was absolute. It was their custom to flatten the heads of the boys of the tribe, from childhood, with tied planks, which gave them a strange appearance. They tilled the land, wove beautiful material and made fine pottery.

De Soto had been well informed of the Natchez' industry and of their advanced culture. He tried to summon enough strength to assemble his men and cross the Mighty River in the small boats he had, before starting to build the bigger boats. When he reached Natchez country, he found several villages, all quite deserted, and decided to pull back to the other bank and return to his headquarters in Guachoya country. He had been sent hostile and threatening messages by Quigualtam every step of the way, whereas the very purpose of his journey had been to find a suitable place to build his boats, a task that required considerable help from the local population.

About May 14, the governor collapsed and his temperature rose sharply. Three days of serious illness brought him to the realization that the end was near. Yet he did not neglect the safety of the camp, and still saw to it that the watches were faithfully kept. He then asked his cousin Friar Luis to give him the sacraments.

The thought of death was no stranger to the adelantado. Death was indeed an old acquaintance, ever since his young days in Darién when he had grown familiar with it in the course of his adventures and battles in Nicaragua and Peru. He had looked death in the face on the extraordinarily long sea voyages and on the fabulous odyssey in Florida. To die was simply to start a long-expected rest, after an accumulation of fatigue, roaming across many continents. At forty-two years of age, he had discovered in the New World more land than any other explorer of his day, traveling over land routes. He had done all this to serve his country in the person of a man of his own age, Emperor Charles the Fifth, who ceaselessly fought for the unification of Europe and then of the whole of the New World. His discovery of Florida was even greater than Pizarro's. Better still, the ground he had covered in North America opened the way to a host of future expeditions. If life failed him before he was able to complete his plan of getting reinforcements, founding cities and settling the country after this first exploratory stage, which may have been too extensive, others would come to carry on his work.

The thought of dying brought with it the realization, too, that he may die far from his beloved Isabel, the dream of his entire life, the romantic ideal of the knight-errant he was. He felt that she was close, perhaps not many miles beyond the place where the waters of the Mighty River met the sea. She might perhaps be looking for him, impatiently sending one boat after another from the Cuba governorship to the ports where he had instructed his sailors to meet him. The idea of death must have carried with it the bitter thought of her absence and the knowledge that she would feel great suffering at learning the awful news of his death. He asked for the copy of the will he carried with him to be read in the presence of his intimate friends. The will, which had been signed in the presence of Francisco Cepero, notary, had been witnessed by some of the people attached to the governor: Baltasar de Gallegos, camp marshal; Captain Juan de Añasco; the steward Alonso de Ayala; his secretary Rangel and Cristóbal de Espíndola, captain of the guard. Other officials mentioned in the document were present at his side at the time the will was read. As Rangel read on,[6] Hernando, half closing his eyes, recalled the course of his life and nodded in assent to each of the clauses he had dictated three years earlier.[7]

The will reaffirmed the testator's Catholic Faith and went on to say that "he was trying to pay the price" of his salvation, "and that, in return for such a great benefit, death being a natural thing, the more he prepared for it, the greater satisfaction it was likely to procure." He wished his body to be buried wherever he may die, until such time as it could be brought back to Jerez, to be laid next to his mother in the Church of San Miguel. He stipulated that a chapel to the Conception be built, and that Masses be said for the repose of his soul, those of his parents and of his wife, Doña Isabel de Bobadilla. He remembered his brother Juan Méndez de Soto, whom he named as "patron" of the chapel in case his wife, Doña Isabel, had no sons, and, failing him, the eldest son of his sister Catalina, or after him, María de Soto's son. He remembered his niece Isabel de Soto, who married the brave Carlos Enríquez, and left her an endowment of 3000 ducats. He then left his effects to his wife, Doña Isabel, with the 7000 ducats she had brought in dowry, as well as the

6000 he had given her as a dowry counterpart. The memory of his adventures in Nicaragua must have brought a smile to his lips, as he heard the clause leaving 400 ducats "to a young boy they say is my son, Andrés de Soto by name" and 1000 "to a daughter I left in Nicaragua, called Doña Marina de Soto, the wife of Hernán Nieto." Other bequests followed: 300 ducats to the steward Ayala, a like amount to Rodrigo Rangel; among others, he remembered his equerry and the ladies-in-waiting of Doña Isabel, María Arias and Catalina Jiménez Mejía y Arellano. Keeping his promise, he left 1000 ducats to Leonor de Bobadilla "for the service that Nuño Tovar and she have rendered to me."

He then remembered his old and fickle friend Hernán Ponce de León who had signed his name next to his on the Letter of Association of the Enterprise of Dreams, a letter he had honored all his life, when it was first drawn up in Panama, later confirmed in Lima and ratified in Havana. He now repeated that his worldly goods belonged by half to Ponce, just as Ponce's belonged by half to him. Finally, as to the proceeds of those revenues from the silk, which he received after lending the Inca gold to Charles the Fifth, he provided that the approximate sum of 300,000 maravedis involved should be delivered, half to Doña Isabel de Bobadilla his wife, in usufruct, and the other half to be used "every year to wed three orphaned young ladies, daughters of gentlemen of my lineage, up to the fifth degree of relationship, of the poorest that shall be found," the matter to be attended to by Doña Isabel herself, and should none of his lineage be found, the bequest should benefit the poorest in Jerez.

He finally named as his executors his wife Isabel, Hernán Ponce de León, his brother Juan Méndez de Soto and Gutiérrez Cardeñosa: his beloved, his friend and his relatives.

When the reading of the will ended, tears ran down the rough faces of the adelantado's valiant companions.[8]

The will very clearly reflected the straightforward nature of de Soto. Feeling that the fever was getting worse and sensing that the end was drawing near, he asked his cousin Friar Luis do Soto to hear his confession and bade the captains return afterward to decide what should be done about the army command.

Captains Moscoso, Tovar, Gallegos, Vasconcelos and Espíndola came back with the secretary Rangel and Ayala, the governor's employees. When everyone was present, including the notary, de Soto slowly, but in a clear voice, thanked them all for their loyalty and their efforts in the interest of the expedition. He told them that, having thought the matter over, he would ask the captains to choose his successor. The senior among them, Gallegos, insisted that it would be preferable for de Soto to name his own successor, asking at the same time that his name be omitted from the choice. In the name of all present, he earnestly requested de Soto to make that decision, since all would accept it and obey the man chosen by the adelantado.

"Since that is your wish," said Hernando, sitting up in bed, "I name as my successor to the posts of governor, adelantado and captain general of "Florida," Don Luis Moscoso y Alvarado, here present. I have, for many years, known his courage and his qualities, ever since we were together in the adventure in Peru. I ask you, for the sake of the affection you bear me, to obey him as you would myself. He will know how to bring our great enterprise to a successful end, since Providence has ordained that I should see it only halfway through. Look upon him as your chief until His Majesty disposes otherwise, and may it so be recorded by the notary. Gentlemen, your word on it!"[9]

"We swear to obey Captain Luis Moscoso," they responded with heightened emotion. After this dramatic decision, de Soto asked that all officers and men of the expedition be allowed in small groups to take his hand. This lasted all day and the following day, until he had said farewell to everyone, urging them to observe the strictest discipline and remain united to ensure the success of the expedition. All felt a sharp pang of sorrow at losing a father, such as Hernando de Soto had been to them during the difficult years of the great adventure.

He lay in his bed for five days, a prey to the terrible malaria. The end was drawing near with every passing day. At the end of each day, the soldiers would comment on the adelantado's grim fight with death and on his victory over illness, until May 21: it was the month, they noted with superstitious comment, that marked the first anniversary of the discovery of the Mississippi and when they began making barges to cross it. On that day, which he seemed to have waited for, Hernando de Soto died, comforted by the affection and solicitude of his captains.

Luis de Moscoso and Tovar, his closest friends, had maintained a veil of secrecy over the seriousness of the governor's condition and now around his death, since they did not want the notion to spread among the Indians that he was mortal after all. They were further concerned with the idea of how to bury him, lest when the expedition left, or even before, the Indians should disinter his body and profane his remains, as had happened in the past. They had themselves witnessed such acts among other abominations committed by the Guachoyas during the raid on Anilco. Those were the men who were now inquiring of the governor's health. They buried him in the greatest secrecy, in a nearby plain, in a large hole that had been dug to procure dirt for other purposes. The brave man from Jerez was buried at dead of night, escorted by a very small retinue of captains, officers, clerics and servants, reciting the Prayers for the Dead in a slow monotone, interrupted by the sobbing of the attendants.

Great demonstrations of military activity, such as changing the guards and galloping detachments, were arranged the following day by the Spanish leaders, in spite of the grief they felt; it was meant to give the Indians the idea that the governor was better and giving orders. The braves, however, began to grow suspicious of these maneuvers and, most of all, of de Soto's absence, and of the tight security that seemed to bar admittance to his quarters. Furthermore, the looks of grief on the faces of his friends were eloquent proof of the governor's death. The Indians would look for his grave. Faced with this situation, the captains met in council and, since it was time for them to leave the camp where they had been for so long, the idea prevailed that they should give de Soto a better burial in an inviolable place. It was Nuño de Tovar who expressed the general feeling,

"Since his memory and his glory are forever bound to this great, ever moving river, let us entrust it with the task of keeping safely, for all eternity, the body of our beloved general. I propose that we find the deepest place and that we lay his body to rest there, at night, without the knowledge of the Indians."[10]

Everyone agreed to this unusual project. To raise de Soto's body and remove it without his potential enemies finding out was worthy of the epic of *The Cid*. After all, the river itself was a symbol of existence. Some may have remembered Jorge Manrique's elegy of the previous century, On the Death of [His Father,] the Grand Master of the Order of Santiago":

> *Our lives are the rivers*
> *flowing into the sea*
> *which is to die;*
> *Thither flow all those*
> *eminent seigniories,*
> *straight to their dissolve*
> *and consummation.*[11]

To carry out their plan, Juan de Añasco and Captains Juan de Guzmán, Arias Tinoco, Alonso Romo de Cardeñosa and Diego Arias, with Juan de Abadía, went down to the river, pretending to go fishing. Halfway across its quarter-league width, they took soundings and found what seemed to be a suitable place, nineteen fathoms deep. Back in camp, they found that they had no stones to serve as ballast, and they therefore decided to cut down a tree trunk of heavy green oakwood and carve a long cavity out of its side, to accommodate the body of the deceased. Having done so overnight, they respectfully opened the grave in the darkness and placed the body in its casket, which they closed with planks nailed to the bottom of the heavy trunk. They then carried their load to the largest boat they had. All told, a dozen mourners traveled with de Soto on his last journey: the captains, the clerics and the close relatives, with other officials following in other boats.

When they reached the middle of the river, they paused for a moment while the oarsmen struggled to keep the boat steady.

Gently, as though fearful of disturbing his slumbers, Hernando's friends and relatives placed the uncommon casket on the gunwale of the boat. In a last loving gesture, they kissed the rough-hewn American green oak. They then let it slip into the waters, which accepted it as their own. The Mississippi, the Father of the Waters, had cast its spell; the man who had intruded on its mystery had returned to pay his tribute. Forever, they were united to one another. In an eternal cycle of renewal, the burial stream would perennially carry de Soto's fame to future generations.

Friar Luis was chanting the requiescat.

The waters, a moment ruffled by their clandestine legacy, now flowed smoothly once again under the skies, reflecting in their mirror surface the peaceful garden of stars.

EPILOGUE

Two days later, Chief Guachoya came to inquire of the White Chief's health. Moscoso replied that he had gone on a visit to his father, the Sun, as he had done on several previous occasions. Guachoya offered to return in the afternoon, and did so, bringing with him two young Indian girls, intended for sacrifice, as was the custom and tradition of the River People, to accompany de Soto on his journey. Moscoso answered that the governor would not think this to be an appropriate gesture, since, after consulting the Sun, he was due to return soon, to ensure the prosperity of the people of the district.

One question remained to be settled: what to do with the expedition. To follow Hernando de Soto's will would require finishing the boats and sailing down the Mighty River until they reached Havana, took on new supplies and returned to settle the country, founding the cities he intended to establish. However, most were inclined to press westward overland, since New Spain could not be far off, and voyages by sea had little appeal for the men of the expedition, who counted neither pilots nor sailors in their midst. This proposal found favor, and Luis de Moscoso gave the order to break camp. The marching columns met with many vicissitudes and suffered many privations. They moved westward, penetrating to the heart of Texas near the approximate site of Bryan, north of

Houston. There, the hard, inhospitable and sometimes hostile country led them to decide to return to the same part of the Mississippi country, this time following de Soto's advice, who could thus in a way be said to be still directing his men. Having wasted a year on this ill-advised chase, they once again had to stop to spend the winter in warm quarters. Moscoso at least managed to persuade the old enemies, Guachoya and Anilco, to make peace with one another, and received help from both chiefs. As for the harsh Quigualtam, he arranged an alliance of all the chiefs of the neighboring districts, to annihilate the expedition. The Spaniards had to fight many battles and lost many men, among them the brave captains Nuño de Tovar and Vasconcelos. They finally built seven boats and fitted them with sails made with leather and cloaks. They still had to face a fearful flood of the Mighty River, which had dire consequences for the Indian populations whose land now lay under water. Only 311 men remained to embark in their small fleet when the level dropped. They were constantly harassed by the Indian confederates, who even pursued them in their canoes.

They fended off attacks with their crossbows and Indian arrows—their harquebuses, unserviceable for lack of powder since the battle of Mobile, had been used to make nails to build the boats. They lived off the salted and dried meat of the hogs and horses they had left. They finally reached the sea, at the delta of the immense Mississippi River, after seventeen days of hazardous navigation. Following the coast, in a fabulous odyssey, they sailed down to New Spain, where they came across the first signs of Spanish settlers at the mouth of the Pánuco River, at the port of Tampico, about the month of September 1543. Aided by the settlers and the Spanish authorities of the villages, they were able to travel to the town of Mexico, with the ever-present benevolent protection of the viceroy, Don Antonio de Mendoza. Serious arguments broke out among them all along the way, generally because of some soldiers' preference for following de Soto's advice, and founding cities on the Mississippi where they would have been their own lords and masters, rather than living on charity in New Spain, a fact that hurt their Spanish pride. They blamed their captains who had decided to lead them into their present situation. Later, some of them returned to Spain, while others, like Moscoso who married a rich heiress, stayed in Mexico. Others still, went to Peru, to join Gonzalo Pizarro's wars and pacification.

Meanwhile, Doña Isabel remained disconsolate in Havana, whence she sent expeditions year after year. Diego Maldonado and Gómez Arias had untiringly set off every summer, laden with supplies, provisions and ammunition, to explore the coasts of the Florida peninsula, both east and west, seeking information about their captain general, but always without success. Every winter they returned to Havana to inform the unhappy spouses of the governor, of Tovar, Enríquez and several others, of their lack of news. Leonor de Bobadilla, who had a daughter by Tovar, waited in great distress for the return of her handsome gallant.[1] In 1543, Gómez Arias and Maldonado's expedition followed the Atlantic coast of Florida up to Cape Cod in Massachusetts. On their way back to the Gulf of Mexico, they called at Veracruz before returning to Havana, and heard of Moscoso's return and of de Soto's death a year earlier. It was at the end of 1543 that the sad news was conveyed to the lady governor, Doña Isabel. Viceroy de Mendoza also sent official communication of the fate of the expedition and the report reached Havana in the first part of December 1543, aboard a ship called the *Santiago*, under the command of the master Ochoa Vizcaíno. The brave daughter of Pedrarias took the blow, which she had in a way expected, with characteristic fortitude.[2] She wept over the death of her hero, and liquidated his estate, doing her best to comply with the last wishes of her beloved Hernando with the limited proceeds of the disposal of his belongings. But the fact remained that her life was empty and she was unable to survive for long the death of her beloved and incorrigible explorer; she died shortly afterward.[3]

The governor's brother, Juan Méndez de Soto, reported to the Crown the services rendered by his brother and he asked and obtained certain favors of Emperor Charles the Fifth, who must have fondly remembered the lively and happy explorer from Jerez, whom he had plied with honors and invested with the necessary authority to undertake the conquest of Florida. This discovery brought to light unknown facts about an immense territory which was now offered to the spirit of enterprise of the future explorers that were to come, first from Spain, then from France and from England.

The Spanish Crown was unable to follow up the plans that the governor from Jerez made for the settlement of Florida, that is to say, the eastern and central part of North America. The subsequent course of history was to a large extent altered by the premature death of Hernando de Soto, of whom Garcilaso de la Vega said, in 1599, on recording the exploit,[4] "If he had lived two years longer, he would have repaired the damage done in the past, with the help of the reinforcements he would have requested and received, via the Mighty River, as he had planned. This could have been the start of an empire that today could have competed with New Spain and Peru. It is inferior to none, either in size or in riches, or in its agricultural possibilities. It may even have been better than others, since we have seen the incredible quantity of pearls and gems that were contained in one single temple, in one single land, not to mention the furs and the pelts of martens and other animals, fit only for kings and mighty princes, or any of the other riches we have enumerated elsewhere. Gold and silver could, doubtless, have been found, had mines been carefully sought, as neither in Mexico nor in Peru were they, at the time of the conquest, as numerous as they are today."

The huge territories visited and reconnoitered by Hernando de Soto's valiant expedition, ranging over ten states of the Union (Florida, Georgia, South Carolina, North Carolina, Tennessee, Alabama, Mississippi, Arkansas, Louisiana and Texas), remained the property of the warlike Indian nations, proud and hostile toward the white man, until well into the nineteenth century. Then, it took the might of fully equipped modern armies to overcome decisively the resistance of tribes that, three centuries earlier, a man had tried to subdue with only a thousand brave Spanish and Portuguese soldiers, mounted on 350 horses: a visionary from Extremadura, an incorrigible temper of fate, Don Hernando de Soto, the discoverer of the Mississippi, keeper of his memory, the memory of the Amadís of Florida, Knight of the Américas.

NOTES

MEM	Montesinos	Memorias Antiguas Historiales del Perú
NAR	Bourne	Narratives of the Career of Hernando de Soto
OND	Ondegardo	Relaciones 1 and 2
OVO	Fernández de Oviedo	Historia General y Natural de las Indias . . .
PRE	Prescott	History of the Conquest of Peru
RAM	Ramusio	Relazione d'un Capitano Spagnuolo
RAN	Rangel	Abridged Journal
ROM	Romoli	Vasco Núñez de Balboa
SAR	Sarmiento de Gamboa	Historia de los Incas
USC	U.S. de Soto Expedition Commission	Final Report to . . . Congress
VEL	Velasco	Historia del Reino de Quito
XER	Xérez	Conquista del Perú
ZAR	Zarate	Historia del Descubrimiento . . .

Prologue
Amadís Once More on Scrutiny

1. Title: It will be recalled that *Amadís of Gaul* was one of the books in Don Quixote's library that was "scrutinized" by his friends the Curate and the Barber. They spared the book from the bonfire, since it was "the best of all books of its kind, unrivaled in its style." Miguel de Cervantes, *Don Quijote de la Mancha*, pt. 1, chap. 6. Translation by Walter Starkie, New York: New American Library, 1964.

Chapter One
The Century of Chivalry

1. Cervantes, *Don Quijote de la Mancha*, pt. 1, chap. 13. Translation by Walter Starkie. New York: New American Library, 1964.
2. The anonymous novel, *Amadís of Gaul*, was variously claimed to be of French, English, Portuguese or Spanish origin. At any rate, the first known printed edition was published in Saragossa, Spain, in 1508, following two centuries of circulation in handwritten form.

3. This city, also known as Jerez de Badajoz, straddled the crests of two hills in the province of Badajoz (*audiencia* of Cáceres, in the captaincy general of Estremadura). It was also the birthplace of Vasco Núñez de Balboa, the discoverer of the Pacific Ocean.

Various cities claimed to be the birthplace of de Soto, including Villanueva de Barcarrota, mentioned in a statement by Garcilaso de la Vega. Though the name of de Soto is seldom mentioned in the records of Barcarrota (whereas it appears conspicuously in those of Jerez de los Caballeros), R. B. Cunninghame Graham mentions that Hernando de Soto was "born at the little town of Barcarrota."

It should be noted, finally, that there was a de Soto from Barcarrota among the companions of Hernando in Florida.

Chapter Two
The Youth from the Sea

1. See no. 4, chap. 11.
2. See CEN, chap. 1.
3. See Gonzalo Fernández de Oviedo y Valdés, *Viaje de Juan de la Cosa*, bk. 3, chap. 8, and bk. 27, chaps. 1 and 3. (Sevilla 1535; Salamanca 1547.) BAE 1959 (Also ROM, chap. 3. BAE: Biblioteca de Autores Españoles, Manuel Rivadeneira Publisher. Madrid 1846–1880. 71 vols.). Also ROM, chap. 3.
4. Now the capital of the Dominican Republic. Hispaniola is the name of the island presently shared by the two independent states of Haiti and the Dominican Republic.
5. See CEN, chap. 1.
6. "The Great Captain" was Gonzalo Fernández de Córdoba, who was sent to Italy as chief of the Spanish armies by the Catholic monarchs of Spain, Fernando and Isabel, known as "the Catholic Kings." There, he took the port of Taranto, defeated the French at Cerignola and Garigliano and consolidated Spain's hold over the kingdom of Naples.

The "wars in Italy" refer to a series of conflicts on Italian territory, which pitted the Spanish against the French armies. The Catholic kings fought one war as a result of a dispute between the Aragonese and Angevin cousins, both claiming the crown of Naples. Charles V, the grandson of the Catholic kings, fought four wars in Italy, in the course of which he conquered Milan and occupied Rome. His son, Philip II, tried to pacify the area by creating the Council of Italy in 1558.
7. Both mother and daughter bore the same name. See n. 2, p. 135, chap. 10.
8. See CEN, chap. 2.

9. See CEN, chap. 2.

10. "Amerigo" refers to Amerigo Vespucci, after whom the American continent was to be named. He held the eminent position of chief pilot of Castile, which his nephew was to hold later.

11. The long delays in sailing were the result of the bureaucratic procedures to which all shipmasters had to submit before sailing, added to the protracted negotiations for the purchase of the many items required for a large fleet, and the recruitment of crews and army participants.

12. Hernando, now fourteen years of age, doubtless identified with the twelve-year-old Amadís, with the physique of a fifteen-year-old.

Chapter Three
The School of the New World

1. From a letter written by Amerigo Vespucci to Lorenzo Pietro di Medici, "Mundus Novus," 1503. *Americo Vespucio, "El Mundo Nuevo": Letters on travels and discoveries.* Preliminary study by Roberto Levillier. Texts in Italian, Spanish and English (Buenos Aires: Editorial Nova, 1951). See also Angelo Maria Bandini, *Vita e Lettere d'Amerigo Vespucci, Gentiluomo Fiorentino* (Florence, 1745).

2. See OVO, chap. 3, as well as ALV.

3. See OVO, chap. 3, and CEN.

4. See OVO, bk. 27. It seems that Diego de Nicuesa, being a pauper, became in six years one of the richest men in Hispaniola.

5. Ibid.

6. Letter from Balboa to King Ferdinand, written on January 20, 1513, quoted in chap. 8; José Toribio Medina, *El descubrimiento del Océano Pacifico*, vol II, pp. 129–39. Santiago de Chile, 1914.

7. See OVO, bk. 27.

8. Correspondence quoted in OVO, bk. 26, chap. 10, and bk. 29, chaps. 1, 6 and 7.

9. The motto displayed on the Spanish flag, after the union of the kingdoms of Castile and Aragón resulting from the marriage of Isabel of Castile and Fernando of Aragón, each a monarch in her and his own right, proclaimed their equality: "Tanto monta, Monta tanto, Isabel como Fernando" (lit.: Like amount, amount alike, Isabel like Fernando). The flag was known as the Banner of the Tanto Monta.

10. In ALV and CEN.

11. Ibid. and in OVO. Gonzalo Fernández de Oviedo y Valdés accompanied Pedrarias on his first journey from Spain to Darién, with the rank of overseer of gold and ransom and major notary of the Crown. He had been a courtier, serving, with the sons of Columbus, the infante (the royal prince) Don Juan. Oviedo not only

depicts the happenings of the time, but he also enlightens us with anecdotes that give life and color to the events he relates. At Governor Pedrarias's side, he attended the meetings with Bishop Quevedo and he had access to all Pedrarias's records; he was thus able to read the logbook recording the daily progress of Balboa's expedition of discovery to the Pacific Ocean, and all documents relating to Balboa's trial.

Chapter Four
The Gateway to the Southern Sea

1. The letter addressed by King Fernando to Pedrarias, dated August 19, 1514, is quoted by Gonzalo Fernández de Oviedo y Valdés, in *Historia General y Natural de las Indias, Islas y Tierra Firme del Mar Océano* (Asunción, Paraguay: Editorial Guarania, 1944–1945). Vol. 29, chaps. 6–8; vol. 50, chaps. 2 and 3. Also quoted in HI, vol. 3, chaps. 65–68.
2. See ALV, chap. 2; and L. Villanueva, *Hernando de Soto*, chap. 3.
3. These instructions given by King Fernando to Pedrarias are related by Manuel Serrano y Saenz in *Preliminares del Gobierno de Pedrarias Dávila en Castilla del Oro* (Madrid, 1918), pp. 279–88.
4. See OVO.
5. The castilian (castellano) exactly matched the peso de oro or ounce of gold (avoirdupois, weighing 28.35 grams), which represents one-sixteenth part of a pound. Today, the unit for weighing precious metals is the troy ounce of 31.10 grams. Using gold prices quoted at the end of June 1985 ($325 per troy ounce), the sixteenth-century castilian would be the equivalent of $290 in 1985 U.S. dollars.

    More specifically, the "value of the booty" mentioned in this passage would exceed two million 1985 dollars. (See also nn. 1 and 3, chap. 13.)
6. See Kathleen Romoli, *Vasco Núñez de Balboa*, pp. 243–46.

Chapter Five
Captain of Lancers

1. From Raimundo Lulio, *Libro del Orden de Caballería. Principes y Juglares* (1275).
2. See CEN, OVO and ALV.
3. See HI, bk. 3, chaps. 69–72, and OVO, bk. 10, chap. 3, and bk. 12, chap. 7.
4. In "Report from Pedrarias to the King," dated November 20, 1515. Medina II, *Relación de Balboa*, chaps. 72–73; Angel de Altolaguirre, *Vasco Núñez de Balboa*, "Relación de Balboa," chaps. 36–37; OVO, bk. 29, chaps. 8 and 9; HI, bk. 3, chaps. 60–61.

There was indeed reason for disappointment: the poor results of Pedrarias's first months in the colony, probably due to his change of policy compared with Balboa's, make for sorry reading. There was not sufficient food to feed the large numbers of Spaniards who came in with the fleet and epidemics soon broke out. There was no money to meet essential expenses. Corpses lay unattended in the streets of Darién. Relations with the Indians lost all of the friendly character and the spirit of cooperation which Balboa had managed to establish and nurture. By December 1514, Pedrarias's administration had accumulated a deficit of 16,000 gold pesos. Oviedo writes of Spaniards dying at the rate of twenty every day and Andagoya reports seven hundred deaths in a month.

5. For accounts of de Soto's fencing, see Antonio del Solar y José de Rújula, *El Adelantado Hernando de Soto,* and Lummis, *Los Exploradores Españoles del Siglo XVI.*

6. See CEN, chap. 8, p. 60: de Bry's painting of Indians torturing Spaniards with molten gold.

7. The fact that Pedrarias and some of his associates hid the letters and deeds from the king of Spain, appointing Balboa adelantado of the Pacific coast, and governor of Panama and Coiba, is reported by all the historians of the day: Oviedo (OVO, bk. 29); Pedro Mártir, decada 3, chaps. 6, 10; Las Casas (HI, bk. 3, chaps. 65–68); Medina, vol. II (pp. 73–76, 208–38) et al., such as ROM, chap. 4. So is the fact that Pedrarias's wife, Doña Isabel, as well as Bishop Quevedo, openly denounced such deceit. The bishop inveighed against intercepting royal deeds in his sermon at Sunday Mass and, before the Council of Government, he maintained that all royal letters and deeds should be delivered immediately to the rightful addressee. Pedrarias finally agreed to surrender the documents to Balboa.

8. See ROM, chap. 23.

9. See OVO, HI, Medina et al.

10. The Cenú River, or Sinú, runs in Colombia, from the mountains of Dabaybe (Dabeiba, or Debeiba, or Dabaibe) to the Caribbean Sea, east of the Gulf of Urabá and of Santa María del Darién. It was said by the Cenuan Indians that two large mines, located at Mocri and Tirufi, yielded gold in great abundance.

11. See OVO.

12. Ibid.

13. See ROM; OVO; Mártir; HI; Andagoya; Medina, vol. II, *Letters from Balboa,* pp. 142, 217–20. A letter from Balboa to the king describes the expedition to Dabaybe and the reasons for the failure, mainly attributed to the lack of food for the troops, as a consequence of the destruction by a cloud of locusts of all crops in the Atrato River basin.

14. Doña Isabel's favorable disposition toward Balboa, and Bishop Quevedo's suggestion to marry him to one of her daughters, is mentioned by most contemporary historians of Panamá.
15. See CEN.
16. See HI, vol. 3, chaps. 64–67; OVO, bk. 19, chap. 8; bk. 29, chaps. 10–12. Some of the incidents related by Las Casas are confirmed by references in "proofs of merit," made by several former soldiers years later.
17. See HI, vol. 3, chaps. 64–67. Mártir, decada 3, bk. 6; HER, decada 2, bk. 1, chaps. 1–4. Though still a junior officer, de Soto showed a marked repugnance for Morales's abuse of the Indians, as is clearly evidenced by all contemporary references to him. He later in life displayed the same equity in his treatment of the indigenous population, following Balboa's example of straightforward and just dealing, in contrast to the mainstream of political practice of the day at Santa María del Darién.
    Most of de Soto's service was spent in the column assigned to Pizarro, where he earned his chief's appreciation. Pizarro's favorable report to Morales was a requisite for de Soto's promotion.
18. See above n. 17.

Chapter Six
The Triumph of the Gods

1. From Johann Schiller, "The Veiled Image of Saïs," *The Poems and Ballads of Schiller*, trans. Sir Edward Bulwer-Lytton, Bart. (Leipzig: Bernhard Tauschnitz, 1844.)
2. See HI, vol. 3, p. 34. See the "Report" made by Gaspar de Espinosa, mayor of Castilla del Oro, to Pedrarias Dávila, lieutenant general of these provinces, containing a description of all that happened during his expedition, in compliance with Pedrarias's orders (1516). (Unpublished documents of the Archives of the Indies.) HER, decada 2, chaps. 1 and 9.
3. See OVO, vol. 4, chap. 2, and vol. 29, chap. 13, HI, vol. 3, chaps. 2, 74, 75; G. B. Muñoz, "Informe de Espinosa," *Transcripts*, (New York).
4. See ROM, chap. 30.
5. Balboa's relationship with Anayansi was used by his enemies, who wrote to Pedrarias condemning the affront his son-in-law, Balboa, was thus publicly committing vis-à-vis Pedrarias and his daughter, though she remained in Spain.
6. See HI, bk. 3, chaps. 47 and 48. OVO, bk. 29, chap. 3.
7. See OVO.
8. The astrologer Messer (or Micer) Codro had given Balboa a warning, based on a reading of the stars. The quotation is mentioned

in several chronicles of the Indies. See also ROM, chap. 30, p. 362.

9. See ROM, chap. 30, p. 363.
10. Ibid., p. 363.
11. See CEN, chap. 6, p. 49.
12. See ROM, bk. 29, chap. 12; HI, bk. 3, chaps. 75, 76, 141.
13. See ROM, chap. 31; HI, bk. 3, chaps. 74, 76, 132, 152; OVO, bk. 6, chap. 61, bk. 29, chap. 12. Octavio Méndez Pereira, *El Cacique Careta*: "La Estrella de Panamá"; CEN, chap. 6, p. 48.
14. See HER, decada 2, bk. 2, chap. 22; OVO, bk 10, chap. 3, and bk. 29, chap. 10.
15. See HI, bk. 3, chaps. 74, 76, 106, 132; CEN, chap. 6.

Chapter Seven
The Romance of Isabel

1. Vasco Loheyra, *Amadís of Gaul*, vol. 1 (London, 1803).
2. See CEN, chap. 7. Oviedo and Angleria describe the Pedrarias family in Darién. Doña Isabel de Bobadilla y Peñalosa is referred to as an "illustrious lady, of courageous character" most distinguished by her aristocratic dignity, prudence and kindness. Blanco Castilla refers to the "anxiety with which both Pedrarias's daughters would wait for Hernando's return whenever he was sent on inland expeditions." Young Isabel in particular, who was to wait for him for so many years, used to "warn him at all times against the treacherous natives . . . The mother, far from opposing such legitimate feelings, would justify them and, in due time, would even protect them."
3. Fitzmaurice-Kelly, *Historia de la Literatura Española*. Madrid, 1913. For material on this, see CEN.
4. "You must know, Sancho, that the famous Amadis of Gaul was one of the most perfect of all knights-errant. I was wrong to say 'one': he was alone, the first, the unique, the lord of all who in his age were in the world." Cervantes, *Don Quijote de la Mancha*, pt. 1, chap. 25.
5. See L. Villanueva, *Hernando de Soto*.
6. See CEN, chap. 7.
7. See P. de Sandoval, *Vida y Hechos del Emperador Carlos V* (Valladolid, 1604).

Chapter Eight
The Scourge of God

1. From HI.
2. A peso was the equivalent of 450 maravedis. Two thousand mar-

avedis were therefore the approximate equivalent of four ounces of gold avoirdupois, or, at 1985 prices, about 1200 U.S. dollars.

3. Hernán Cortés had been appointed captain general by the governor of Cuba, Diego Velázquez, to lead the expedition that was to explore Yucatán and Mexico. However, the governor changed his mind at the last moment and decided to give the command to another. This caused Cortés to leave Cuba clandestinely, for which Velázquez never forgave him.

4. It was impossible to sail from the Caribbean (the Northern Sea) to the Pacific (the Southern Sea), since no passage was known at the time. The results of the voyage of discovery of Magellan (who was killed in the Philippines in the autumn of 1521) were not yet known. Moreover, the arduous task of dismantling ships on the Caribbean side and carrying the pieces to the Pacific coast for reassembly would probably have ended in failure, since the wood, being of foreign origin and therefore less resistant to local molds and insects, would probably have become useless.

Chapter Nine
The Enterprise of Dreams

1. The deed of ratification of the de Soto–Ponce de León Company was signed in 1539 by de Soto and Ponce de León only. Campañón, the third party, had died in 1528, in León, Nicaragua, naming his two friends as his legatees.

2. See CEN, pt. 2, chap. 9.

3. See CEN, chap. 9, pp. 68, 69 and 70.

Chapter Ten
The New Kingdom of León

1. Rubén Darío (1867–1916), an eminent Nicaraguan poet, regarded as the foremost Latin American innovator in modern Spanish poetry. The poem from which the quoted excerpt is taken refers to the Nicaraguan volcano Momotombo, overlooking Lake Managua. The full Spanish text is as follows:

Momotombo

Ya estaba yo nutrido de Oviedo y Gómara
y mi alma florida soñaba historia rara,
fábula, cuento, romance, amor,
de conquistas, victorias de caballos bravos
incas y sacerdotes, prisioneros y esclavos,
plumas y oro, audacia, esplendor.
Y llegué y vi en las nubes la prestigiosa testa

de aquel cono de siglos, de aquel volcán de gesta
que era ante mí de revelación.
Señor de las alturas, emperador del agua,
a sus pies el divino lago de Managua,
con islas todas de luz y de canción.

Momotombo

I had already been nurtured on Oviedo and Gomara
And my blossoming soul was dreaming a strange story,
A fable, a tale, romance and love,
Of conquests, victories of valiant knights,
Incas and priests, prisoners and slaves,
Feathers and gold, daring and splendor.

And I arrived and saw, in the clouds, the prestigious head
Of that peak of ages, that volcano of legend
Standing before me—a true revelation.
Lord of the heights, Emperor of the waters;
At its feet, the divine lake of Managua,
With islands filled with light and song.

Selection and foreword by Jaime Torres Bodet, *Biblioteca Americana* (Mexico, National University of Mexico, 1966).
2. Most of the expeditions under the Spanish Crown were financed by their captains, who customarily set up their own businesses, importing products from Spain to trade for gold, in the hope of turning a quick profit.
3. See CEN, chaps. 9 and 10. Also ALV.
4. See XER, bk. 3, p. 181; also, Naharro, "Relación Sumaria," MS; MAN; and PRE, chap. 3.
5. See Prescott et al.
6. Pedrarias Dávila and Doña Isabel de Bobadilla had five sons and four daughters.
7. For material on this page, see CEN, pt. 2, chap. 12.
8. See Solar y Rújula, *El Adelantado Hernando de Soto.*

Chapter Eleven
The Fascination of the South

1. From Pedro de Cieza de León, *Relación de la Sucesión y Gobierno de los Incas y Otras Cosas Tirantes a Aquel Reino* (Madrid, 1877).
2. See CEN, chap. 12.
3. See Pedro Pizarro, "Descubrimiento y Conquista"; also Naharro, "Relación Sumaria"; Montesinos, "Anales," year 1528.
4. Francisco's father, Colonel Gonzalo Pizarro of Trujillo (c. 1442–c. 1518), a legendary one-eyed veteran of the Italian Wars (nicknamed

"El Romano"), fathered ten children of various maidens. The eldest son and heir, Hernando Pizarro (c. 1465–c. 1560), joined Francisco Pizarro (c. 1471–c. 1541), with two half brothers (Juan Pizarro [?–1536]—later one of the regidors of Cuzco—and Gonzalo Pizarro [c. 1506–1548], the future governor of Quito and a skillful lancer who, in the interminable Italian Wars, became the First Lance of Italy, like his father whose name he bore) to go to the New World with one of Francisco's half brothers on his mother's side, Francisco Martin de Alcántara, as well as a nephew, Pedro Pizarro (c. 1514–c. 1571), who later wrote a valuable chronicle.

5. See OVO, pt. 3, bk. 8, chap. 1.
6. See PRE, chap. 4, and CSN, chap. 24.
7. *Llautu* was the name given in Quechua (the language of the Incas) to a headdress with a woolen red tassel which fell over the forehead of the Inca, reaching almost to his eyes. It was the symbol of the reigning Inca emperor.
8. See Benjamin Carrion, *Atahualpa*.
9. A translation of Orejones, the name the Spaniards gave to all men of royal blood at the Court of the Inca, because of the long lobes of their ears, inserted in which they carried large pieces of gold, "as large as an orange," to the astonishment of visitors. The larger the distortion, the greater the gentleman. See Pedro Pizarro, "Descubrimiento y Conquista," pt. 3, bk. 8, chap. 3. Montesinos, "Memorias Antiguas Historiales del Perú, bk. 2, chap. 6. Also Garcilaso de la Vega, *Comentarios Reales*, pt. 1, chap. 22.
10. See OVO, pt. 3, bk. 8, chap. 3.

Chapter Twelve
The Child of the Sun

1. R. Palma, *Tradiciones Peruanas* (Lima, 1918).
2. XER, bk. 3, p. 197, and Naharro, "Relación Sumaria."
3. See PRE, chap. 4.
4. See XER, bk. 3, pp. 200–5.
5. See Pedro Pizarro, "Descubrimiento y Conquista," and XER, bk. 3, pp. 196–205.
6. See PRE, chap. 4, based on the *Relación* (the work mentioned in n. 1, chap. 11, above, and contained in CSN), which was attributed by Prescott to Juan Sarmiento, president of the Council of the Indies, to whom the *Relación* was dedicated, and properly (it seems) assigned to Cieza de León by Ballestero, the editor of CSN—see his introduction, p. 20—as well as by Mario Balotta, the editor of CDC—see his introduction, p. 51, for an account of the Sarmiento-Cieza confusion.
7. See PRE, chap. 4.

8. Ibid.
9. See Prescott et al.
10. See Prescott et al.
11. XER, bk. 3, p. 197. Also Naharro, "Relación Sumaria."
12. See Naharro, ibid.
13. Ever since Columbus first landed in 1492 and, on his fourth trip, explored Panama in 1502, rumors of the Europeans' presence spread throughout the Indian kingdoms, carried by Indian merchants. These rumors were promptly retold by the priests who turned them into "prophecies" which they used to gain influence with their rulers. Atahualpa's father, the great Inca Huayna Capac (who was born in Cuenca, a city now in southern Ecuador, and died in Quito in 1526), was haunted, even on his deathbed, by reports that strange men had come over the waters, conveyed to the shores of the Great Sea in floating houses, with tall white wings. They had pale faces, grew abundant hair, were dressed in shining metal and carried powerful canes which would hurl fire, thunder and death at great distances. They also brought monstrous animals never seen before.
14. See Prescott et al.
15. GOM, pt. 1, p. 199, "Imprisonment of Atahaliba" (Atahualpa).
16. GOM, pt. 1, p. 199, "Imprisonment of Atahaliba" (Atahualpa).
17. PRE, chap. 5.
18. Pedro Pizarro, "Descubrimiento y Conquista," quoted by Prescott, chap. 5.
19. Prescott et al.
20. See Pedro Pizarro, "Descubrimiento y Conquista." Also HER, decada 5, bk. 2, chaps. 12 AND 13. Further, RAM, bk. 3, pp. 375 and 407, and PRE, chap. 6.
21. See Prescott et al.
22. See Prescott et al.

Chapter Thirteen
Gold, Crime and Treachery

1. From OVO, pt. 3, bk. 8, chap. 22.
2. The "metal value" of Atahualpa's ransom as weighed and recorded in The Act of Partition, totaled 1,326,539 pesos of gold, or approximately 400 million 1985 U.S. dollars. To this should be added 51,610 marks (each weighing 8 ounces avoirdupois) of silver, with an estimated present-day value (calculated at 8 dollars per ounce) of 3.3 million 1985 U.S. dollars. (See also n. 5, chap. 4, and n. 4, below.)
3. See OVO pt. 3, bk. 8, chap. 16. Also, XER, bk, 3, p. 232, and CEN, chap. 16.

4. According to estimates made in 1847 by William Prescott (see PRE, p. 966), based on Xerez ("Act of Partition of the Atahualpa Ransom," in XER, bk. 3, p. 232), as well as on Señor Clemencin, secretary of the Royal Academy of History of Madrid, the approximate commercial value of the ransom was "nearly four times as great" as its specific value. The ransom would thus come to over 1.5 billion in 1985 U.S. dollars.
5. See OVO, pt. 3, bk. 8, chap. 22.
6. See Prescott et al.
7. See Prescott et al.
8. See Prescott et al.

Chapter Fourteen
The Pacifier of Cuzco

1. See PRE, chap. 8, "Carta de la Justicia y Regimiento de Xauja" (Letter of the Municipality of Xauja to the King) MS.
2. See Prescott et al.
3. See Prescott et al.
4. See CEN, chap. 18. Also PRE, chap. 8.
5. Years later, Doña Leonor de Soto, who married a Captain García Carrillo and lived in Peru, requested a grant of land and an annuity before the Royal Council of Indies in Madrid. Her petition met with partial success when, on July 20, 1587, she was granted an annual allowance of 2000 pesos.
6. See CEN, chap. 19. Leonor Toctochimbo Coya, daughter of the Inca Huayna Capac, bore de Soto a daughter (the same Leonor de Soto who later married García Carrillo, as mentioned in the above note) whom she made her legatee: "I leave as my inheritor a daughter of mine and of Captain Hernando de Soto, called Leonor." (Seville: Archives of the Indies, "Patronato" number 1091.5-20.4.)

Chapter Fifteen
Imperial Knight

1. Garcilaso de la Vega (nicknamed "El Inca"). See FLI, bk. 1, chap. 1.
2. The title given in the Catholic Church to the religious authority ruling over all the churches, monasteries and convents of a province of his own order.
3. The surname given by Western historians to four Turkish pirates, including Arouj, or Horush, and his brother and successor (1518), Khair-ed-Din. The Barbarossas were the "owners" of the territory of Algiers, which Khair-ed-Din placed under the protection of the

sultan of Constantinople, Selim I the Grim (1512–1520), receiving in exchange the title of pasha and becoming the founder of the regency of Algiers (1516). (Khair-ed-Din) Barbarossa unified the country and ensured its welfare by the practice of piracy and the slave trade along the coast of the Barbary States (North Africa).

4. Charles I, king of Spain, lived from 1500 to 1558. He ruled over the Low Countries and later inherited Austria and southern Germany. In 1519, he was elected Holy Roman Emperor, the secular head of Christendom, and took the name of Charles V. With his vast domains in America, Sicily and Naples, as well as in Germany and Brabant, he was the most powerful monarch on earth.

It is a thought worth pondering that, from the date of the discovery of America by Columbus in 1492, until 1600, more than eight million ounces of gold, that is, 35 percent of the world's gold production for that period, came from South America. Atahualpa's ransom alone represented 1.32 million ounces of gold.

5. See Prescott et al.

6. See OVO, pt. 3, bk. 9. Also CEN, chap. 20.

7. The high standing accorded to Pedrarias's wife, Doña Isabel, was due to the fact that her aunt, Doña Beatríz de Bobadilla, marchioness of Moya, was the closest friend and the confidante of Queen Isabel the Catholic. It was a common saying at the Court that, "after the Queen of Castilla, the Bobadilla."

An idea of the size and splendor of de Soto's wealth, including his jewelry, may be gathered from a perusal of the inventory of his belongings, as recorded in the General Archives of the Indies, Seville (Sign. 50-2-55.10, Papers of Justice, no. 750(a), pt. 1, pp. 306–33). Moreover, the Library of Congress in Washington has an impressive list of de Soto's household goods, as well as an interesting collection of his Sevillian tailor's bills.

8. See CEN, chap. 20. Also Solar y Rújula, *El Adelantado Hernando de Soto.*

9. See CEN, chap. 20.

10. See RAN: Rodrigo Rangel was a close friend of de Soto's, who was regularly seen at his side in Madrid and Seville. He later accompanied de Soto to Florida, acting as his private secretary.

11. From the file on "Admissions to the Order of Santiago" (Madrid: National Historical Archives, Section of Military Orders, Santiago, file no. 7855).

12. See CEN, chap. 20, pp. 166–67.

13. De Soto had never been to Segovia, but he had heard—from members of the Pedrarias family, natives of Segovia—of the classical elegance of its monuments and he must naturally have looked forward to this visit.

14. See Deeds relating to the Dowry and Arras of Doña Isabel de

Bobadilla, General Archives of the Indies, Seville (Papers of Justice, number 750 (a) pt. 1, pp. 64–69). The dowry was supplied by the bride's family at the time of the marriage and the *arras* were a down payment or token payment made by the bridegroom-to-be, before the wedding, not to exceed one-tenth, or one-eighth (depending on the stipulations of provincial laws) of his fortune. The arras were forfeited if the engagement was broken off.

Chapter Sixteen
The New Temptation

1. The young Doña Isabel had been schooled in the courtly manners and protocol of the Spanish Court by her mother, who held a position of great eminence in the royal entourage. De Soto, for his part, had spent most of his time traveling under rough conditions, and living a soldier's life on various military campaigns and explorations. He was now entering a new world, that of the grandees of Spain, the process being rendered all the more difficult by the fact that he was now a stranger in his own land.
2. See CEN, chap. 20, where the hero is described as follows:
    Hernando de Soto was then in the prime of his life, in all his manhood and the dream-inspiring figure of a handsome conqueror. He was tall, strong and athletic, with a broad forehead and dark hair. His features, tanned by the sun, were handsome, and his well-groomed black beard gave his countenance a martial air. The gaze of his large, deep, black and shining eyes seemed to be set upon some distant horizon, as befitted a victorious captain, inhabited by a poetic spirit—for Hernando de Soto was, if any, the first romantic figure of the Conquest.
3. All chroniclers agree in stating that de Soto wanted to take back his wife to the American lands where she had spent some of her early years. They owned property in Panama and had the chance of acquiring new kingdoms. Such was his wish, to compensate her in some way for the long years she had waited for him. It is safe to assume that Isabel discussed the matter with her mother, who probably encouraged her: indeed, another daughter of Doña Isabel's, María, Balboa's widow, was then married to Rodrigo de Contreras, who, in Nicaragua, ruled over a large tract of land, worked by two thousand Indians, and later became governor of Nicaragua. The general interest and source of income of the family was clearly the New World.
4. See note above.
5. Now, four and a half centuries after the start of the quest for the Fountain of Youth, can it not be said that the state of Florida itself

has richly fulfilled its early advocation? This State of the Radiant Sun, with its growing Spanish-speaking population, fully one-third of its ten million inhabitants, is a vacation resort and a land of retirement, where visitors and permanent residents alike continue to seek youth and the good life, and a new generation of explorers at Cape Canaveral prepares to discover the universe.

6. See FLI, bk. 1, chap. 2.
7. Ibid.
8. See CEN, chap. 24. In fact, the land entrusted to de Soto's governorship, comprised that previously awarded to Vázquez de Ayllón and Pánfilo de Narváez, that is to say, the territory bordering the Atlantic Ocean from Cape Florida, or Corrientes, to Newfoundland, running west as far as the Palmas River and New Mexico, and extending north into the uncharted Terra Incognita.
9. See FLI, bk. 1, chap. 5.
10. See EL3, chap. 2. Cabeza de Vaca's friends explained to de Soto that the strange captain, "being reluctant to march under the standard of another," preferred to solicit another government. This, after de Soto, though wanting Cabeza de Vaca's company, had demurred at purchasing a ship the latter had bought.
11. See EL3, chap. 1, in which Elvas says, "The emperor made him governor of the island of Cuba and adelantado of Florida, with the title of marquess over such part of the territory he was to conquer."
12. Although she was a tactful courtier, adept at concealing her feelings, Doña Isabel was, nevertheless, a person of strong character and a caring mother, concerned for the happiness and success of each of her children. She doubtless was interested in the home life of her daughter Isabel, yet she could not fail, at the same time, to be interested in assisting at the launching of a new adventure, which would likely bring added wealth, fame and power to the family.
13. See EL3, chap. 1.
14. See EL3, chap. 1. The inner circle of friends of de Soto were "Juan de Añasco, of Seville, Luis Moscoso de Alvarado, Nuño de Tovar and Juan Rodríguez Lobillo. All, except Añasco, came with him from Peru."
15. See note 3, above.

Chapter Seventeen
The Great Fleet

1. From HER, decada 6, chap. 9, pp. 129, 130. It is clear, from this and other chroniclers, that "since the failure of Pánfilo de Narváez, no one had yet dared to attempt such an undertaking, deeming it too difficult and expensive."

2. The king's enthusiasm may be judged from the authority and favors bestowed on de Soto, as related in the *Concession* made by the king of Spain to Hernando de Soto of the government of Cuba and conquest of Florida, with the title of adelantado, in Valladolid, April 20, 1537. *Archives of Indies* at Sevilla, Colección Muñoz, vol. 71, page 105. Printed in Colección Torres de Mendoza, vol. 22, pp. 534–46.
3. Ibid.
4. See the *Final Report* of the U.S. De Soto Expedition Commission, 76th Cong. 1st sess., House Document no. 71, p. 76, chap. 6, "The Beginnings of the Expedition and Its Personnel."
5. The jurisdiction of Adelantado de Soto, as established by the Royal Provision given in Valladolid on May 4, 1537, is kept in the Archives of the Indies ("Patronato") and has been published by the Royal Academy of History of Madrid (*Colección*, vol. 4, pp. 431–37).
    The creation of the gobernación and capitanía general of Florida represented the establishment of a civilian authority in the governorship, with the captaincy referring to the establishment of a military authority, also vested in the same person. In the Spanish system of colonial administration, the *audiencias* were the major provinces where the government functions were centralized. An *audiencia* had a president and a council of *oidores*, vested with judiciary responsibilities. The *audiencias* were divided in governorships, or minor provinces, and these, in turn, consisted of *corregimientos* and *tenencias de gobernación*. The general captaincies' functions were to subdue such groups of rebellious Indians as may exist. Unlike the *audiencias*, which reported to the viceroy, the general captaincies were autonomous. The fact that the captaincy of Florida, bestowed on de Soto, was not to be under the authority of any *audiencia*, but would be directly answerable to the Council of the Indies in Madrid, was one more example of King Charles's favorable disposition toward de Soto.
6. In 1525, the richly endowed Isabel of Portugal, at age twenty-two, married Charles V, who had asked Henry VIII of England to release him from his engagement to Mary, the nine-year-old daughter of Queen Catherine of Aragon, first wife of the English king.
7. Religion, particularly the expansion of the Catholic Faith, was the main motivation of all Spanish explorations. This was so from the very first of Columbus's voyages.
    Even Garcilaso de la Vega's description of de Soto's request to Charles V for permission to explore and conquer Florida begins thus:
    It is for the glory and honor of the Most Holy Trinity, God Our Lord, and with a desire to augment His Holy Catholic Faith and the Crown of Spain that we now attempt to record

in these pages the story of many Cavalier Spaniards and Indians, and especially that of Hernando de Soto, Governor and Captain General of the provinces and seigniories of the great Kingdom of Florida.

In the letter of agreement signed by the king on April 20, 1537, whereby authority was granted to de Soto over the province of Tierra-Nueva, the stipulation was made that the governor should carry and provide for those "persons, religious and secular, who shall be appointed by us for the instruction of the natives of that province in our Holy Catholic Faith." De Soto was also commanded "to obey and to give due regard to that country, and to the good treatment and conversion to our Holy Catholic Faith of the natives thereof." He was expected to "promise and declare" that he would adhere to those instructions.

8. Garcilaso de la Vega, nicknamed "El Inca," is the author of one of the four main narratives of de Soto's Florida expedition. He was born in Cuzco, the son of a conquistador and of an Inca princess, and his works, *The Florida of the Inca* and the *Comentarios Reales,* recount the history of the Incas.

   The three other accounts of de Soto's exploration are a chronicle by an officer of the expedition called The Gentleman of Elvas, the *Relación,* by Luys Hernández de Biedma, and the diary kept by Rodrigo Rangel, the commander's private secretary, which appeared in the *Historia General y Natural de las Indias,* by the Spanish historian Oviedo (Gonzalo Fernández de Oviedo y Valdés).

Chapter Eighteen
Fernandina Island

1. *Columbus' Letter on His First Voyage.* Official Report on his First Voyage to Ferdinand and Isabella, par. 2. 1st ed. New York Public Library. (Cathay is the medieval name of China. Columbus named Cuba the Isla Juana, in honor of the Infante Don Juan, heir to the throne of Castile and Aragon.
2. See CEN, chap. 21.
3. See FLI, chap. 7.
4. See CEN, chap. 22.
5. See FLI, bk. 1, chap. 7.
6. See CEN, chap. 22.
7. See FLI, chap. 8.
8. Ibid.
9. See FLI, bk. 1, chaps. 8 and 9.
10. See FLI, bk. 1, chap. 12.
11. Tovar's alienation was certainly a blow for de Soto. Nuño de Tovar, his countryman, a native of Jerez de Badajoz, was, with Moscoso,

according to Garcilaso, among the group of close friends who with Hernando enjoyed life in Seville upon de Soto's return from the Indies. Tovar's office of lieutenant general was given by de Soto in Cuba to Vasco Porcallo de Figueroa. Sometime later, Tovar appears listed as a captain in the cavalry. He died at Aminoya in the winter 1542–43. U.S. De Soto Expedition Commission, p. 369. Rangel, pp. 67, 85, 127. EL3, pp. 7, 11, 30, 31, 221. FLI, pp. 8, 45, 152, 153, 155, 157, 167, 221, 266.

12. Nicolas de Ovando was appointed governor and supreme justice of the islands and mainlands of the Indies in 1501, thereby to a great extent curtailing the rights and privileges of Columbus as viceroy and admiral of the islands and mainlands of the Ocean Sea. A spiteful enemy of Columbus, he was, in fact, governor of Hispaniola (see n. 4, chap. 2), whence he sent exploratory parties to Cuba.

The expression "Ocean Sea" used in Columbus's title was the name given at that time to the expanse of water that Columbus had just crossed. The name evidently derives from Okeanos, the river which in Greek mythology was said to circle the land mass of the world.

13. See HI, vol. 1, chap. 43.
14. See OVO and FLI for Mendoza's letter to de Soto.
15. See CEN, chap. 23, p. 189.
16. See FLI, bk. 1, chap. 15.

Chapter Nineteen
North America

1. From Theodore Irving, *The Conquest of Florida under Hernando de Soto* (London, 1835).
2. See FLI.
3. See FLI.
4. See CEN, chap. 24, p. 201.
5. See FLI, pt. 1, bk. 2, chaps. 5, 6.
6. See FLI.
7. See EL3, chap. 8.
8. See EL3, chap. 8.
9. See CEN, chap. 24, p. 207.
10. "The Great Captain" was Gonzalo Fernández de Córdoba; see n. 5, chap. 2.
11. FLI, p. 36.
12. Porcallo de Figueroa was named to replace Tovar. See n. 11, chap. 18.
13. See FLI, bk. 2, chap. 11.
14. See EL3, chap. 17.

15. See FLI, OVO and HER, decada 6, chap. 10, p. 141.
16. See FLI, pt. 1, bk. 2, chap. 23.
17. Ibid.
18. See USC, chap. 15, p. 161; also FLI and EL3, p. 235.
19. See FLI and OVO, chap. 25.
20. See EL3, chap. 13.
21. Ibid.
22. CEN, chap. 28, pp. 254, 255.
23. See CEN, chap. 29, pp. 261, 262.
24. See CEN, chap. 29, p. 262, and EL3, chap. 14.
25. See FLI and EL3, chap. 16.
26. See FLI, bk. 3, chaps. 23 and 24.

Chapter Twenty
The Father of the Waters

1. From Walt Whitman, "Earth's Most Important Stream" Specimen Days. Vol. I. *The Collective Writings of Walt Whitman*, Prose Works, 1892. Edited by Floyd Stovall, (New York: New York University Press, 1963).
2. See EL3, chap. 17.
3. See FLI, *Florida of the Inca*, chap. 25.
4. USC, chap. 18, p. 213, describes the battle thus:

   The battle lasted all day and resulted in the death of about twenty Spaniards and the loss of the greater part of their property. On the side of the Indians, the destruction was terrible, including, according to our authorities, almost the entire fighting force. The estimates of Indian dead run from 2500 by Elvas, to 11,000 by Garcilaso. A number of horses also perished in this encounter, much of the clothing was lost, the pearls they obtained at Copitachequi and other places, and the vessels used in celebrating Mass.

5. The memory of de Soto is kept alive in several states and cities of the Union, such as Memphis, Tennessee, where the belief is held in certain quarters that de Soto was an early founder (or a precursor of the founder) of the settlement near the Chickasaw Bluffs, above the Mississippi River.

   De Soto's landing at Tampa Bay is now a landmark and an attraction. The present-day Knights of de Soto commemorate the landing in Bradenton with colorful ceremony.
6. See RAN, "Events of March 3." Also CEN, chap. 32, p. 293.
7. De Soto was a man who took stern decisions, which he would not subsequently change. He acted in such a manner toward his friend and alternate, Luis Moscoso de Alvarado, whom he stripped of

his office as *maestre de camp* or camp marshal (a title given in the sixteenth and seventeenth centuries to a chief of staff, entrusted with special responsibilities and holding a rank equivalent to a present-day colonel).

Such was also the treatment meted out to Nuño de Tovar, whom de Soto relieved of his duties as lieutenant general when in Cuba. But his affection for these old friends and comrades of the days in Peru, or at the Court of Spain, remained unaltered. They, in turn, with exemplary loyalty, stood by him at all times, including the hours of danger. Lance at the ready and sword in hand, they jealously defended him and shared his fate.

In return, de Soto, on his deathbed, appointed Moscoso governor, adelantado and captain general of Florida. Moscoso thus assumed the leadership of the expedition, until the survivors reached Mexico.

8. See CEN, chap. 33, p. 302. "It is understood that the river was sighted by de Soto from Sunflower Landing, south of Memphis."
9. See RAN; OVO; CEN, chap. 33, p. 303; EL3, chap. 22, p. 103.
10. See EL3, chap. 24.

Chapter Twenty-One
The Spell of the River

1. From Homer, *Odyssey*, bk. 5, v. 445 ff.
2. De Soto needed comforting in such circumstances, as "he sank into deep despair at the sight of the difficulties that faced him upon his reaching the sea." Moreover, "he was worried about the possible shortage of food for his men, which would keep him on the march, in search of new territory and booty—specially food." EL3, chap. 29, p. 140.
3. The bald eagle (*Haliaeetus leucocephalus*), a sea eagle native to North America, used to be abundant over the Mississippi area, from Florida to Alaska. See Oliver L. Austin, *Birds of the World*, Golden Press. New York: University of Florida, 1983.
4. EL3, chap. 29, pp. 139, 140.
5. See EL3, chap. 29.
6. Rodrigo Rangel was not only a close personal friend of de Soto's and his personal secretary, but he was also the author of a diary, in which he recorded the events of the expedition, now the basis of any study of the route of the Florida adventure. He wrote his entries in the diary at intervals. His manuscript was reproduced in Oviedo's *Historia General y Natural de las Indias*. His description of events is considered to be superior to that of Elvas, with regard to sequence "and an accurate placing of the route" as the U.S. De

Soto Expedition Commission puts it. Rangel can justifiably be called the official historian of the expedition.

Rangel was a native of the village of Almendralejo, in Badajoz, Estremadura. He was at de Soto's side at the hour of his death, and he accompanied Moscoso on the final lap of the expedition to Mexico.

7. See EL3, chap. 30; also FLI, pt. 1, bk. 5, chap. 7.
8. See CEN, chap. 37, p. 338.
9. See FLI, pt. 1, bk. 5, chap. 7.
10. See CEN, chap 37, p. 338. Also FLI.
11. Jorge Manrique, "Elegy on the death of the Grand Master of Santiago" (his father) (1440–1478). In *Coplas*, vol. 3, critical edition. Edited by R. Foulché Delhose. Madrid: Biblioteca Oropesa, 1912.

Epilogue

1. See CEN, chap. 38, p. 353.
2. Ibid.
3. Ibid.
4. See FLI, bk. 6, chap. 21.

SELECTED BIBLIOGRAPHY

Abbreviations used in Notes

Abbott, John Stevens Cabot. *Ferdinand de Soto*. New York: Dodd, Mead, 1898.

Acosta, Friar José de, S.J. *Historia Natural y Moral de las Indias, en que se tratan las cosas notables del cielo y elementos, metales y plantas y animales dellas, y los ritos y ceremonias, leyes y govierno y guerras de los Indios*. Addressed to the Most Serene Infanta Doña Clara Eugenia of Austria. Madrid: Casa Alonso Martin, 1608.

Alvarez Rubiano, P. *Pedrarias Dávila*. Madrid: Consejo Superior de Investigación Cientifica, 1944. ALV

Amadís de Gaula, El Caballero Cifar, Tirant lo Blanc. Books of Spanish chivalry. Madrid: Editorial Aguilar, 1960.

Andagoya, Pascual de. *Narrative of the Proceedings of Pedrarias Dávila in the Provinces of Tierra Firme or Castilla de Oro, and of the Discovery of the South Seas and the Coasts of Perú and Nicaragua*. Translated and edited by Clements R. Markham. London: Hakluyt Society, 1865.

Andrade, Martín, Luciano. *Llanganati*. Quito, 1936.

Andrews, Daniel Marshall. *De Soto's Route*. Lancaster, Pa.: New Era Printing Co., 1917.

Arciniegas, Germán. *Amerigo y el Nuevo Mundo*. Mexico City: Editorial Hermes, 1955.

Bandin, Louis. *El Imperio Socialista de los Incas*. Santiago de Chile: Zig-zag, 1962.

Barcia. *Historiadores Primitivos de las Indias Occidentales*. Madrid, 1749.   **BAR**

Bayle, Constantino. *Hernando de Soto*. Madrid: Editorial Razón y Fe.

Biedma, Luys Hernández de. *Relación de la Isla de la Florida*. 1865. Translation included in Smith below.

Blanco Castilla, F. *Hernando de Soto, El Centauro de las Indias*. Madrid: Editorial Carrera del Castillo, 1955.   **CEN**

Borbolla, Daniel Rubin de la. *Los Tesoros Artisticos del Perú*. Mexico City: Universidad Nacional Autónoma de Mexico, 1961.

Bourne, Edward Gaylord. *Narratives of the Career of Hernando de Soto*. 2 vols. New York: A. S. Barnes, 1904.   **NAR**

Brandel, Fernand. *The Mediterranean and the Mediterranean World in the Age of Philip II*. New York, London: Harper and Row, 1949.

Cabeza de Vaca, Álvar Núñez. *Naufragios y Comentarios*. Madrid: Editorial Historia 16, 1984.

Carles, Ruben D. *Crónicas de Castilla del Oro*. Panama City: 1960.

Carrion, Benjamin. *Atahualpa*. Quito, Ecuador: Editorial Casa de la Cultura Ecuatoriana, 1956.

Casas, Friar Bartolomé de las. *Historia de las Indias*. Mexico City: 1875; Mexico City Fondo de Cultura Económica, 1951.   **HI**

Chadwick, Mara Louise Pratt. *Columbus and De Soto*. Chicago: Educational Publishing Company, 1891.

Citri de la Guette. *Of the anon. Portuguese "Relaçam verdadeira": Two journeys of the present emperour of China*. London: F. Collins for J. Lawrence, 1686.

Cieza de León, Pedro. *Crónica del Perú (Antwerp, 1514)*. Edited by Manuel Ballestero Gaibrois. Madrid: Editorial Historia 16, 1984.   **CRO**

———. *Descubrimiento y conquista del Perú*. Madrid: Editorial Zero, 1984.   **CDC**

———. *El Señorio de los Incas*. Madrid: Editorial Historia 16, 1985.   **CSN**

Colón, Fernando. *Historia del Almirante de las Indias, Don Cristóbal Colón*. Mexico City: Editora Latino Americana, S.A., 1958.

Cotterill, R. S. *The Southern Indians*. Norman: University of Oklahoma Press, 1971.

Daly, Dominick. *Adventures of Roger l'Estrange*. London: S. Sonnenshein, 1896.

Day, A. Grove. *Coronado's Quest*. Berkeley and Los Angeles: University of California Press, 1940.

Elvas, Fidalgo de. *Expedición de Hernando de Soto a Florida* (1557). EL1
Colección "Austral." Buenos Aires: Espasa-Calpe, 1952.

Elvas, Fidalgo de (Gentleman of Elvas). *Virginia*. London: F. Kynston for M. Lownes, 1609.

Elvas, Fidalgo de (Gentleman of Elvas). *Discovery of Florida*. NY, 1864. Translation included in Smith below.

Fernández de Navarrete, Martín. *Colección de los Viajes y Descubrimientos que hicieron por Mar los Españoles*. Buenos Aires: Editorial Guarania, 1945.

Fernández de Oviedo y Valdés, Gonzalo. *Historia General y* OVO
Natural de las Indias, Islas y Tierra Firme del Mar Océano, 4 vols. Madrid: Editorial José Amador de los Ríos, 1851–55.

Fernández Flores, Darío. *The Spanish Heritage in the United States*. Madrid: Publicaciones Españolas, 1971.

Fitzmaurice-Kelly, James. *Historia de la Literatura Española*. Madrid: 1913.

French, Benjamin Franklin. *Historical Collections of Louisiana*. New York: Wiley and Putnam, 1846–53.

Garcilaso de la Vega, El Inca. *Commentarios Reales*. Madrid: COM
Espasa-Calpe, 1942.

Garcilaso de la Vega, El Ynca. *Historia General del Perú*. 2d ed. GAH
Madrid: Oficina Real, 1722.

Garcilaso de la Vega. *La Florida del Ynca*. Lisbon: P. Crasbeek. FLY
1605.

————. *The Florida of the Inca (Lisbon, 1605)*. Translated by Grier FLI
Varner and Jeannette Varner. Austin: University of Texas Press, 1951.

Gentleman of Elvas. See all entries under Elvas.

Gómara. See López de Gómara.

González Suárez, Federico. *Historia General del Eduador*. Quito, Ecuador: Imprenta del Clero, 1915.

Graham, R. B. Cunninghame. *Hernando de Soto*. New York: The Dial Press, 1924.

Hagen, Victor W. von. *El Imperio de los Yncas*. Mexico City: Editorial Diana, 1964.

Hare, Cristóbal. *La Reina de las Reinas, Isabel la Católica*. Mexico: Editorial Nacional, 1957.

Hemming, John. *La Conquista de los Incas*. Mexico City, 1982. Fondo de Cultura Económica. In English: *The Conquest of the Incas*. London: Macmillan, 1970.

Herrera, Antonio de. *Historia General de los Hechos de los Cas-* HER
tellanos en las Islas y Tierra Firme del Mar Océano. Madrid, 1726;

Buenos Aires: Editorial Guarania, 1944. Also, Madrid: Academia de la Historia, 1936.

Hewitt, John Hill. *Shadows on the Wall.* 1877.

Hodge, Frederick Webb. *Handbook of American Indians North of Mexico.* Washington, D.C.: Government Printing Office, Smithsonian Institution, 1907.

Holford, Castello N. *Cofachiqui and Other Poems.* Bloomington, Ill.: L. D. Holford, 1984.

Horgan, Paul. *Conquistadors in North American History.* New York: Farrar, Straus, 1963.

Humboldt, Baron de. *Narración personal de Viajes a las Regiones Equinocciales de América durante los años 1799–1804.* Paris, 1808–1834 (30 vols.).

Jameson, J. Franklin. *Original Narratives of Early American History.* New York: Charles Scribner's Sons. 1907.

Jaramillo Alvarado, Pío. *La Nación Quiteña y otros ensayos.* Quito, Ecuador: Imprenta Fernández, 1947.

———. *La Presidencia de Quito.* (A note on the origins of the Ecuadorian nationhood and its territorial defense, from an historical and legal standpoint.) Quito, Ecuador: Editorial El Comercio, 1938.

Jennings, John Edward. *The Golden Eagle.* New York: Putnam, 1959.

Keating, Bern. *The Mighty Mississippi.* Washington, D.C: National Geographic Society, 1971.

Kirkpatrick, F. A. *Los Conquistadores Españoles.* Colección "Austral." Mexico City, 1958.

Knowles, Charles Edward. *In Quest of Gold.* New York: John Lane, 1912.

Littleton, Mary Brabson. *By the King's Command, a Romance of Ferdinand de Soto.* New York: P. J. Kenedy & Sons, 1928.

López de Gómara, Francisco. *Historia General de las Indias* (1522), 2 vols. Barcelona: Editorial Iberia, 1954.   GOM

Lozoya, Marqués de. *Segovia.* Barcelona: Editorial Noguer, S. A., 1963.

Lulio, Raimundo. *Libro del Orden de Caballería. Príncipes y Juglares* (1275). Buenos Aires: Espasa-Calpe Argentina, 1949.

Lummis, Carlos F. *Los Exploradores Españoles del Siglo XVI.* Mexico City: Editorial Porrúa, S. A., 1981.   LUM

McCullough, David. *The Path between the Seas.* New York: Simon and Schuster, 1977.

McIntyre, Loren. *The Incredible Incas and Their Timeless Land.* Washington, D.C.: National Geographic Society, 1975.

Madariaga, Salvador de. *Carlos V.* "Dimensiones hispanicas." Barcelona: Ed. Grijalbo, S. A., 1984.

————. *Cristóbal Colón*. Madrid: Espasa-Calpe, S.A., 1975.

————. *Hernán Cortés*. Mexico: Editorial Hermes, 1955.

Majó Framis, R. *Vida de los Navegantes y Conquistadores Españoles del Siglo XVI*. Madrid: M. Aguilar, 1945.

Mártir, Pedro. *Peter Martyr Anglerius "De Orbe Novo" Compluti*. Spain: Alcala de Henares, 1530. Trans. Frank A. MacNutt. 2 vols. New York, 1912.

Medina, Jose Toribio. *El Descubrimiento del Océan. Pacifico*. Vols. I and II. Santiago de Chile: 1914.

Menéndez Pidal, Ramón. *Idea Imperial de Carlos V*. Buenos Aires: Espasa-Calpe Argentina, 1949.

Mirsky, Jeannette. *The Gentle Conquistadors*. England: Karze & Ward, 1972.

Montesinos. "Anales." MS.   MAN

————. "Memorias Antiguas Historiales del Perú." MS.   MEM

Morison, Samuel Eliot. *Admiral of the Ocean Sea*. Boston: Little, Brown, 1942.

Morris, Wright. *The Mississippi River Reader*. New York: Doubleday, 1962.

Muñoz de San Pedro, Miguel. *Diego García de Paredes*. Madrid: Espasa-Calpe, 1946.

Naharro, Fray Pedro Ruiz. "Relación de los hechos de los españoles en el Perú, desde su descubrimiento hasta la muerte del Marqués Francisco Pizarro." Colección de Documentos ineditos para la historia de España, ed. M. Fernandez Navarrete. Madrid: 1827–95.

Ondegardo, Licentiate Polo de. "Relación Primera" and "Relación Segunda." MSS.   OND

Oviedo: See Fernández de Oviedo y Valdés.

Palma, Ricardo. *Tradiciones Peruanas*. Colección "Austral." Mexico City: Espasa-Calpe, 1956.

Pareja Diezcanseco, Alfredo. *Historia del Ecuador*. 2 vols. Quito, Ecuador: Casa de la Cultura Ecuatoriana, 1958.

Pereira Jiménez, Bonifacio. *Historia de Panamá*. Panama: Agencia Internacional de Publicaciones, 1963.

Pereyra, Carlos. *Francisco Pizarro y el Tesoro de Atahualpa*. Madrid, 1930.

————. *Las Huellas de los Conquistadores*. Madrid: M. Aguilar, 1929.

Pfandl, Ludwig. *Introducción al Siglo de Oro*. Barcelona: Casa Editorial Araluce, 1929.

Pierce, Frank. *Amadís de Gaula*. Boston: University of Sheffield, Twayne Publishers, 1976.

Pizarro, Pedro. "Relación del Descubrimiento y Conquista de los Reynos del Perú." MS. Included in a collection of unpublished documents for the History of Spain, Academy of History, Madrid (1965).

Pizarro y Orellana, Fernando. *Varones Ilustres del Nuevo Mundo*. Madrid, 1639.

Preble, John. *The Darién Disaster*. London: Secker & Warburg, 1968.

Prescott, William H. *History of the Conquest of Mexico* (1843) and *History of the Conquest of Peru* (1847). New York: Random House, the Modern Library, 1950.   PRE

Quintana, M. J. *Vida de Francisco Pizarro*. Madrid: Espasa-Calpe, S.A. 1959.

Ramusio, Giovanni-Battista. "Relazione d'un Capitano Spag-   RAM
nuolo." In *Navigazioni e Viaggi*. Venice, 1565.

Rangel, Rodrigo. "Abridged Journal." In *Narratives of the Career*   RAN
of Hernando de Soto, translated by Edward Gaylord Bourne. New York: A. S. Barnes, 1907.

Ranke, Leopold von. *La Monarquia Española de los Siglos XVI y XVII*. Mexico City: Editorial Leyenda, 1946.

Robertson, James Alexander. *True Relation of the Hardships Suffered by Governor Fernando de Soto*. No. 8, Florida. De Land: The Florida State Historical Society, 1932.

Romoli, Kathleen. *Vasco Núñez de Balboa, Descubridor del Pacífico*.   ROM
A translation of her English book, *Balboa of Darién*. Madrid: Espasa-Calpe, 1955

Rubio Orbe, Gonzalo. *Rumiñahui, Ati II*. Quito, Ecuador: Talleres Gráficos de Educación Pública, 1944.

Sáenz, Herlinda Treviño. widow of. *Perú Joyas, telas y cerámica*. Mexico City, 1946-47.

Sahagún, Friar Bernardino de. *Historia General de las Cosas de Nueva España*. Mexico City: Editorial Porrúa, S.A., 1982.

Santamarina, Luys. *Cisneros*. Buenos Aires, Argentina: Espasa-Calpe, 1953.

Sarmiento de Gamboa, P. *Historia de los Incas (1572)*. Edited by   SAR
R. Pretschmann. Published by author, Berlin, 1906.

Schoolcraft, Henry R. *Scenes and Adventures*. Philadelphia: Lippincott, Grambo, 1853.

Shipp, Barnard. *The History of Hernando de Soto*. Philadelphia: Collins, 1881.

Simms, William Gilmore. *Vasconselos: A Romance of the New World*. New York: A. C. Armstrong & Son, 1882.

Smith, Buckingham. *Narratives of de Soto in the Conquest of Flor-   EL3
ida, as Told by a Gentleman of Elvas, and a Relation by Luis Hernández de Biedma*. Gainesville, Fla.: Palmetto Books, 1968.

Solar y Taboada, Antonio del. *El Adelantado Hernando de Soto: Breves Noticias*. Badajoz, Spain: Ediciones Arqueros, 1929.

Solar y Taboada, Antonio del, y Rújula, José. *El Adelantado Hernando de Soto.* Badajoz, Spain: Ediciones Arqueros, 1933.

Steele, William O. *De Soto, Child of the Sun.* New York: Aladdin Books, 1956.

Syme, Ronald. *De Soto, Finder of the Mississippi.* New York: Morrow, 1957.

Toland, Mary B. *The Inca Princess.* Philadelphia: J.B. Lippincott, 1886.

U.S. De Soto Expedition Commission. *Final Report of the United States De Soto Expedition Commission to the U.S. Congress.* Washington, D.C.: U.S. Government Printing Office, 1939.   USC

Valbuena, Prat Angel. *Historia de la Literatura Española.* Barcelona: Gustavo Gili, 1937.

Vázquez de Espinosa, Antonio. *Compendium and Description of the West Indies.* Washington, D.C.: Smithsonian Institution. 1942.

Velasco, Padre Juan de, S.J. *Historia del Reino de Quito.* Quito, Ecuador: Biblioteca Ecuatoriana Mínima, 1960.   VEL

Villanueva, L. *Hernando de Soto.* Badajoz, Spain, 1892.

Viú, José. *Estremadura: Colección de sus inscripciones y monumentos, seguida de reflexiones importantes sobre lo pasado y el porvenir de estas provincias.* Madrid, 1852.

Walsh, W. T. *Isabel la Cruzada.* Buenos Aires: Espasa-Calpe Argentina, 1945.

Wilmer, Lambert A. *The Life, Travels and Adventures of Ferdinand de Soto.* Philadelphia: J. T. Lloyd, 1858.

Wolf, Teodoro. *Geografía del Ecuador.* Leipzig, 1892. Quito, Ecuador: Casa de la cultura 8 Ecuatoriana, 1975.

Wyndham Lewis, D. B. *Carlos de Europa, Emperador de Occidente.* Colección "Austral." Buenos Aires, 1946.

Xérez, Francisco de. "Conquista del Perú." In Barcia, above.   XER

Young, John Preston. *De Soto and Chickasaw Bluffs.* Publications of the Mississippi Historical Society, vol. 2. Centenary Series. Memphis, Tenn., 1918.

Zarate, *Historia del Descubrimiento y Conquista del Perú.* (Amberes, 1555) (Sevilla, 1577.)   ZAR

Zweig, Stefan, *Américo Vespucio.* Buenos Aires: Editorial Claridad, 1942.

INDEX